WORLD LEADER OF SANITATION

BINDESHWAR PATHAK

Praise for the Book

"I have many beautiful memories of summers spent in my native place. But the one thing I would rather forget is the toilet. It was a raised platform with a hole. No flush, no sanitation, no escape from that awful stench. For days, I simply would not use the toilet. But how long could one hold back? Thoughts like these cross my mind on a beautiful February morning under a gorgeous blue sky. I am at the Sulabh complex near Palam in New Delhi, home to the world's only museum dedicated to toilets."

—Rashmi Bansal

WORLD LEADER OF SANITATION

BINDESHWAR PATHAK

VINAY RAJATH D.

RUPA

Published by
Rupa Publications India Pvt. Ltd 2021
7/16, Ansari Road, Daryaganj
New Delhi 110002

Sales Centres:
Allahabad Bengaluru Chennai
Hyderabad Jaipur Kathmandu
Kolkata Mumbai

ISBN: 978-93-90547-20-3

First impression 2021

10 9 8 7 6 5 4 3 2 1

Printed at Thomson Press India Ltd., Faridabad

CONTENT

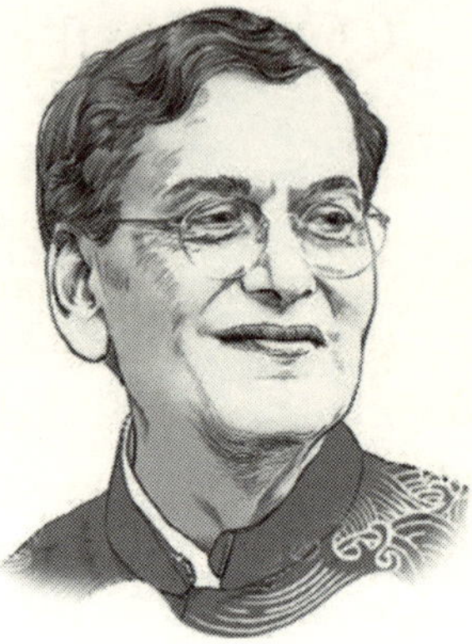

Dr Bindeshwar Pathak

A young Brahmin boy was once made to eat cow-dung by his grandmother to purify himself after contact with an untouchable. The same boy grew up to lead a movement 'Sulabh'. A revolution in toilets and a rightful place in society, for those who once cleaned them. This is the life story of Dr Bindeshwar Pathak the world leader in Sanitation. This man made it his mission to bring sanity to this country's archaic systems, both social and sanitary.

FOREWORD

It gives me immense pleasure to write the foreword to the book *World Leader of Sanitation: Bindeshwar Pathak* by Dr Vinay Rajath. One of the complex issues that bothers modern contemporary Indian society is sanitation, with all its related components as pollution, environmental degradation, waste management, water scarcity, etc. on the physical part; and caste, gender, scavenging, open defecation etc., on the cultural side. Pioneers and celebrities in many areas have raised their voices and opinions; however, this particular area, sanitation, did not gain enough currency in policies, publicities and propaganda until Dr Bindeshwar Pathak initiated his Action Sociology, in the footsteps of Mahatma Gandhi. The author, in this book, has highlighted different areas of sanitation: the concept, culture, technology and the social practices. The units presented in the book echoed all these aspects. The author has attempted to focus more on the diverse activities of Dr Bindeshwar Pathak. By concentrating on these issues he tries to unveil the philanthropic profile of the world Sanitation Leader. Many activities of Dr Bindeshwar Pathak are systematically mapped in this volume, more in a sociological perspective.

Bindeshwar Pathak was born in a respectable Brahmin family, a prosperous and well-respected family. His thirst and desire for knowledge and understanding the reality earned him the education qualifications, M.A., Ph.D and also D.Litt for his work on Sanitation. In his experience, young Bindeshwar Pathak noticed discrimination and untouchability and wished to seek some solution to this problem. Even though he is a Brahmin he lived in a colony of untouchables and faced all kinds of taunts and insults.

Sulabh is his brain child, the application of mind and technology. The model he designed is simple; low cost, needs only a little water, and turns waste into a resource. Sulabh is a twin-pit, pour-flush compost toilet. A deeply sloping toilet pan connected to two pits by a Y-shaped channel;

to use the pits alternatively. He has made pans with his own hands and polished them. Five things are most important in his life: *vision, mission, commitment, capabilities* and *efficiency*. The public toilet complexes in cities and lakhs of two-pit toilets in homes all over the country and the toilet museum are the lasting contributions of Dr Pathak to Sanitation. This is a Sanitation Revolution; and his mission is to fulfil the dream of Mahatma Gandhi, to make India scavenger free.

Dr Pathak did not restrict himself to sanitation activities. His vision is broad, encompassing the whole humanity. This made him to extend his helping hand to the needy in any walk of life. In the journey of sanitation spanning nearly five decades, Dr Pathak has taken the help of truth, honesty, integrity, ethics and morality, to create confidence among different cultures and communities, political parties, the government and the people in general. In this direction Dr Pathak has also made earnest request that sanitation should be included as a discipline in sociology because the core problem areas of sanitation require sociological intervention.

Dr Bindeshwar Pathak is a great humanist and social reformer of contemporary India. He is the icon of sanitation and social reform who has made a difference in the lives of millions of people. His boundless love for the downtrodden finds expression in innumerable and tangible ways. Dr Pathak is the first person in India who is instrumental in constructing more than 7,500 public toilets in slums and at public, religious and tourist places and maintained them on a pay-and-use basis. After Gandhiji, Dr Pathak is the man, in India, who has championed the cause of adequate sanitation and upliftment of the untouchables. For his exemplary work Dr Bindeshwar Pathak has been honoured nationally and internationally; including the Padma Bhushan.

The entire book gives the reader glimpses of varied aspects of the personality of Dr Bindeshwar Pathak. In almost all units, like the History of Sanitation, Sanitation and Culture, Manual Scavengers, Open Defecation, Sulabh Sauchalay and Sanitation Research, the profile of the Sanitation Leader has been narrated in a prolific manner.

I am happy to note that this book comes out as a mark of reverence to a great and versatile world leader of sanitation, Dr Bindeshwar Pathak, who is an intellectual personality in sociology and known for his humble character. The book will be of great interest for the people who are interested in continuing the dream of Mahatma Gandhi and Dr Bindeshwar Pathak in making India clean, hygienically, culturally and spiritually; in making India free from manual scavenging and open defecation.

Dr Mahipathsinh D. Chavda
Vice Chancellor
Maharaja Krishnakumarsinjhi
Bhavnagar University

PREFACE

The present volume, *World Leader of Sanitation: Bindeshwar Pathak,* mainly focuses on Dr Bindeshwar Pathak as a world sanitation leader, his efforts in eradicating the practice of scavenging, contribution to sociology of sanitation and the founding of Action Sociology. After presenting a brief profile of the leader in the first chapter, the second chapter gives a broad outline of the sociology of sanitation, its nature, scope and importance and the various sociological perspectives in understanding the concept of sanitation.

The chapter on the history of sanitation in India narrates its growth from the Indus Valley Civilisation to the present society, covering various stages like sanitation in Mohenjo-Daro and Harappa, during the Colonial Period, post-Independence, and organisation leaders in sanitation in India. A Section unit analyses the cultural bearing of sanitation. It focuses on the socio-cultural structure and its impact on the sanitation concept and system. Caste, religion and environmental sanitation are interrelated aspects. It brings home how caste, untouchability and sanitation are intrinsically connected in the Indian context.

The measures for social upliftment of manual scavengers in India are covered significantly. There have been several attempts made at different stages to improve the social conditions of the scavenging community in India. Many of these are policy matters. The chapter discusses the different policy interventions by governments and involvement by social service organisations, especially Sulabh. In continuation of this, the book discusses the problem of open defecation in India and the origin of the Sulabh Shauchalaya, as a technological intervention to eradicate open defecation and also manual scavenging.

The Sanitation Movement by the leader has brought about social transformation in the whole sanitation system itself. The innovations by Sulabh and its leader in this direction are discussed with concrete illustrations. Various Sulabh initiatives like new methods in sanitation, biogas technology, sanitation research and the growth of Sulabh activities are highlighted. A separate chapter focuses on the World Leader in Sanitation, Dr Bindeshwar Pathak. Dr Pathak believes in and practises the philosophy of Mahatma Gandhi. The work of Gandhiji in relation to sanitation is seen as a motivating factor by the leader. The objectives and achievements of the leader through Sulabh are brought in focus. Dr Pathak is seen as a visionary with a global concern.

One unique and special feature in the approach of Dr Pathak is his Action Sociology. Drawing inspiration from pure sociology and its research, going beyond applied sociology, he has introduced the new concept of Action Sociology; that is, sociology with actual principles and practices. A chapter therefore discusses the nature of Action Sociology of Dr Pathak. Similarly, aspects of sanitation research are discussed in the following section. Dr Pathak has, over decades, brought about several technological innovations in the field of sanitation, mainly through research. Low-cost sanitation technology, planned sanitation development and the purpose of the unique sanitation museum are explained. And, finally, the volume envisions the future of the sanitation mission of Dr Pathak.

Dr Pathak's contributions to the field of sanitation, eradication of manual scavenging and rehabilitation initiatives for manual scavengers are widely acknowledged worldwide. His Action Sociology of eradication of manual scavenging does not function by knocking down dry latrines but by providing an alternative, new technology which does not require manual scavenging. Having earned his Master's in Sociology, Dr Pathak wanted to become a professor of Sociology; unfortunately, his wish was not fulfilled. However, he has achieved it in action; he has professed and lived sociology in action. Truly, he is the founder of sociology of sanitation in India; and the founder of Action Sociology with his unique technological initiatives to transform society regarding sanitation. Dr Pathak fought against not only the eradication of manual scavenging but also against the feminisation of manual scavenging and the caste basis of the sanitation work.

Dr Pathak is a model to the present generation, in bringing about social change, in breaking the shackles of caste exploitation without violence; his strategies were directly issue based, not against any caste, any religion or region. There is a dangerous trend among young scholars today, of reductionism. Reducing a person or his contribution to one particular thing;

leaving aside the whole range of thinking and debates at wider perspective. For example, Gandhiji is reduced to Swachhata and Dr BR Ambedkar to Constitution; and debunking their noble thoughts on democracy and humanism. Similarly, we should not reduce Dr Pathak only to sanitation. His vision does not end with the construction of toilets; his aim is to reach the message to all, and education is a powerful means to communicate this message. Therefore, along with teaching of sociology of sanitation at the colleges and universities, his target of establishing one separate university for sociology of sanitation is well articulated.

He is a visionary of humankind; and began a (silent) war against caste and gender discrimination. He has come out with technological solutions to the problems of sanitation; with alternatives which are non-violent, affordable and replicable. That was his beginning, but now he has focused on other concerns of humanity; extending activities to the destitute, victims of violence and natural disasters and also the widows of Vrindavan. To reach the target, Sulabh is giving importance to education of the young and the adults. I sincerely thank Dr Bindeshwar Pathak, Sulabh and Rupa Publications for giving me this opportunity to bring out this material in a book form. I also place on record the support and encouragement I received from Prof. Richard Pais and Prof. Niel Rathan. Let us join hands to take further the message of the "World Leader of Sanitation".

Vinay Rajath D.

Chapter 1

WORLD SANITATION LEADER: A PROFILE

Bindeshwar Pathak was born on 2 April 1943, in a respectable Brahmin family of Rampur Baghel village in Vaishali district of Bihar. His grandfather was a famous astrologer and his father an Ayurvedic doctor; a prosperous and well-respected family. His thirst and desire for knowledge and understanding reality motivated him to earn an M.A. in sociology and in English. His doctoral thesis was on "Liberation of Scavengers through Low Cost Sanitation", submitted to Patna University, Bihar. Dr Bindeshwar Pathak was also awarded a D.Litt. for his work on "Eradication of Scavenging and Environmental Sanitation in India—a Sociological Study", by Patna University.

Young Bindeshwar Pathak had no idea what he wanted to do in life. In fact, like many young people, his ambitions were guided by circumstances. Education was the escape route. Pathak took up sociology in 1961 as one of his subjects in B.A., Part-I programme, in Patna University and later opted for the same in the Honours class. He stood first in the college and decided to become a lecturer; a career with respectability and stability. After a B.A. in sociology (Honours), he wanted to specialise in criminology because it was a new subject and people said it would help him to join the Indian Police Service (IPS) or the Criminal Investigation Department (CID). Besides, there were no lecturers in the field of criminology then. So it seemed likely that he would get his dream job.

Pathak was at the top of the class up to the terminal exam. But in the finals, somehow, he scored very low marks in three papers and stood fourth. In fact, he could not even get a first class overall. And his dream of becoming a lecturer remained unfulfilled. He was shattered and perhaps this was the turning point of his life. He first became a school teacher, then worked at various odd jobs and eventually joined the family business, selling ayurvedic medicines. At that time, businessmen were not held in high esteem; despite money and luxury. In 1967, he decided once again to pursue his dream. He applied to study his favourite subject, criminology, at Sagar University in Madhya Pradesh, and got selected. However, due to delay in reporting, the seat was allotted to someone else.

Pathak grew up in an extensive house with a large compound. There were nine rooms, but no toilet. Every morning at 4 a.m., there was chaos in the house. All the women in the house had to complete their ablutions before sunrise. In case a woman in the house fell sick, she would have to relieve herself in a straw basket or a mud pot/container lined with ash. Pathak noticed all this, and felt something was not quite right. He studied in four different schools, none of them had a toilet. Millions of people experienced these very same things, yet it was only him who wished to seek an alternative or a solution. In fact, he was led by the thoughts of Mahatma Gandhi.

A woman of the untouchable caste, referred to as 'Dom', used to come to their house to deliver utensils made from bamboos. After she left, his grandmother used to sprinkle holy water over the area to purify it. Pathak was told that she was an untouchable and whoever touched her would be polluted. Being a curious child, when his grandmother was not around, he would touch the woman to see whether he became polluted and if his complexion changed. One day, as usual, when the woman came to deliver the utensils and was leaving, his grandmother had started her usual sprinkling of water and cleansing ritual when she saw Pathak touching the woman. She made a hue and cry about it and asked the boys in the neighbourhood to catch hold of him and then forced him to swallow cow dung and cow urine. Then she gave him Ganges water to drink to purify him. It was traumatic for him and it remained with him.

Bindeshwar Pathak narrated two incidents that had a lasting impact on him. A young bride, on the very first day of reaching her marital home, was forced to clean latrines. In the second incident, a bull charged towards a young boy in a marketplace. At first several people rushed forward to rescue him. Then someone shouted that the boy was from the scavenger colony. And suddenly the crowd dispersed. Pathak and his friend tried to intervene and rescue the boy but he died on the way to the hospital. These incidents had a lasting impact on him and he decided to dedicate his life to fulfilling the dream of Mahatma Gandhi.

In 1968, by coincidence, Pathak joined the Bihar Gandhi Centenary Celebration Committee as a social worker. During this time, he read the autobiography of Mahatma Gandhi as well as other books related to Gandhiji which had a profound influence on him. The Gandhi Centenary Committee was formed in 1967 to celebrate the birth centenary of Mahatma Gandhi. This committee had taken up numerous programmes, one of which was to restore the human rights and dignity of the untouchables who used to clean human excreta manually, carrying it as head-load for disposal. These people were referred to as human scavengers. Later on, he came to know that this subhuman practice stemmed from the genesis of untouchability and had been continuing for centuries through the Vedic, Buddhist, Mauryan, Mughal and British periods.

The general secretary of the Centenary Committee, having seen Pathak's commitment and work for the Committee, advised him to engage himself fully to fulfil the dreams of Mahatma Gandhi, and his unfinished agenda to restore the human rights and dignity of untouchable scavengers. This would be the best tribute by the Centenary Committee to Mahatma Gandhi. Being born in the Brahmin caste, this was unthinkable to Pathak; and he already had one traumatic experience after associating with an untouchable.

However, the general secretary patiently said, "I do not know your caste or whether you are an engineer or not, but by seeing your performance, your dedication as well as commitment in this short period that you have worked with us, I see light in you and strongly feel that you can fulfil the dreams of Mahatma Gandhiji to bring the untouchables to the mainstream of the society on a par with others."

In 1969, when Gandhiji's birth centenary was celebrated, Pathak worked with the subcommittee, 'Gandhi Sandesh Prachar'. Due to some internal politics he was transferred to the scavenger cell. A punishment posting, it was the starting point of Bindeshwar Pathak's journey. He was told, "*Gandhiji ka ek sapna tha, tum usko pura karo*" (Gandhiji had a dream, you complete it.) For having taken up that post the Brahmin community used to make fun of him, "Haan bhai, bhangiji, aa jaaiye. We have heard that these days you are doing the work of a bhangi."

And that is how a Brahmin went to live in a colony of untouchables in Bettiah. He faced all kinds of taunts and insults, but bore it all quietly.

Origin of Sulabh

Two books made a significant impact on Pathak. One was the volume published by WHO titled, *Excreta Disposal for Rural Areas and Small Communities.* And the second was the book authored by Rajendra Lal Das, who was part of the Sarvodaya Movement. The book outlined *What a Better Toilet System Should Be Like.* The WHO handbook had a sentence which struck Pathak in particular. It noted that out of the heterogeneous mass of latrine designs produced all over the world, the pit privy (The Indian-style toilet) was the most practical and universally applicable type. Whatever Pathak took from the book and whatever he added to it became an innovation. Many things which were not in it were created and became inventions. This was given to people and to the government and it became development.

Application of the mind is the basis of all the technology created at Sulabh. The model is simple; low-cost, needs little water, turns waste into a resource, can be built quickly, locally and needs no scavengers to maintain it. Sulabh is a twin-pit, pour-flush compost toilet. A deeply sloping toilet pan was developed to enable effective flushing with just a mug of water. The pan is connected to two pits by a Y-shaped channel. As soon as one pit is filled up (it may take months or years, depending on usage), the excreta is removed to the second pit. There is no need of a sewer line or a septic tank. The waste in the first pit turns into valuable fertiliser during the rest period. No odour, no pathogens and no manual cleaning is required.

Pathak said, based on his experience, five things are most important in life: *vision, mission, commitment, capabilities* and *efficiency*. You need all five to come together to make a success of any idea. He has made pans with his own hands and polished them. The initial work happened over a few months; perfecting the design took 2–3 years. Over the decades, it got a little better with more variations and different building material. But the essential idea remained the same.

When Bindeshwar Pathak approached the government with his initial prototype, the first reaction was: "This won't work, *phalthu hai, humbug hai*". Yet, he did not give up easily. The local administrator in Patna rejected the Sulabh design outright. However, the second officer he approached permitted him to build 200 Sulabh shauchalayas in Patna saying, "If it works, it will create history, if it doesn't, we will shut it down." And thus it was in 1970 that the government of Bihar agreed in principle to build Sulabh toilets and a circular was sent out. By then, Pathak had formed his own sanstha under the name of Sulabh. Generally, NGOs have a love-hate relationship with the government. But with Sulabh, it was different. From the very beginning, they worked hand-in-hand.

The second and most crucial direction came in 1971, when Pathak applied for a grant of ₹70,000. An amount of ₹50,000 was sanctioned. But then, the government fell. He did not get the money sanctioned and was given only advice—"Don't ask for grants, charge money for doing your work"; and the permission was given without any grant. And this is the model Sulabh has adopted ever since; pay per use from beneficiaries for maintaining; no grants, subsidies, loans or donations. Sulabh is a self-sustaining organisation.

Unfortunately, the next officer opposed the idea and the file was returned. With constant efforts and the intervention of the then prime minister, Indira Gandhi, the permission was granted to start a pilot project in Saran district (Bihar). In 1973, ₹25,000 was sanctioned for the project. But just as the work was about to begin, the officer-in-charge was transferred. The new secretary once again halted the work. This was the most difficult period of Pathak's life; from extreme wealth to near poverty, Pathak had experienced it all growing up. Two things came to his rescue: first, he sold the little property he still owned in his village; second, he sold his wife's jewellries. Hence, his wife had to depend on a few ornaments, when Sulabh was in its struggle phase. And further, Pathak also borrowed ₹50,000 as loan, a large sum in those days.

Pathak went back to the family business of selling medicines; he had to earn a living. He had nothing to show in terms of Sulabh shauchalayas as the government did not sanction it. Apart from his wife, every single person opposed his choice of work. Later, when he became successful, they all flocked back. A special officer, Ramakant Mishra, provided the funds to start two shauchalayas; he wrote out a cheque for ₹500. This was how the very first Sulabh Shauchalaya came into existence in August 1973. But selling the twin pit concept remained difficult. He went from door-to-door, explaining the benefits, but most people wanted a septic tank.

Sulabh had its effect in Patna in 1974 when a circular was sent out acknowledging it as a catalytic agency, between the government, local bodies and beneficiaries. So far, Sulabh had focused on converting bucket toilets in homes into pit privies. As a chance to venture into the public domain, the actual toilet block was up and ready. It was a pay-for-use toilet, 10 paise per visit. The government agreed to provide the land free of cost, and pay for the construction. The maintenance was to be covered by charging users. The toilets were kept spotlessly clean and quickly, they set up pay-for-use toilet blocks across Patna city and then across the state. In 1977, Sulabh had 40,000 twin pit latrines installed in individual homes. And pay-for-use Sulabh shauchalayas had sprung up all over the state. WHO, UNICEF and the Government of India conducted a seminar in 1978 for chief engineers and bureaucrats across the country and recommended the Sulabh toilet model to be adopted across India. From 1978, Sulabh spread to West Bengal, Odisha, Uttar Pradesh and then all over India. Today, Sulabh has a presence even in other countries like Afghanistan and has trained professionals from 14 African countries to replicate the model.

The important job was to go door-to-door, explain the benefits and motivate people to adopt the new system which did not require manual scavenging. Sulabh would collect the signatures of interested parties, get their papers processed, expedite release of funds and build the toilet. It also provided a guarantee card for a five-year period. If anything went wrong within that period, repair and replacement would be done free of cost. Since the technology was simple, it did not require engineers or other highly educated professionals.

The Organisation

The founder created the culture of the organisation. There was love, compassion, nurturing and a sense of pride and generosity of spirit as well as actual resources. Sulabh, as a self-sustaining entrepreneurial social organisation, has annual revenues. On the one hand, it earns income from building toilets in homes and in public places; on the other, it is paid to maintain them. This income goes out to different directions; money is used towards physical infrastructure, to build and maintain facilities; and for salaries of people who are associate members on a full-time basis and on a project basis. There are also welfare activities. Sulabh runs its own school, vocational classes for young men and women and does other such activities, mainly for the benefit of manual scavengers and their families. Hence, there is no concept of profit, only sustainability.

Pathak's lasting contribution is the public toilet complexes in cities and lakhs of twin pit toilets in homes all over the country. This is only the outward manifestation. This is a sanitation revolution. And his mission is to fulfil the dream of Mahatma Gandhi, to make India manual scavenger-free. It is his mission to educate these scavengers, get them into new occupations, make them part of the mainstream. This dream has been realised. The same people who were once considered untouchables, dirty and unfit to be a part of society are now human beings. Women, who once had only scavenging as a source of livelihood, are now running small businesses. They can enter the houses of people for whom they did the scavenging work, sit on a sofa and share a cup of tea with the lady of the house. They enter temples, where they were earlier, never allowed.

Insights from Sociology

Pathak's knowledge and insight of sociology has instilled in him a multifaceted approach, and it came to his help here. Social research teaches that if somebody wants to work for the cause of a community then first and foremost, one has to build a rapport with the community to know in detail their attitudes, lifestyle, behaviour and share food with them so that one could come up with knowledge and information about the community in-depth and also in detail. Thus, towards this end, to build a rapport with the untouchables, Pathak went and lived in the colony of untouchables in Bettiah, a small town in Bihar, for three months; coincidentally the same place from where Mahatma Gandhi had started his freedom movement.

When he was going to live with these untouchables, his father was upset and sad. The Brahmin community turned against him and his father-in-law was furious. He was absolutely against Pathak's living with the untouchables in their territory and also working in the field of sanitation and building toilets. But Pathak was determined, "So far as untouchability is concerned, either I will be successful or I will get lost. But I cannot just sit and watch," he said.

It was certainly a very oppressive situation that a person, once born as an untouchable, will die as an untouchable. There is no scheme for these untouchables to escape from the social prison where they have to remain imprisoned for life. One can be released from actual prison someday, but not from this social prison created by society. If they take to selling vegetables or anything else, no person will buy things from them. They have no alternative and are destined to do this job for life. Pathak was in two minds whether to continue this work or not, because of the opposition from his family and the Brahmin community. But he ignored his family, his caste, his community and took a solemn vow to fulfil the dream of Mahatma Gandhi to rescue the untouchables.

Once again, the tools of sociological research came to his rescue. Sociology teaches that for doing any research, there should be some tools developed to test the hypothesis of the research. Here, the tool required was a flush toilet which did not require manual cleaning, which could replace the bucket or dry toilets cleaned by human scavengers.

In those days, hardly any house or schools in rural areas had toilets.. Pathak studied in four village schools, none of them had toilets. Women were the worst sufferers because they had to go for defecation in the open, either before sunrise or after sunset. Sometimes, they were bitten by snakes or scorpions and at other times, they were subjected to criminal assault and also molestation. Further, a large number of children used to die because of diarrhoea, dehydration, cholera and dysentery. In fact, his sister died because of diarrhoea while she was being taken to a hospital. In urban areas, 85 per cent of the houses used to be served by the bucket toilets cleaned by manual scavengers; and public places had no facilities of maintained toilets and baths. The general picture was miserable.

Hence, Pathak had to find a suitable technology which would be appropriate, affordable, indigenous and culturally acceptable. The technology available at that time was the sewerage system which was costly in construction as well as in maintenance, and required an enormous quantity of water to flush. So, by this sewer technology, it was not possible to stop open defecation or manual cleaning of human excreta by the untouchables. Very little work had been done in this sphere and only rudimentary literature was available on the subject. Pathak went through the literature. Here, application of the mind was more important than knowledge. Knowledge can be borrowed but we need to apply our minds in such a way that there is a breakthrough.

To overcome these constraints, Pathak innovated and developed the twin pit pour-flush compost toilet and gave it the name 'Sulabh Shauchalaya'.

Sulabh Shauchalaya also helped to economise the use of water which was the need of the time. Sulabh toilets require only one litre of water for flushing while the conventional toilet requires 10 litres. More important, in this kind of toilet, manual scavenging is not required. Thus, the Sulabh toilet became a tool of social change. Mahatma Gandhi got freedom for the country through the tool of the spinning wheel the Industrial Revolution in Europe started from the tool of the Spinning Jenny. Similarly, this Sulabh Shauchalaya has become a tool of social change and has brought about transforming society and the social system. In fact, this technological innovation was a landmark in the history of sanitation, marking a quantum leap and paradigm shift from the conventional centralised system (the sewerage system) of treatment of human waste to the decentralised system (Sulabh Shauchalaya), which is affordable, accessible, easy to construct and suits a country like India.

The third tool of sociology which Pathak used was methodology. He used methodology to get the bucket toilets converted to Sulabh shauchalayas. It was decided that Sulabh International Social Service Organisation will work as the catalytic agency between the government, local bodies and the beneficiaries. Sulabh workers will go house-to-house to motivate and educate the beneficiaries and if they agree, get the form filled up to obtain loan and grant from the local bodies and then build the toilets as per the design and specifications. To convince the government, local bodies and beneficiaries, a five-year guarantee card would be issued to rectify the defects if any, free of cost.

The job of the government and local bodies was to mobilise resources, to do monitoring and supervision; while the work of motivation, education, communication, training, designing, estimation, implementation, maintenance and follow-up would be done by Sulabh. Consequently, with close cooperation and collaboration, the programme became very successful. So far, Sulabh alone has converted 1.3 million bucket toilets into Sulabh flush toilets and lakhs of manual scavengers have been freed from manual cleaning of human faeces and the shackles of untouchability.

Rehabilitation of Manual Scavengers

After the manual scavengers were relieved from this subhuman occupation, to rehabilitate and to bring them in the mainstream of society (which was the dream of Mahatma Gandhi), Dr Pathak took the help of the other tool enunciated by Gandhiji, the tool of non-violence. Here, he took the help of the upper caste people and persuaded them to sit with these scavengers and dine with them. For attaining the goal, he did not agitate against the social order of the upper caste. He did not tear or burn the books of the Manusmriti or other scriptures. He did not say a single word against anybody. Rather, he persuaded the upper caste people to have social interaction with the manual scavengers. He changed their mind, thoughts, behaviour and attitude towards toilets, sanitation and those who used to work cleaning the toilets.

When Pathak started his work in 1960, nobody used to talk about toilets. It was a cultural taboo, especially with regard to sharing of food and there was no question of sitting, meeting and eating food with the untouchables. First, he started educating them on how to read, write and how to put their signatures wherever required because education is the key to human development.

As Gandhiji had given emphasis on basic education, Pathak also started giving them vocational education in different trades like making pappadam, noodles, pickles; stitching, tailoring, embroidery; and beauty parlour training so that they could earn their livelihood and be self-reliant. The products made by them are being sold in markets and hotels and they also sell pappadams and noodles in the same homes where earlier they used to go and clean toilets. Apart from stitching, tailoring, fashion designing and carpet weaving, they also do beauty care jobs and go house-to-house to do facials for the same women in whose houses they used to clean toilets. Most of their clients provide them with tea and breakfast and chat with them.

Pathak invoked sociology and decided to help them to perform rites, rituals and ceremonies of the upper caste people. He took these untouchables to temples where their entry was banned. He accompanied them to the famous Nathdwara temple, worshipped with them alongside upper caste people, and the then president, R. Venkataraman and prime minister, Rajiv Gandhi, also gave them an audience.

These untouchables were also taken on a trip to Varanasi to see the sacred Ganges which they had never seen before, where they got a chance to worship Lord Shiva; most important, 200 Brahmin men with their wives and children shared food with these untouchables in the holy city of Varanasi. That had never happened earlier in history. Pathak also took them to pay obeisance at the dargah of Ajmer Sharif, the Convent of Jesus and Mary at Delhi and the Gurudwara Sahib at Rakabganj so that they may have a feel and experience of other religions as well.

They were active participants in the World Toilet Summit held in New Delhi in 2007 where delegates from all over the world had participated. They went to the United States and participated in the proceedings of the United Nations General Assembly where they also walked the ramp along with top Indian and American fashion models in a fashion show before a galaxy of diplomats from all corners of the globe. They also went to see the Statue of Liberty, a symbol of equality, liberty and freedom; that they are no longer untouchables. They also went to France to attend the Summit at Le Havre and Marseilles and finally, they visited the Phoenix Ashram of Mahatma Gandhi in Durban, South Africa, where Gandhi lived and started his movement. And on that visit they proudly proclaimed, "Oh Bapu, because of you we are free from bondage and the shackles of untouchability and social discrimination."

Education holds the key to any major change and development. With the objective of imparting quality education, Sulabh Public School, a premium English-medium school, was set up in Delhi in 1992. The school aims at preparing children from the weaker sections of society for a better life by bringing quality education within the reach of boys and girls from manual scavenger families. Apart from academic activities, co-curricular activities are regularly organised in the school to promote social integration among students.

Nai Disha, a vocational training centre, has also been set up by Sulabh for the women liberated from manual scavenging so that they can acquire skills in various trades, engage in gainful employment, start a new life and can easily assimilate to mainstream. At one point of time when they were engaged in manual scavenging, people looked at them with contempt. But now, the same people are using goods, articles and eatables prepared by these women gladly and treat them at par with others. Besides establishing neat and clean toilet complexes and liberating manual scavengers, Sulabh has also set up a number of vocational training institutes throughout the country. The purpose of imparting vocational training to them is to give them new means of livelihood, alleviate their poverty and bring them into the mainstream of society.

Sulabh Expansion

Dr Pathak did not restrict himself to sanitation activities. His vision is broad, encompassing the whole of humanity. This made him extend a helping hand to the needy in any walk of life. The Hon'ble Supreme Court in an order, directed the National Legal Services Authority (NALSA) to contact Sulabh International Social Service Organisation to find out whether it could come forward to help the 1,780 elderly widows living in four government shelters in Vrindavan. Vrindavan has become host to widows from all over India, shunned by society when their husbands die, not for religious reasons but because of tradition as well as the financial drain on their families. They pass their days in abject poverty and beg in the streets; and wait on the steps outside temples for scraps of food and alms. Even when they die there is nobody to take care of their cremation. On getting this request, without giving a second thought, Pathak went to Vrindavan and was terribly moved by the plight of these widows and the conditions that they live in. Immediately, he gave them the necessary monetary help and within a month thereafter, each of these widows gets an honorarium of ₹1000 a month for their needs from Sulabh. Sulabh has also provided five ambulances to each of the five widow shelter homes along with doctors and nurses; eye and medical check-ups are also held regularly. Nearly 500 widows have been provided with spectacles as well as other health requirements by the organisation. Above all, Sulabh has given them what they required most—affection, compassion, respect and dignity.

Another area in which Sulabh has played a pioneering role is the development of the concept of community latrines by constructing public toilets on pay-and-use basis. Dr Pathak took the initiative in reviving and giving concrete shape to the concept of public toilets, which already had a place in the Bengal Municipal Act, 1876 (amended in 1878), on 'pay-and -use' basis in Bihar in the year 1974. This was a landmark in the history of sanitation. The system of operating and maintaining community toilets with bathing and urinal facilities (popularly known as Sulabh Shauchalaya Complex), with attendants round the clock, was initiated in Patna on 'pay-and-use' basis with people's participation. This Patna experiment has been replicated throughout the country. Besides toilets, bathing and urinal facilities, some more amenities like public telephone, primary healthcare, drinking water etc. have also been provided at Sulabh Shauchalaya complexes.

Sulabh toilet complexes have electricity, 24 hours' water supply and soap powder supplied free to users for washing hands. The complexes have separate enclosures for men and women. Children, differently-abled persons and those who cannot afford to pay the fee are allowed to use the facility free of charge. These toilet complexes are being constructed at public places like bus stands, markets, railway stations, hospitals, etc. Sulabh has constructed more than 8,000 public toilets at important places all over the country which are being used by more than 15 million people every day; 200 of them are linked with biogas plants.

Sulabh International Social Service Organisation has also worked in Afghanistan and Bhutan. At the request of the External Affairs Ministry, Government of India, Sulabh constructed five toilet complexes with biogas plants in Kabul. These projects have been executed and completed in collaboration with Kabul Municipality. These toilet complexes have been handed over to Kabul Municipality and are in operation. In collaboration with the Royal Government of Bhutan, Sulabh International Social Service Organisation has also constructed public toilets in Bhutan and is planning to do the same in Uganda and 50 other countries.

Recycling and reuse of human excreta for biogas generation is an important way to get rid of health hazards from human excreta. Sulabh is a pioneering organisation in the field of biogas generation from public toilet complexes. The human excreta-based biogas technology design developed by Sulabh does not require manual handling of human excreta and there is complete recycling and resource recovery from the wastes. Biogas is utilised for cooking, lighting mantle lamps, electricity generation and is being converted into energy to be used for lighting street-lights and such other uses. The sludge at the bottom of the digester can be used as fertiliser.

Sulabh has also provided training and orientation courses to government employees, especially local bodies. Some government departments in India and abroad have been sending their employees to learn this technology. The Sulabh model has been adopted by a number of countries including China, Bhutan, Bangladesh, Afghanistan, Burkina Faso, Ghana, Kenya, Mali, Nigeria, Senegal, Tanzania and Zambia for expansion and promotion of sanitation facilities.

The Sulabh International Museum of Toilets, located in the Sulabh International Social Service Organisation campus, is a rare museum in the world. A large number of visitors, both from within the country and abroad, have shown keen interest in the toilet museum and they have found it very informative, fascinating and useful. The museum has a rare collection of artefacts, pictures and objects detailing the historic evolution of toilets since 2500 BCE. It gives a chronology of developments relating to toilet technology, toilet-related social customs and etiquettes, and the sanitary conditions and legislative efforts of many countries. It has an extensive display of privies, chamber pots, toilet furnitures, bidets and water closets in use from 1145 CE to modern times.

In the journey of sanitation, spanning nearly five decades, Pathak has imbibed truth, honesty, integrity, ethics and morality to create confidence among different cultures and communities, political parties, the government and the people in general. Gandhiji said, "An ounce of practice is worth more than tons of preaching." True, knowledge and action are both important. In this direction, Dr Pathak has made the earnest request that sanitation should be included as a discipline in sociology because the core problem areas like social deprivation, hygiene, ecology, water, public health, poverty, gender equality, welfare of children etc., require sociological intervention with spiritual and philosophical knowledge. Hence, he has termed it Sociology of Sanitation.

Pathak is a great humanist and social reformer of contemporary India. He has the vision of a philosopher and the undying zeal of a missionary. He is an icon of sanitation and social reform who has made a difference in the lives of millions of people. In fact, he has turned the pages of history. With his efforts, the formerly untouchables have been allowed by society to mingle with others, to live on par with them, dine with them and offer prayers in temples. He has created a new culture which embraces the poor and upholds the dignity of labour. His boundless love for the downtrodden finds expression in innumerable and tangible ways. Dr Pathak is the leader of an international crusade for restoration of human rights and dignity to millions of manual scavengers; and for providing a safe and hygienic human waste disposal system which can benefit 700 million Indians who go for open defecation, even along the roads and railway tracks. It is a far grimmer scenario when womenfolk have to go out to defecate in the open, at the cost of their dignity and risking criminal assault.

Dr Pathak's multi-pronged efforts in bringing manual scavengers, the worst victims of institutionalised caste discrimination, who are engaged in a subhuman occupation, to the mainstream of society, have taken the shape of a movement for social justice. Moreover, he is an internationally acclaimed expert on sanitation and has developed and implemented, on a pan-Indian scale, a low-cost and appropriate toilet technology which has been recommended as a Global Best Practice. To him goes the credit of sensitising Indians towards sanitation and those engaged in the sanitation work. Apart from low-cost sanitation, his contributions are widely known in the areas of bioenergy and biofertiliser, liquid and solid waste management, poverty alleviation and an integrated rehabilitation programme for the liberated scavengers. In fact, he is a Renaissance man and combines in himself the traits of a social scientist, an engineer, an administrator and an institution-builder. What is remarkable is that he has ingeniously utilised all this expertise to enrich and empower the oppressed classes, improve community health and hygiene and the environment. Thus, he is fulfilling the dreams of Mahatma Gandhi.

Dr Pathak is the first person in India instrumental in constructing more than 7,500 public toilets in slums and at public, religious and tourist places, maintaining them on a pay-and-use basis, without putting a burden on the public exchequer. More than 10 million people are using these facilities daily. The practice of untouchability due to scavenging, which is centuries old, has almost been removed. Earlier, talking about a toilet was taboo in Indian society, but now, people talk freely about Sulabh toilets. Because of his painstaking efforts and untiring zeal, he has been able to bring about a change in the thoughts, behaviour and attitudes of Indians about sanitation and those engaged in sanitation work.

Environmental cleanliness and sanitation were subjects closest to Mahatma Gandhi's heart; he had proclaimed, "Cleanliness is next only to godliness". Gandhi also said, "There are many things to do, let each one of us choose our task and stick to it through thick and thin. Let us pick up that position which we can handle best." Gandhiji had two ideas in mind while talking about sanitation. The first was that no one should clean and carry excreta of others, just to earn livelihood. There must be some scientific method of human waste disposal. Finding no other affordable alternative during his lifetime, Gandhiji had suggested "*Tatti par mitti*" (cover human excreta with soil) or use of a trench which he himself did while living in Phoenix Ashram in South Africa. Secondly, Gandhiji wanted those engaged in sanitation work not to be treated as untouchables. He took pains to emphasise that they should get equal respect in society; and in his typical style went on to declare, "The Bhangi (scavenger) is as important as the Viceroy."

After Gandhiji, Dr Pathak is the man, more than any other in India, who has championed the cause of adequate sanitation and made uplifting the untouchables his mission in life. For the past five decades, he has been working relentlessly to keep the ecosystem clean and bring the marginalised sections of society to the mainstream. He has given a new dimension to the Gandhian movement and broad-based his principled fight against all kinds of discrimination. The *New York Times*, in its article, "Untouchables Gain the Help of a Brahmin" (13 November 1989), hailed Dr Pathak as a "fulltime crusader against the humiliations of untouchability".

In 1996, the Sulabh technology was declared one of the Global Urban Best Practices at the Habitat-II Conference held at Istanbul. The UN Economic and Social Council granted Special Consultative Status to Sulabh in recognition of its outstanding service. "You are helping the poor;" lauded Pope John Paul II while honouring Dr Pathak with the International Saint Francis Prize for the Environment in 1992. The President of India conferred on him the Padma Bhushan, a very prestigious national award for his distinguished service to the nation. The United Nations Environment Programme (UNEP), while electing Dr Pathak for the Global 500 Roll of Honour, 2003, wrote about him: "As a staunch defender of the environment, UNEP is honoured to pay tribute to your commitment and we hope that this recognition will encourage you to continue your work. Please accept our heartfelt congratulations." Honours and acclaim, both national and international, have become a dime a dozen for Dr Pathak. What inspires him is the deep love of his country, its people and their problems.

Among the prominent awards Pathak received are the Padma Bhushan in 1991 and the International Saint Francis Prize for the Environment "Canticle of All Creatures" in 1992. He also received the Bombay Citizens' Award in 1992, the Indira Gandhi Priyadarshini Award in 1994, the Babu Jagjivan Ram Award for abolishing scavenging in 1997, and the Indira Gandhi Paryavaran Award in 2003. Here is the list of awards and honours conferred on Pathak at different times in recognition of his service in the field of sanitation.

Awards and Honours Conferred on Dr Bindeshwar Pathak

1. K.P. Goenka Memorial Award, 1984
2. Prabandhak Mahan Muzzaffarpur, 1990
3. Builders' Information Bureau Award, 1990
4. Civic Betterment Award at Bombay, 1990-91
5. Padma Bhushan, 1991
6. National Citizens' Award,1991
7. The International Saint Francis Prize for the Environment "Canticle of All Creatures", at Assisi, Italy, 1992
8. Dr Pinnamaneni and Smt Seethadevi Foundation Award, 1992
9. Bombay Citizen's Award, 1992
10. Shahid Bhup Singh Award for Social Work, 1992
11. Anne Mukhopadhya Award for Social Work, 1992
12. Rotary International Spectra-93, Par Excellence Award for Protection of Environment, 1993
13. Ratna Shiromani Award given by India International Society for Unity, 1993
14. Indira Gandhi Priyadarshini Award, 1994
15. NRI Gold Award, 1994
16. Manav Sewa Puraskar, 1995
17. Vikas Ratna Award, 1995
18. Limca Book of Records' Man of the Year Award, 1995
19. Global Urban Best Practices by United Nations Centre for Human Settlements (UNCHS) at Istanbul, 1996
20. Babu Jagjivan Ram Award for Abolishing Scavenging, 1997
21. Michael Madhusudan Dutt Award, 1997
22. Distinguished Leadership Award, 1997
23. Samaj Ratna Award at Lucknow, 1999
24. Dubai International Award for Best Practices, 2000
25. Global 500 Roll of Honour Award by UNEP at Beirut, Lebanon, 2003
26. Scroll of Honour by UN Habitat at Rio de Janeiro, Brazil, 2003
27. Indira Gandhi Paryavaran Puraskar, 2003
28. Good Corporate Citizen Award, 2005
29. Sakshi Bharat Award, 2006
30. International Human Rights Award, 2006

31. One India One People Foundation Award, 2006
32. Maharana Uday Singh Award, 2006
33. Lifetime Achievement Award for Leadership in the social sector by Dr P.N. Singh Foundation, 2007
34. Bharat Gaurav Award by Citizen Forum of Human Rights, New Delhi, 2007
35. Aryavart Shikhar Samman by The Indian Nation Publication, 2007
36. Hindi Vachaspati Award by Rashtriya Hindi Parisad, Meerut, 2008
37. National Energy Globe Award, by Energy Globe, Belgium, 2008
38. Rashtriya Gaurav Award by Institute for Environment Yoga & Social Security, Delhi, 2008
39. Hall of Fame Award by World Toilet Organization at World Toilet Summit at Macau, China, 2008
40. Stockholm Water Prize by Stockholm International Water Institute at Stockholm, Sweden, 2009
41. Vishwa Bhojpuri and Indian Diaspora Sammaan, 2009
42. Sat Paul Mittal Award at Ludhiana, 2009
43. FACE Award 2008 by FACE magazine, 2009
44. Sanitation Visionary Award by World Toilet Organization at Singapore, 2009
45. Bihar Ratna Award at Patna, 2010
46. National Award for Innovations in the Services for the Urban Poor by The India Urban Space Foundation, 2010

Fellowships

1. International Biographical Research Foundation (Nagpur, India) recognised Dr Bindeshwar Pathak's work and selected him as a Fellow for his distinguished standing and outstanding contribution in the field of 'Social Reforms, Low-Cost Sanitation and Rural Development.'
2. Honorary Fellow of The Institution of Public Health Engineers (Kolkata, India)
3. Honorary Fellow of Indian Water Works
4. Honorary Fellow of Indian Public Health Association, Kolkata, India
5. Senior Fellow of Ashoka Innovators for the Public, a global association of leading social entrepreneurs
6. Fellow, American Biographical Research Association, USA

7. Fellow, International Biographical Association, England
8. Fellow, the National Academy of Sciences, India

Membership in Organisations

1. Life Member, Indian Science Congress
2. Life Member, Museum Association of India
3. Member, International Water Academy (Norway)
4. Member, Indian Association of Action Sociologists
5. Member, Council for Advancement of People's Action and Rural Technology (CAPART)

Nomination as Member of Various Committees of the Government of India

1. Task Force on Problems of Scavenging, Planning Commission, Government of India
2. Socially Oriented and Rural Energy Programmes, Ministry of Non-Conventional Energy Sources,, Government of India
3. High-Power Committee on Urban Solid Waste Management in India, Ministry of Urban Affairs and Employment, Government of India
4. Steering Committee on Drinking Water Supply and Sanitation (Rural and Urban). The Committee was constituted by the Planning Commission for formulation of the Tenth Five-Year Plan (2002-2007)
5. Working Group on Urban Development–Urban Water Supply and Sanitation and Urban Environment for the Tenth Five-Year Plan, Planning Commission, Government of India
6. Tenth Plan Steering Committee on the Empowerment of Scheduled Castes, other Backward Classes and Minorities, Planning Commission, Government of India
7. National Environmental Council, Ministry of Environment and Forests, Government of India
8. National Waste Management Council, Government of India.
9. Steering Committee for UN Habitat-II, Ministry of Urban Affairs and Employment, Government of India
10. Monitoring Committee on the Liberation and Rehabilitation of Scavengers. Ministry of Social Justice and Empowerment, Government of India

11. Central Advisory Council, Ministry of Industry, Government of India
12. Advisory Committee for Non-Conventional Energy Sources, Government of India
13. Sub-Group of Environment and Health, Ministry of Health, Government of India
14. Committee for Evolving a Co-ordinative System for Implementing Low-Cost Sanitation and Scavengers' Liberation Programme, constituted by Housing and Urban Development Corporation, Government of India

Conferences and Seminars attended:

- International—over 70
- Conferences, seminars and workshops in India—over 250

What other Leaders Say...

> "I congratulate you for what you have achieved, which you richly deserve, for which there is no comparison. You have done such a great job and I would like to tell you that Dr Bindeshwar Pathak has brought about a revolution, a very big revolution. Financial revolution can come about and can be brought about, but to bring a revolution in the mindset of people is a very big achievement, a very difficult job which Dr Pathak has brought about. He increased your self-respect, your self-confidence and not only your own self-confidence but also showed to society what you are worth and what you can do. Whatever he has shown everyone sees. The whole country looks at it and every village looks at it and tries to do what he has done. If Mahatma Gandhi was watching today's function from heaven, his eyes would be brimming with tears of joy. I do not think any other programme in the country would give so much happiness to Mahatma Gandhi as this one."
>
> —**Pratibha Devi Singh Patil,** former Hon'ble President of India.

On the occasion when the liberated scavenger women of Alwar visited the President after their visit to the UN and the US to participate in Mission Sanitation, at Rashtrapati Bhawan, New Delhi (25 July 2008).

◆

Timothy J. Roemer, former US Ambassador to India, while addressing students at the University of Notre Dame, Indiana, USA, on 21 May 2011, told them a motivational, inspiring story, giving the example of Sulabh and Dr Pathak. The relevant extract is stated here:

> "To motivate you, let me tell you a story about…toilets! India is a country with many inspiring people. There is, of course, Mahatma Gandhi, the father of the nation. His teachings of tolerance really are the key to the success of democracy in India and he has influenced civil rights movements around the world including in the United States. There is Mother Teresa, who lived and worked in India although her legacy now touches the lives of children, women, and the poor all over the world. There is Rabindranath Tagore, the first non-European to win the Nobel Prize for Literature.
>
> But there are also many inspiring people, lesser known to the world, like Dr Bindeshwar Pathak. Dr Pathak, although from a very high caste, knew at a very young age that there was nothing wrong with touching the untouchables. He has dedicated his life to restoring the human rights and providing dignity to scavengers, which is the bottom-rung caste in India responsible for cleaning up human waste.
>
> To do so, he used technology to develop a safe and environment-friendly toilet to replace pit latrines, reducing the need for scavenging and improving sanitation and hygiene for both rural and urban poor. He provided education to the children of scavengers, helping to break the never-ending family cycle of scavenging. He provided alternative economic opportunities so that women no longer have to clean toilets for the rest of their lives to provide for their families.
>
> All this has helped tackle a bigger problem—breaking down the caste system in India.
>
> As you leave Notre Dame today, I hope you will remember the story of Dr Pathak. He did not start out to change the world. He started out to help some scavengers in a few villages in Bihar, a small state in the north of India on the Nepal border. As you start out today, you do not have to change the world overnight. But I encourage you to try to make a difference. As you walk out these doors and leave this campus for your final time as a student, follow

the counsel of President John Quincy Adams, who said, 'March then with firm, with steady, with undeviating step, to the prize of your high calling. Consecrate above all, the faculties of life to the cause of truth, of freedom, and of humanity.'"

◆

Prof. Raj Mohan Gandhi, the grandson of Mahatma Gandhi, visited the Sulabh campus in 2010 with students of the University of Illinois, USA. He was so overwhelmed that he stated:

"I am the son of the son of Mahatma Gandhi but Dr Bindeshwar Pathak is the son of his soul. If we were to go to meet Mohandas Karamchand Gandhi, he would first greet Dr Pathak for the noble work that he is doing and then meet me. Dr Pathak has restored human rights and dignity to people engaged in the manual cleaning of human excreta which they carried as head-load."

◆

"The Sulabh movement is indeed a reminder and jolt to conscience. It is performing the double task of socially rehabilitating the suffering segment of our society and providing healthy and clean municipal life. It deserves all support."

—**I.K. Gujral**, former Prime Minister of India.

◆

"I read with great sympathy your account of the situation of the scavengers' community, and I congratulate you on the work which you are doing on its behalf. I am sure your International Saint Francis Prize for the Environment was richly deserved."

—**Boutros Boutros-Ghali**, former UN Secretary General (after Dr Pathak was awarded the International Saint Francis Prize for the Environment—"Canticle of All Creatures"—in 1992).

◆

"The centre of Sulabh is everything I imagined and much more. A centre of inspiration, liberation and human vitality. I will remember forever this visit and remain a disciple and willing promotee of their wonderful ideas and activities in an area most people are too shy even to talk about. Nearly everything which works began with an idea and a small group of people committed to work to realise it. Thank you, Dr Pathak and your co-workers, for your inspiration and achievements."

—**Sir Richard Jolly**, Special Advisor to the Administrator, UNDP and Chairman, Collaboration Council for Drinking Water and Sanitation.

◆

"As a staunch defender of the environment, UNEP is honoured to pay tribute to your commitment and we hope that this recognition 'Global 500 Roll of Honour' will encourage you to continue your work. Please accept my heartfelt congratulations."

—**Klaus Toepfer**, Executive Director, UNDP.

◆

"Technology from Sulabh can help alleviate the water and sanitation problems in a big way if replicated in other countries. We can achieve the MDGs within the prescribed period with the help of a social organisation like Sulabh."

—**Margaret Catley-Carlson**, Global Water Partnership.

◆

"One organisation which works to improve the state of sanitation in the country is Sulabh, founded by Dr Bindeshwar Pathak in 1970. Sulabh is the largest internationally recognised pan-Indian social service outfit with over 35,000 volunteers. It began through Pathak's desire to help scavenger men and women who carry and dispose of human excreta. He developed a two-pit pour–flush toilet (known as the Sulabh Shauchalaya) which did not require scavenging to clean. Subsequently, Sulabh also started pay-and-use public toilets, popularly known as Sulabh Complexes, with bath, laundry and toilet facilities. These are used by about 10 million people every day. Sulabh has also pioneered the production of biogas and biofertiliser from excreta-based plants."

—**Dr A.P.J. Abdul Kalam**, former President of India.

◆

"Now that the world is shrinking, leaders of the world unite to initiate a global approach to the problems of sanitation and water supply which have also become a tool for social change. In this field, the role of Sulabh International Social Service Organisation is crucial. Sulabh is a known name not only in India but also in other countries. I have read about Sulabh and now I know how Sulabh makes things happen."

—**Dr Jan P. Pronk**, Chairman, Water Supply and Sanitation Collaborative Council.

◆

"The Sulabh technology is revolutionary. The efficacy of the system lies in its cost effectiveness and hence can be accepted globally. We are definitely going to mention Sulabh technologies and initiatives in our report."

—**Roberto Lenton**, Chairman, UN Millennium Development Goal Task Force on Water and Sanitation.

◆

"Pathak founded the organisation Sulabh International in 1970. It is now India's largest charity, with 50,000 on its staff. Millions of Indians have installed the Sulabh Shauchalaya latrine. Of more interest to non- Indians will be the half a million public toilets that Sulabh had built all over India. Every day, 10 million Indians, and plenty of relieved foreign travellers use a Sulabh toilet, because they are in railway stations, airports, on the main streets of India's cities. Pathak's toilet blocks are so common, Indians now say 'I'm going to the Sulabh,' and the word toilet can be left silent."

—**Rose George**, A noted writer in *Doing Good Well.*

◆

"In India we have already witnessed the dramatic impact that ordinary citizens can have. Bindeshwar Pathak's invention of the toilet—the Sulabh shauchalya, built to function with little water and a self-cleaning pit—has done more than any bans on discrimination in helping put an end to the sordid work of manual scavenging that the Dalit Bhangi caste had been forced into for centuries."

—**Nandan Nilekani**, Co-chairman, Infosys Technologies Ltd., in *Imagining India.*

◆

"Sulabh created a low-cost toilet technology that not only helped maintain sanitation but also restored the dignity of millions of 'scavengers', the cleaners of human excreta who are traditionally untouchables. The West's toilet technology, composed of sewage and septic tanks, was unaffordable for India's teeming millions. Pathak's technology relies on two simple pits and sealed covers. While one pit is in use, the other is left to decompose, forming a fertiliser that can be used in agricultural fields. Equally important, human waste no longer requires manual cleansing."

—**Jorge Paulo Lehmann**, Professor, Harvard Business School, in *Billions of Entrepreneurs.*

◆

"Dr Pathak's contributions are unparalleled and only one of its kind in the world."

—**Prof. Hidemi Yoshid**, Associate Professor, Hosei University, Tokyo, Japan, on 11 March 2015.

◆

"Homage to Sulabh International, for vision of liberation of millions of scavengers. Abraham Lincoln liberated five million black slaves, Sulabh dreams of liberating 20 million rejected for handling dirt. All honour to Dr Bindeshwar Pathak for actualising Gandhiji's dream of abolishing untouchability.

As author of a novel, Untouchable, written in Sabarmati Ashram, I am proud to be associated with this liberation movement. I congratulate Dr Pathak and his associates for the persistent, organised and imaginative initiatives in the struggle to free the untouchables from bonded labour. May the dream be realised in the whole of our country."

—**Mulk Raj Anand**, noted writer, novelist, on 2 March 1989.

◆

"We appreciate the efforts the Sulabh International and its Founder, Dr Bindeshwar Pathak are taking to make India a scavenging-free country, which was the dream of Gandhiji. We would like to collaborate with Dr Pathak in our youth programmes."

—**N. Radhakrishnan**, Director, Gandhi Smriti Anad Darshan Samiti, on 3 November 1990.

◆

"Sulabh International showed me a good example. This organisation has proved how effective small-scale solutions can be and how they can be extended all over India within a short time span. Thousands of 'Pay and Use' public toilet-cum-bath complexes and more than a million pour-flush latrines in private houses have been built (and are maintained) and they are used by more than 10 million people every day. By doing so, Sulabh has restored human dignity and given a new future to thousands of untouchables."

—**HRH Willem-Alexander**, the Prince of Orange of the Netherlands and Chairman of the United Nations' Secretary-General's Advisory Board of Water and Sanitation (UNSGAB) at launch of International Year of Sanitation in New York on 21 November 2007.

What the Leader said....

The distance is long and the day is short; let us hurry home, travellers, before sundown; target to liberate all scavengers in the country is still too far away and, hence, we have to speed up work. Scavengers and their families look to us for their salvation; let us not disappoint them, or else we shall be accountable to history and future generations.

◆

A society cannot long endure half touchable, half untouchable. Scavengers are more sinned against than sinning. They carry human excreta on their head, flitting between the dark lanes and bylanes, only to live far out of colonies where they suffer only because, in the hoary past, their forefathers lost in wars against foreigners while defending the country. And were later made captives to carry human excreta on their heads. This is the history of the scavengers which we refuse to remember and continue to punish them for no fault of theirs. This is a guilt we are living with.

◆

"It was certainly not as crucial as the invention of the wheel, nor as important as the making of the lever which 'could lift the globe'." (Dr Pathak added a pit and water sealed the pan to produce a technology which promises to free over half a million scavengers who still carry human excreta on their heads, besides providing clean toilet for the people).

◆

When the water closet (WC) was invented for the first time in England, its inventor, a courtier, was banished from the Elizabethan court for discussing as profane a thing as the human excreta disposal system. But, after London was sewered and most houses were fitted with WCs, it was discovered that Harrington was the harbinger of modern civilisation.

◆

The bhangis (scavengers) go about practising their profession of carrying human excreta on the head, generation after generation, without protest or representation to the power that be. They have no forum, no union nor any caste leader to plead for their salvation. These are the defenceless people, almost perpetually waiting for a redeemer who doesn't seem to be coming.

◆

Who says untouchability is a thing of the past? In many parts of the country it still exists, though lawfully banned, due to the need for "scavengers" to service the hundreds of dry latrines used by the population. Institutionally as well as traditionally, untouchables have always been hired to do the job; therefore, no amount of government policies to uplift this section of society has helped eradicate this deeply ingrained caste bias.

◆

I fulfilled the dreams of Mahatma Gandhi by restoring the human rights and dignity of untouchables and brought them into the mainstream of society on a par with others. Tell scavengers after they are freed; we gave our today for their tomorrow.

Chapter 2

SOCIOLOGY OF SANITATION: AN INTRODUCTION

Sanitation is generally understood as the hygienic means of promoting health through prevention of human contact with the hazards of wastes as well as the treatment and proper disposal of sewage or wastewater. Hazards can be physical, microbiological, biological or chemical agents of diseases. Wastes that can cause health problems include human and animal excreta, solid wastes, domestic wastewater (sewage or grey water), industrial wastes and agricultural wastes. Hygienic means of prevention can be by using engineering solutions (e.g., sanitary sewers, sewage treatment, surface runoff management, solid waste management, excreta management), simple technologies (e.g., pit latrines, dry toilets, urine-diverting dry toilets, septic tanks), or even simply by behaviour change in personal hygiene practices, such as hand washing with soap.

Providing sanitation to people requires a system approach, rather than only focusing on the toilet or wastewater treatment plant itself. The experience of the user, excreta and wastewater collection methods, transportation or conveyance of waste, treatment, and reuse or disposal, all need to be thoroughly considered. Therefore, the main objective of a sanitation system is to protect and promote human health by providing a clean environment and breaking the cycle of disease.

For any social and economic development, adequate sanitation in conjunction with good hygiene and safe water are essential. Lack of proper sanitation causes diseases. Most of the diseases resulting from sanitation have a direct relation to poverty. The lack of clean water and poor sanitation cause and spread many diseases and the spread of disease. It is estimated that inadequate sanitation is responsible for 4 per cent of deaths and 5.7 per cent of the disease burden worldwide.

In developing countries, sanitation is a necessity for a healthy life. Lack of sanitation is a serious issue affecting most developing countries and countries in transition. Studies show that the effect of sanitation has impacted human society throughout history. The combination of direct and indirect deaths from malnutrition caused by unsafe water, sanitation and hygiene practices is estimated by WHO to lead to 8,60,000 deaths per year in children under five years of age. The multiple interdependencies between malnutrition and infectious diseases make it very difficult to quantify the extent of malnutrition caused by infectious diseases which are in turn caused by unsafe practices.

Relevant diseases and conditions caused by lack of sanitation and hygiene include:

1. Waterborne diseases, which can contaminate drinking water;
2. Diseases transmitted by the faecal-oral route. Infections with intestinal helminths (worms)--approximately two billion people are infected with soil-transmitted helminths worldwide; they are transmitted by eggs present in human faeces which in turn contaminate the soil where sanitation is poor;
3. Stunted growth in children; and
4. Malnutrition, particularly in children.

The list of diseases that could be reduced with proper access to sanitation and hygiene practices is very long. In India, the following diseases have been listed which could be stamped out by improving sanitation: anaemia, malnutrition, ascariasis (intestinal worm infection), campylobacteriosis, cholera, cyanobacteria toxins, dengue, hepatitis, Japanese encephalitis (JE), leptospirosis, malaria, ringworm or tinea (intestinal worm infection), scabies, schistosomiasis, trachoma, and typhoid and paratyphoid enteric fever. Polio is another disease which is related to improper sanitation and hygiene.

All over the world, 2.6 billion people lack adequate sanitation, the safe disposal of human excreta. In the past, government agencies have typically built sanitation infrastructure, but sanitation professionals are now concentrating on helping people to improve their own sanitation and to change their behaviour. Improved sanitation has significant impacts not only on health, but also on social and economic development, particularly in developing countries.

The health sector has a strong role to play in improving sanitation in developing countries through policy development and the implementation of sanitation programmes. In addition to its impact on health, improved sanitation generates both social and economic benefits. Householders understand these wider benefits; scientists study the motivations of individuals for improving sanitation and changing sanitation behaviour. While the main goal of agencies in sanitation programmes is to improve health, householders rarely adopt and use toilets for health-related reasons. Instead, the main motivations for sanitation adoption and use include the desire for privacy and to avoid embarrassment, wanting to be modern, the desire for convenience and to avoid the discomforts or dangers of the bush (e.g., snakes, pests, rain), and wanting social acceptance or status. For women, the provision of household sanitation reduces the risk of rape and/ or attack experienced when going to public latrines or the bush to defecate, and for girls, the provision of school sanitation facilities means that they are less likely to miss school by staying at home during menstruation.

The economic benefits of improved sanitation include lower health system costs, fewer days lost at work or at school due to illness or caring for an ill relative, and convenience time-saving (time not spent queuing at shared sanitation facilities or walking for open defecation). In total, the prevention of sanitation and water-related diseases could save millions per year in health system costs; the value of deaths averted, based on discounted future earnings, adds to another advantage.

Concept of Sanitation

The ecological approach to sanitation seeks to contain, treat and reuse excreta, minimising contamination and making optimum use of resources. The key issue here is that each community, region or country needs to work out what is the most sensible and cost effective way of thinking about sanitation in the short and long term and then act accordingly.

Professionals opine that sanitation as a whole covers:

1. Safe collection, storage, treatment and disposal/reuse/recycling of human excreta (faeces and urine)

2. Management/reuse/recycling of solid wastes (trash or rubbish)
3. Drainage and disposal/reuse/recycling of household wastewater (often referred to as grey water)
4. Drainage of storm water
5. Treatment and disposal/reuse/recycling of sewage effluents
6. Collection and management of industrial waste products and
7. Management of hazardous wastes (including hospital wastes, and chemical/radioactive and other dangerous substances)

Providing environmentally safe sanitation to millions of people is a significant challenge. The task is even more difficult in a country like India where the introduction of new technologies can challenge people's traditions and beliefs. Inadequate sanitation is a major cause of disease world-wide and improving sanitation ensures significant beneficial impact on health, both in households and across communities.

Progress in sanitation and improved hygiene has greatly improved health, but many people still have no adequate means of disposing of their waste. This is a growing nuisance for highly populated areas, carrying the risk of infectious disease, particularly for vulnerable groups such as the very young, the elderly and people suffering from diseases that lower their resistance. Poorly controlled waste also means daily exposure to an unpleasant environment. The build-up of faecal contamination in rivers and other waters is not just a human risk; other species are also affected, threatening the ecological balance of the environment.

The discharge of untreated wastewater and excreta into the environment affects human health in several ways:

a. By polluting drinking water
b. Entry into the food chain, for example via fruits, vegetables or fish and shellfish
c. Bathing, recreational and other contact with contaminated water
d. By providing breeding sites for flies and insects that spread diseases

The word "sanitation" is derived from the Latin word "Sanitas", which means to protect and promote human health by providing a clean environment and breaking the cycle of disease. It refers to the principles and practices relating to the collection and treatment of refuse as they impact people and the environment (Mullegger, Lanergraber and Lechner: 2011). The word hygiene comes from "Hygeia", the Greek goddess of health, who is the daughter of Aesxulapius, the god of medicine. Since the advent of the Industrial Revolution and the discovery of the germ theory of disease in the second half of the 19th century, hygiene and sanitation have been at the forefront of the struggle against illness and disease (Williams, 1981).

Sanitation is the hygienic means of promoting health through prevention of human contact with the hazards of wastes. WHO states: Sanitation generally refers to the provision of facilities and services for the safe disposal of human urine and faeces. Inadequate sanitation is a major cause of disease world-wide and improving sanitation is known to have a significant beneficial impact on health both in households and across communities. The word "sanitation" also refers to the maintenance of hygienic conditions through services such as garbage collection and wastewater disposal.

The term sanitation can be applied to a specific aspect, concept, location or strategy (Nagla 2015) such as:

1. Improved sanitation refers to the management of human faeces at the household level. This terminology is the indicator used to describe the target of the Millennium Development Goal (MDG) on sanitation, by the WHO/UNICEF Joint Monitoring Programme for Water Supply and Sanitation.
2. On-site sanitation—the collection and treatment of waste is done where it is deposited. Examples are the use of pit latrines, septic tanks and Imhoff tanks.
3. Food sanitation—refers to the hygienic measures for ensuring food safety.
4. Environmental sanitation—it helps the control of environmental factors that form links in disease transmission. Subsets of this category are solid waste management, water and wastewater treatment, industrial waste treatment, and noise and pollution control.
5. Ecological sanitation—it is an approach that tries to emulate nature through the recycling of nutrients and water from human and animal wastes in a hygienically safe manner.

The MDGs included a target to reduce by half the proportion of people without access to basic sanitation by 2015. In December 2006, the United Nations General Assembly declared 2008 "The International Year of Sanitation" in recognition of the slow progress being made towards the MDGs' sanitation target. The year aimed to develop awareness and action to meet the target. The Joint Monitoring Programme (JMP) for Water Supply and Sanitation of WHO and UNICEF (2012) include the following in the improved sanitation: flush toilet, connection to a piped sewer system, connection to a septic system, flush/ pour-flush to a pit latrine, ventilated improved pit (VIP) latrine, pit latrine with slab and composting toilet.

However, according to the JMP report (2012), the world remains off-track for the sanitation target of the MDGs in terms of the percentage of people using improved sanitation. If current trends continue (as quoted in Nagla, 2015), billions of people will lack access to improved sanitation facilities; 15 per cent of the population still practises open defecation (in fields, forests, bushes, bodies of water or other open spaces). Though the proportion of people practising open defecation is decreasing, the absolute number has remained at over one billion for several years, due to population growth. This outcome presents substantial public health risks as the waste could contaminate drinking water and cause life-threatening forms of diarrhoea in infants. Most cities can neither afford a sewage drainage system nor a sewage treatment system.

Though sanitation was a part of human life since ancient times, it gained importance with the development of human civilisation. As human civilisation started to expand with diversity, sanitation became one of the necessities of human society. Social scientists thought that developing sanitation was a major social aspect of life. Now, sanitation has developed as a major subject of study. Thus, socio-cultural aspects of human life forced social thinkers to develop sanitation as a subject of study rather than just as a health science. Sanitation is not only the need of an individual; it is the requirement of society.

According to Bindeshwar Pathak (as quoted in Pais, 2015), in ancient civilisations, there was no problem of sanitation because humans were not provided with latrines or particular places, inside or outside the houses, for defecation. People used open spaces, riverbanks and outskirts of habitats for defecation. With the development of human civilisation, there cropped up the problem of the disposal of human excreta. Further, with the development of the latrine system in civilised societies, people started facing the problem of disposal of human excreta. With the advancement of knowledge, humans implemented different kinds of technologies as a solution on the basis of different conditions prevailing in their habitats. In this way, different kinds of technologies developed throughout the world for protecting the surroundings to maintain better health and hygienic conditions. Hence, sanitation gained importance in human society. Sanitation gained public policy importance only recently in India.

The Seventh Five Year Plan (1985–1990) launched a rural sanitation programme in India that aimed to provide 25 per cent of rural households with individual household sanitary latrines by 1995. Consequently, households with individual sanitary latrines increased from 1 per cent in 1981 to 9 per cent in 1991. In 1999, the Central Rural Sanitation Programme was restructured into a demand-responsive community-led Total Sanitation Campaign (TSC). The Zila Parishads and other district-level project implementation agencies currently implement TSC as a district-level project model. While the UN declared 2008 the International Year of Sanitation, the Ministry of Urban Development, Government of India, launched the National Urban Sanitation Policy (NUSP) that same year. November 19 is celebrated as World Toilet Day to raise awareness on the use of toilets, sanitation and clean water.

Sanitation in India

India may be on-track in achieving the MDGs' sanitation target of 2008. MDGs simply represent achievable levels if countries commit the resources and power to accomplish them. They do not necessarily represent acceptable levels of service. This is especially true of India's sanitation situation. Despite recent progress, access to improved sanitation remains far lower in India compared to many countries. An estimated 55 per cent or close to 600 million people still do not have access to any kind of toilet. Among these, those who live in urban slums and rural areas are affected the most. In rural areas, the gravity of the problem is particularly disappointing, as 74 per cent of the rural population still defecates in the open. Household income is very low and the idea of building a facility for defecation in or near the house is not affordable. Where facilities exist, they are often inadequate. The sanitation landscape in India still consists of 13 million unsanitary bucket latrines, which require manual scavenging. Over 7,00,000 Indians still make their living this way (Sulabh 2013).

The situation in urban areas is not as critical as in rural areas. However, the sanitation problems in crowded environments are typically more serious and immediate. Here, the main challenge is to ensure safe environmental sanitation. Even in areas where households have toilets, the contents of bucket latrines and pits, even of sewers, are often emptied without regard for environmental and health considerations. Sewerage systems, if they exist, mostly are poorly maintained. Today, with more than 20 Indian cities with populations of more than one million people, including Indian megacities such as Kolkata, Mumbai and New Delhi, their antiquated sewerage systems simply cannot handle the increased load (Ibid).

The rapid growth in urban areas, especially in India, has not been backed adequately with basic sanitation infrastructure. This has resulted in inadequacy in services like water supply, sewerage, storm water drainage and solid waste management. Sanitation is intrinsically linked to conditions and processes relating to public health and quality of environment, especially the systems that supply water and deal with human waste. The problem of sanitation gets further worsened in urban areas due to increasing congestion and density in cities resulting in poor environmental and health outcomes.

As per the 2011 Census, households having latrine facility within the premises are 82 per cent which includes 73 per cent households having water closets and 7 per cent households having pit latrines and 2 per cent households having other types of latrine. Out of 73 per cent households, 33 per cent households have water closets with piped sewer system and 38 per cent households have water closets with pit latrines. The remaining households either use public latrines or defecate in the open (Sulabh 2013).

To improve the sanitation situation in urban areas, in October 2008, the Government of India announced the NUSP. This laid down the framework for addressing the challenges of city sanitation. The policy emphasises the need for spreading awareness about sanitation through an integrated city-wide approach, assigning institutional responsibilities and due regard for demand and supply considerations, with special focus on women and the urban poor. All the states in India were requested to respond to the policy and develop their respective State Sanitation Strategies while the cities had to prepare City Sanitation Plans and consider sanitation as a state subject as per Constitutional provisions.

Sanitary Conditions at Public Places

This refers to the sanitary measures at public places like bus-stops, hotels, malls, railway stations, cinemas, stadiums, hospitals, etc. In the past, many public places (markets, bus depots, recreation parks, town centres, etc.) did not have sanitation facilities. The few that were in use under the management of the local authorities were in a state where they were unsuitable for human use. They were filthy and overflowing with human waste. No management system had been put in place for the daily operation of these facilities which were mainly toilet blocks for gents and ladies. These are the places where the public suffers a lot because of lack of sanitary measures. Public places are where disease spreads to individuals. Thus, it is very important to take measures to develop sanitation in public places.

Sanitation at Workplaces

Living without safe drinking water and adequate sanitation is an unacceptable situation for human, social and economic development. This violates basic requirements of human dignity and safety and has enormous impact on people's health, education and capacity to lead fully productive lives. Sometimes it is hard to find separate toilets for males and females in the workplace. It indicates lack of importance given to sanitation. It has been found that lack of proper sanitation measures at workplaces leads to social problems like harassment. Toilets, proper drinking water facility, disposal of wastage, etc., are important in the workplace.

Sanitation and Caste System

Caste-based discrimination leading to human rights violation regarding carrying of night soil makes it an important social issue. The social status of lower caste and ethnic group people in the field of sanitation is a matter of concern. The scavenging castes (also called untouchables) and the others who are related to sanitation work are discriminated against and socially excluded. In spite of legal sanctions and policies, the social conditions prevailing are pathetic.

Gender and Sanitation

Women face problems in society because of lack of sanitary measures. Women in slums are verbally abused, are stalked and physically assaulted while accessing toilets. Effective sanitation and hygiene promotion pays attention to gender differences and the effects of such differences in the process ensure that different groups are treated equitably. No one should be excluded from hygiene and sanitation services on the basis of their sex, age, disability, socio-economic status or cultural/ethnic group. We can see that most sanitation labourers are women and they don't get what they deserve. Every day, 1.3 million people in India are forced to do manual scavenging for little or no wages; out of which more than 80 per cent are Dalit women (Johns 2012).

Social Status of Manual Scavengers

In traditional Indian society, people of a particular section were ordained to carry night soil, and generally regarded as manual scavengers. It was the worst kind of exploitation done against any kind of community. At the same time, these people were hated and shunned for doing this job. It is clearly a denial of social justice. Manual scavenger means a person engaged or employed on a regular or frequent basis by an individual or a local authority or a public or private agency, for manually cleaning, carrying, disposing of, or otherwise handling in any manner, human excreta in an insanitary latrine or in an open drain or pit into which human excreta from insanitary latrines is disposed of, or on a railway track, before the excreta fully decomposes. Development of this community is necessary in the modern world. Sociology of sanitation is goal-oriented towards the development of the social status of manual scavengers. Sulabh has taken remarkable steps in eradicating manual scavenging and rehabilitating people involved in this practice.

Culture of Sanitation

India's enduring shame is clearly rooted in cultural attitudes. More than seven decades after Independence, many Indians continue to relieve themselves in the open and litter unhesitatingly, but keep their homes spotlessly clean.

The state has failed to extend sanitation facilities, but people must also take the blame. In some of the tribal areas, even though the government provided toilets to the families, they are uninterested in using them. To understand the cultural consequences has become one of the important works of sociology of sanitation. Preference for open defecation is a cultural issue in a society where the habit actually perpetuates social oppression. Cultural attitude differs from place to place. Therefore, it is not only lack of knowledge; it is also cultural attitude that leads to sanitation problems.

Sanitation at School or Educational Sector

It is very important to generate knowledge of sanitation and impart the same at school level. It is not only about toilets but also about a healthy environment in the school compound. There should be a proper place for disposal of waste. School is a public place from where disease can spread easily. In co-educational institutions, girls face a lot of problems because of lack of sanitation measures. Some schools don't even have proper drinking water facilities. Schools may be better locations in which to enforce certain behaviours in children than the home, says the World Bank. Schools can also provide an arena where sanitation can be shown at its best, and certain positive hygienic behaviour (hand washing with soap before eating and after going to the toilet) can become an ingrained habit at a young age. Sociology of sanitation finds out problems of sanitation in educational institutions and suggests remedies for the development of sanitation infrastructure.

Disposal of Waste

As cities are growing in size with a rise in the population, the amount of waste generated is increasing and becoming unmanageable. Local corporations have adopted different methods for the disposal of waste like open dumps, landfills, sanitary landfills and incineration plants. Disposal of solid waste depends on the geography of the habitat. In rural places, animal waste is used for biogas and biocompost for agricultural purposes. In urban places, dispose of solid waste of humans and animals is considered a major problem. Urban areas lack disposal places and the municipals or city corporations are struggling with the disposal of waste. Therefore, understanding the measures which are to be followed in the disposal of waste is necessary. Urban society generates different kinds of waste which cannot be disposed together. It has been observed that nowadays, big cities like Mumbai, Delhi and Bangalore are following their own kinds of waste disposal system. They are trying to collect the waste from door-to-door and charging fees for the same.

Public Policies on Sanitation

The Ministry of Drinking Water and Sanitation was created and notified by the Government of India as a separate Ministry, keeping in view the extreme importance of the sector. It is the nodal Ministry for the overall policy, planning, funding and coordination of the flagship programmes of the government for rural drinking water, the National Rural Drinking Water Programme, and the Total Sanitation Campaign. There are three programme divisions, namely, Water, Water Quality and Sanitation, to carry out the functions of the Ministry. It makes policies for the development of sanitation.

Non-Governmental Organisations

As for NGOs, they have been involved in objectively informing the actors (communities, local authorities, media, technical and financial partners) by setting up coalitions to establish stable reference situations and to carry out issue-based advocacy on the basis of rigorously constituted reference documents. In this framework, NGOs work as the pressure group after the government for the implementation of sanitary measures. NGOs spread initiatives related to public health. They specifically focus on sanitation.

Water is intrinsically interconnected to basic sanitation. The provision of safe drinking water and basic sanitation is among the most critical challenges for achieving sustainable development. The provision of safe drinking water and basic sanitation contributes to sustainable improvements in quality of life regarding health and education, the preconditions for productive employment as well as for the eradication of extreme hunger and empowerment of women. A favourable environment policy is essential for the success of projects that aim to improve hygiene, sanitation and water supply. Political commitment to education and health creates an environment that is conducive to implementing, operating and maintaining such projects effectively. Advocacy and information sharing can be an important tool to build political commitment that can help national and local governments put priorities and policies in place and change political attitudes and mobilise activities for hygiene, sanitation and water.

A multifaceted approach is required to deal with the plethora of the issues embodying sanitation. Dr Bindeshwar Pathak has been working in the area of sanitation for more than five decades. He has propounded his concept of sociology of sanitation: "Sociology of sanitation is a scientific study to solve the problems of society in relation to sanitation, social deprivation, water, public health, hygiene, ecology, environment, poverty, gender equality, welfare of children and empowering people for sustainable development and attainment of philosophical and spiritual knowledge to lead a happy life and to make a difference in the lives of others" (as quoted in Nagla 2015).

Sanitation refers to the safe disposal of human excreta. This entails the hygienic disposal and treatment of human waste to avoid affecting the health of people. The most affected countries are in the developing world. Population increase in the developing world has posed challenges in the improvement of sanitation. According to Zawari, Sowers, and Weinthal (as quoted in Nagla 2015), lack of provision of basic sanitation is estimated to have contributed to the deaths of millions of people annually from waterborne diseases. Mullegger, Lanergraber and Lechner (2011) of EcoSan Club have discussed the issue of sanitation at length.

The standard sanitation technology in urban areas is the collection of wastewater in sewers, its treatment in wastewater treatment plants for reuse or disposal in rivers, lakes or the sea. Sewers are either combined with storm drains or separated from them as sanitary sewers. Combined sewers are usually found in the central, older parts or urban areas. Heavy rainfall and inadequate maintenance can lead to combined sewer overflows or sanitary sewer overflows, i.e. more or less diluted raw sewage being discharged into the environment. Industries often discharge wastewater into municipal sewers, which can complicate wastewater treatment unless industries pre-treat their discharges (Ujang 2003).

Origin of Sociology of Sanitation

Sociology of sanitation is a sub-branch of medical sociology that emerged in the US during the 1940s. This discipline was to investigate the social causes and consequences of health and illness and inspired by the health and sanitary reforms that took place in western society. It was well recognised that the relations between sociology and sanitation are extremely intimate. The individual is the essential element of society; his social values depend largely upon his health. Good health is a prerequisite for the adequate functioning of an individual or society.

On the other hand, health is partly determined by the conditions which society imposes. Social factors play a critically important role in health. Social conditions and situation not only promote the possibility of illness and disability, they also enhance prospects for disease prevention and health maintenance. The disheartening status of mankind today is undoubtedly the result of the sanitary and social conditions of past ages and previous generations. Clean food, adequate supply of clean water, sanitary schools, public baths, adequate housing, etc. are sanitary measures which are most effective in both sanitary and social results. Hence sanitation and sociology must go hand in hand in their effort to improve the race and now, their relations have been openly recognised.

Sociology, as a vast subject, includes almost everything of society which human beings deal with. Sociology has developed rapidly since World War II, resulting in an increase in specialisations within the field.. In recent years, the importance of sanitation in human society forced social scientists to improve sociology of sanitation as a specialised study in sociology. Thus, the relationship of man and human society enabled further development of the sociology of sanitation.

The extension of the study of sanitation was a requirement to improve the physical life of human beings in society. It is understood that sanitation process should begin with the individual itself and the work of sanitation is acknowledged to be of greater scope. Further, sanitary reforms should not be restricted to the physical life of man, but to all the activities that affect human beings. When the physical condition and the moral attitude of human beings are identified, the study of sanitation becomes important. So, a more rational and practical view of sanitation is gaining ground.

The relationship of sociology and sanitation is considered equally important. The individual is the essential element of society, his social values depend largely upon his health, while in turn his health is partly determined by the conditions of the society where he lives and which are imposed by society. The disheartening status of mankind today is undoubtedly the result of the unsanitary social condition of past ages. However, the influences under which men of the present generation place themselves are more or less within their control and may be made to work for both the present and future good of society. Sanitation shows what steps should be taken by society, individually and collectively, to secure good health. Sanitation and sociology must go hand in hand in their effort to improve humankind. The value of the relation which exists between them will be greater in proportion as its importance is consciously and openly recognised.

Sociology of sanitation is a necessity of the present world. It is very difficult to survive in the modern world without proper sanitation measures. From home to the larger social life, everywhere, man is facing the problem of sanitation. We are developing in almost everything but forgetting the basic requirement of human life. And lack of sanitation is the enemy of human health and good social life.

Sanitation in public life is the responsibility of an individual, community and the state (Akram 2015). Leaders in sanitation movements opine that sanitation can only be brought in by changing the attitude or personal habits of the individual and thus the public to itself. When habits don't change, the people are blamed for their own poor surroundings. It is a waste to construct public toilets where we hardly get water. Public policies go waste if the state is not interested in maintenance it. Technical solutions are often suggested without understanding the habits or social life of the people; sometimes they go unnoticed and often they create more problems than they solve. Hence, sanitation needs to be seen as an integral component of public health programmes, individuals and communities.

The first challenge for countries seeking to solve the problem of access to sanitation is to understand what "sanitation" really means. The requirement of sanitation in public life developed the concept of sanitation as a subject. The key issue here is that each community, region or country needs to work out what is the most sensible and cost-effective way of thinking about sanitation in the short and long term and then act accordingly. Since it's a part of both man and society, we understand that human habits, lifestyle, cultural and social behaviour is the major reason for the problem of sanitation. Thus, it has been found that sanitation should be understood within sociological method. Sociological study enables in depth analysis of the subject for better results. Scientific study of sanitation was one of the requirements for its development as a subject.

Nature and Subject Matter of Sanitation

Sanitation refers to formulation and application of measures designed to protect public health. It also refers clean and safe water supply, clean and safe ambient air, efficient and safe disposal of animal, human and industrial waste, protection of food from biological and chemical contaminants and adequate housing in clean and safe surroundings. According to WHO, sanitation generally refers to the provision of facilities and services for the safe disposal of human urine and faeces.

The word "sanitation" also refers to the maintenance of hygienic conditions, through services such as garbage collection and wastewater disposal. According to UNICEF, sanitation literally means measures necessary for improving and protecting the health and well-being of people. Sanitation is any system that promotes proper disposal of human and animal wastes, proper use of toilets and avoiding open defecation. Sanitation is not to be restricted to one particular act of human civilisation; it is the cluster of acts which a human being does for a clean, safe and healthy environment. Adequate sanitation, together with good hygiene and safe water, are fundamental to good health and to social and economic development. It is very important to remember the words of Mahatma Gandhi: "Sanitation is more important than independence." In other words, sanitation refers to conditions relating to public health, especially the provision of clean drinking water and adequate sewage disposal.

Nature of Sociology of Sanitation

Sociology of sanitation includes human beings and their social life, interaction and behaviour with reference to sanitary conditions. Sociology of sanitation is a social science; a study of society and human social action for sanitation activity. It generally concerns itself with the social norms and processes that bind and separate people from sanitary conditions as individuals, and also as members of associations, groups and institutions. Sociology of sanitation ranges from the analysis of individuals on the street to the study of global social processes. It is a science which is the implementation of scientific measures for better understanding of sanitation conditions in society.

The nature of sociology of sanitation is concerned with the scientific status of the discipline. Being a specialised area of sociology, its nature also has a bearing closer to sociology proper. Hence, as a discipline, it should include all the features a typical science would have—objectivity, generality, verifiability, rationality, predictability and systematicity. Any body of knowledge, to be regarded as a science must have objectivity. The objectivity helps different researchers to reach the same conclusion. Generality implies that a science is not interested in individual objects or individual groups of objects. It seeks to ascertain common characteristics of types of objects and general laws or conditions of events. Scientific findings are based on empirical evidence. Therefore, speculation and imagination have no place in science. The empirical findings and the scientific generalisations should be verifiable or tested. The empirical conclusions are guided by logic and rational arguments. Hence they should be properly organised to arrive at the general truth. Logical reason and inferences establish the cause and effect of relationship among different phenomena. This provides for prediction of social phenomena or social happenings in society. Finally, a science should be a systematic method of analysis and generalisation. Therefore, it is argued that sociology of sanitation, a branch of sociology, is a systematic study of sanitation aspects.

Sociology of sanitation is a branch of knowledge distinct from other subjects. The following are the main characteristics of sociology of sanitation (Pais 2015):

1. *Sociology of sanitation is not an independent subject:* Till date, it is treated and studied as a branch of sociology with the implementation of sociological knowledge and methodology.
2. *Sociology of sanitation is a social science and not a physical science:* As a social science it concentrates its attention on man, his social behaviour, social activities and social life and cultural life regarding sanitation. It studies human habits of cleanliness.
3. *Sociology of sanitation is a positive discipline:* It confines itself to statements about what is and what can be. As a social science, we can study about sanitation in groups and societies and suggest remedies.
4. *Sociology of sanitation is a pure and applied science:* The main aim of pure science is the acquisition of knowledge and this knowledge is applied to groups and communities to solve their sanitary problems.
5. *Sociology of sanitation is abstract in nature:* Sociology of sanitation does not confine itself to the study of toilets or disposal of waste. It deals with

complete sanitation activity of human society without the restriction of any group or community.

6. *Sociology of sanitation is general and not particular in nature:* Sociology of sanitation tries to find out the general laws or principles about human attitude towards sanitation. It tries to find out the relationship of human groups and societies in sanitation. It tries to make generalisations on the basis of the study of some selected events.
7. *Sociology of sanitation is general and not special in nature:* The area of inquiry of sociology of sanitation is general and not specialised. It is concerned with human interaction and human life with or without sanitation in general. It only studies human activities in a general way.
8. *Sociology of sanitation is both rational and an empirical study in nature as sociology:* There are two broad ways of approach to scientific knowledge; empiricism and rationalism. Empiricism is the approach that emphasises experience and the facts that result from observation and experimentation. Rationalism stresses reason and the theories that result from logical inference. Sociology of sanitation uses both for its epistemology.

Subject Matter of Sociology of Sanitation

Sociology of sanitation is the study of human action which includes the individual, community and public policies for the betterment of sanitary measures in the environment. It studies the present infrastructure of sanitation and the development required in sanitation, from the individual household to the whole community. Sociology of sanitation is a field of study that seeks to analyse and explain important matters that affect our everyday sanitation problems in society, and the world in which we live.

At the personal level, it investigates the causes and consequences of such things as lack of toilets in the houses and in public places, lack of drainage facilities, lack of proper drinking water facilities, and gender and sanitation issues, behavioural approach towards sanitation, disposal of waste, and cultural practices of various ethnic groups and management of sanitation. At the societal level, sociology of sanitation examines and explains such matters as the existence of night soil carriers, prejudice and discrimination of night soil carriers in society, the construction of toilet as business, sanitation in schools and education, and social movements with regard to sanitation. At the global level, sociology of sanitation studies such things as the contribution of WHO, UNICEF and other organisations. It studies economic contribution towards sanitation development policies.

One of the important things that sociology of sanitation can offer to its students is the ability to grasp a connection between broad behavioural patterns of individuals and the community towards sanitation. This provides personal experience regarding the unknown faces of sanitation problems. This is an extremely important preparation for living effective personal lives in a changing and complex world. It is also equally important for the future development of society.

Some of the areas sociology of sanitation studies includes:

1. The sanitary measures in household
2. The sanitary conditions at public places
3. Sanitation at workplaces
4. Relation of sanitation with caste
5. Gender and sanitation
6. Social status of manual scavengers
7. Culture of sanitation
8. Sanitation in schools or educational sector
9. Disposal of waste
10. Public policies of sanitation
11. Non-governmental organisations

Scope of Sociology of Sanitation

"Great cities, when badly administered, cannot be sold or abolished; they simply become dirty, unhealthy, unsafe, disgraceful, and expensive" (Saxena 2015). Sanitation is a very important index of socio-economic development in any society. It is an integral part of human ecology and is understood as safe handling of excreta in the human environment. It can also be simply labelled as people's approach to taking care of their primal needs. Achieving and maintaining a healthy community environment requires control of activities which may adversely affect that environment.

According to Dr Bindeshwar Pathak (2013), sanitation should be included as a discipline in sociology. He defines sociology of sanitation as "a scientific study to solve the problems of society in relation to sanitation, social deprivation, water, public health, hygiene, ecology, environment, poverty, gender equality, welfare of children and empowering people for sustainable development and attainment of philosophical and spiritual knowledge to lead a happy life and to make a difference in the lives of others".

In a broader sense, sanitation implies management, operation and maintenance of human/social ecology involving greater hygiene and referring to people's capability to fulfil their primal physical, biological, psychological, philosophical, social and economic needs and entitlements. It involves the well-being of individuals through exclusion or neutralisation of elements dysfunctional to them and their community. Good sanitation is a way of life and an effective tool for progress of one's mind, body and surroundings in terms of health, scientific temper and secular behaviour in an acceptable, affordable and sustainable way.

Sanitation constitutes as interplay between man, society and environment. And hence the subject matter of sociology of sanitation includes:

1. Creation of a healthy society. It seeks to analyse the factors and forces promoting health and well-being of the individuals in society.
2. Study of primary units of social and environmental life. It is concerned with the social acts and social relationship, varied groups and institutions, organisations and associations as well as ecological milieu in a cultural framework.
3. It deals with various social processes such as co-operation, competition and conflicts in the sustainability of the environment as well as holistic development of man in society.
4. It involves the study of research methods and theorisation of issues of health and well-being of man in society.
5. It deals with the remedial measures for eradication of various social evils in a society.

Sociology of sanitation being an applied discipline, the scope of sanitation is basically the study of social, physical and physiological pathology with all its complexities. Primarily, its aim is to make a scientific, systematic and comprehensive study of health and hygiene in relation to the social organisation and its associated functioning. It being an interdisciplinary entity, it incorporates the broader areas under its framework, thus widening its scope. It may incorporate a variety of issues in a national and global framework.

In its scope of application it is applied to a wide range of subjects as:

a. Improved sanitation, in management of human faeces at the household and the community level.
b. On-site sanitation, in the collection and treatment of waste from where it is deposited.
c. Food sanitation, ensuring food safety.
d. Environmental sanitation, protection of the environment from different pollutants.
e. Ecological sanitation, handling human and animal wastes in a hygienically safe manner.

Importance of Sociology of Sanitation

Sociology of sanitation provides a number of benefits:

1. Sociology of sanitation allows the researcher to do a scientific study of sanitation issues in society. It enables him to collect data in a prescribed format. It suggests remedies for the identified problems of sanitation. Scientific study of sanitation highlights sanitation as of greater importance among other social aspects.
2. It studies the role of institutions in sanitary conditions and in the development of sanitation. It is through sociology of sanitation that a scientific study of social institutions and the relation of the individual are made. It enables providing the individual and the society with better sanitation solutions.
3. Study of sanitation is important for understanding and planning of a healthy society. Society is a complex phenomenon with a multitude of intricacies. It is impossible to understand and solve its numerous problems without the support of sociology. Sociology of sanitation helps in understanding problems related to sanitation, hygiene and health and in framing social policies related to health and sanitation.
4. Sociology of sanitation is of great importance in the solution of social problems. Its task is to study sanitation problems through methods of scientific research and to find solutions to them. The scientific study of human affairs will ultimately provide the body of knowledge and principles that will enable us to control the

conditions of sanitation and improve them. It is very important to bring the problem of sanitation into the mainstream.

5. Sociology of sanitation has drawn our attention to the effects of lack of sanitation: It has been instrumental in understanding the need for sanitation. The problem of sanitation conditions in society also affects our social life directly or indirectly in the form of harassment, school dropout rate and social injustice. In order to have insights into the problem of sanitation, the existence of knowledge through sociology of sanitation is essential.
6. Sociology of sanitation has changed our outlook with regard to the problems of manual scavengers. Manual scavengers are now treated as equals in social relationships.
7. Sociology of sanitation has made great contributions to the culture of sanitation. Sociology of sanitation has taught us to have a rational approach to questions regarding sanitation concerning oneself, one's religion, customs, morals and institutions. By comparative study of societies and groups, life becomes healthier.
8. Sociology of sanitation is of great importance in the global understanding of sanitation. The progress made by physical sciences has brought the nations of the world nearer. Sociology of sanitation provides knowledge about policies for sanitation at the global level.
9. Every nation has to think for the global future. The value of sociology of sanitation lies in the fact that it keeps upgrading sanitation conditions. It contributes to improving the environment and finding solutions to community problems. It helps the individual grasp his relation to sanitation. Sociology of sanitation pulls people away from older sanitation measures.
10. Sociology of sanitation conceptualises how people perceive and experience sanitation within informal settlements. It contextualises existing sanitary practice and explores it in relation to potential sanitation interventions by the state and civil society and it relates urban sanitation experience, perception and coping strategies to debates in urban theory and development studies.
11. Sociology of sanitation provides an understanding of social issues and patterns of sanitation. It helps us to identify the social rules that govern our lives with or without sanitation. Social scientists study how these rules are created for human society, maintained,

changed, passed between generations, and shared between people living in various parts of the world.

12. Sociology of sanitation helps us to understand the working of the social systems of sanitary conditions. Social scientists bring sanitation into a social context. This means social scientists look not only at sanitary equipment or measures, but also at behaviour and relationships, and also how the larger world influences these things.
13. Sociology of sanitation helps us understand why we are in need of proper sanitation. Sociology helps us examine behavioural pattern, cultural attitudes and geographical influence regarding sanitation.
14. Sociology of sanitation helps us identify what we have in common within and between cultures and societies. Social scientists know that although people in different parts of the city, country or world dress differently, speak differently and have many different beliefs and customs, the requirement for sanitation is the same among all people. Social scientists look for what sanitation and hygiene mean to various groups. They look at how various groups follow sanitary measures.
15. Sociology of sanitation provides us theoretical perspectives within which to frame these understandings and research methods that allow us to study sanitation scientifically. The theories focus on how social institutions operate sanitation. Scientific methods provide ways of generating accurate research results.
16. Sanitation is important for the health and well-being of all people. Without good, clean sanitation systems, disease can break out very quickly and spread easily. Sanitation is an important way of promoting good health and preventing disease. It is a hygienic means of promoting good health through prevention of contact with hazards such as waste.
17. Sanitation lies at the root of many other development challenges, as poor sanitation impacts public health, education and the environment. Girls are more likely to drop out of school or are vulnerable to attacks if proper functioning toilets are unavailable. Globally, poor sanitation leads to premature deaths annually. Study analysis shows that ending open defecation can save children's lives by reducing disease transmission, stunting and under-nutrition,

which are important for childhood cognitive development and future economic productivity.

18. The economic losses are mainly driven by premature deaths, the cost of healthcare treatment, time and productivity lost seeking treatment, and finding access to sanitation facilities. Pollution resulting from improper disposal and treatment of wastewater and domestic faecal sludge also affect both water resources and the ecosystem. At the same time, faecal sludge and wastewater can provide valuable resources (water, nutrients, energy) and economic opportunities, especially in urban areas and in water-scarce environments.
19. Pictures of public places in India would instantly convey the need for clean toilet facilities. The lack of clean sanitation facilities has been a common cause of many diseases in India. Most of the places where a large number of people assemble, such as schools, railway stations, bus stations, hospitals, parks, beaches, markets and places of worship, lack adequate toilet and urinal facilities for public use.

Sociological Perspectives in Sociology of Sanitation

A perspective is simply a way of looking at the world. To understand the reality, sociologists analyse social phenomena at different levels and from different perspectives. From concrete interpretations to generalisations on society and social behaviour, sociologists study everything, from the micro level of analysis of small social patterns to the macro level of analysis of large social patterns.

Sociological theories help us to explain and predict the social world in which we live. The theoretical perspectives that sociologists today employ may be broadly viewed in three parts: the functionalist perspective, the conflict perspective and the symbolic interactionist perspective. Each perspective offers a variety of explanations about the social world and human behaviour. These perspectives offer sociologists theoretical paradigms for explaining how society influences people, and vice versa. Each perspective uniquely conceptualises society, social forces and human behaviour.

1. Functionalist Perspective

According to the functionalist perspective, each aspect of society is interdependent and contributes to society's functioning as a whole. The functionalist perspective is based largely on the works of Herbert Spencer, Emile Durkheim, Talcott Parsons and Robert Merton. According to functionalism, society is a system of interconnected parts that work together in harmony to maintain a state of balance and social equilibrium of the whole. For example, each of the social institutions contributes important functions for society: family provides a context for reproducing, nurturing and socialising children; education offers a way to transmit a society's skills, knowledge and culture to its youth; politics provides a means of governing members of society; economics provides for the production, distribution and consumption of goods and services; and religion provides moral guidance and an outlet for worship of a higher power. If all goes well, the parts of society produce order, stability and productivity. If all do not go well, the parts of society then must adapt to recapture a new order, stability and productivity.

The functionalist perspective emphasises the interconnectedness of society by focusing on how each part influences and is influenced by other parts. Functionalists use the terms functional and dysfunctional to describe the effects of social elements on society. Elements of society are functional if they contribute to social stability and dysfunctional if they disrupt social stability.

Functionalists believe that society is held together by social consensus and cohesion, in which members of the society agree upon, and work together to achieve what is best for society as a whole. Durkheim explains social consensus takes one of two forms: mechanical and organic solidarity. Mechanical solidarity arises when people in a society maintain similar values and beliefs and engage in similar types of work. This occurs in traditional and simple societies. In contrast, organic solidarity arises when the people in a society are interdependent, but hold varying values and beliefs and engage in varying types of work. This commonly occurs in industrialised, complex societies. Further, sociologists have identified two types of functions: manifest and latent (Merton 1957). Manifest functions are consequences that are intended and commonly recognised. Latent functions are consequences that are unintended and often hidden.

A sociological approach in functionalism is the consideration of the relationship between the functions of smaller parts and the functions of the whole. However, functionalism neglects the negative functions of an event. Critics also claim that the perspective justifies the status quo and complacency on the part of society's members. This does not encourage people to take an active role in changing their social environment, even when such change may benefit them. Instead, functionalism sees active social change as undesirable because the various parts of society will compensate naturally for any problems that may arise.

The functional theory is very important in the context of maintenance of society which is also applicable to the problem of sanitation. A typical functional perspective justifies the social order as good. For instance, its outlook justifies the working of the caste system as it fulfils definite functions for society. Therefore, sanitation and caste are directly related.

2. Conflict Perspective

In contrast to the functionalist perspective that views society as composed of different parts working together, the conflict perspective views society as composed of different groups that are unequal and competing for power and resources. The conflict perspective explains various aspects of the social world by analysing groups in relation to power and benefit from a particular social arrangement.

The origin of the conflict perspective can be traced to the classic works of Karl Marx. Marx suggested that all societies go through stages of economic development. In this process, as societies evolve from agricultural to industrial, concern over meeting survival needs is replaced by concern over making a profit, the hallmark of a capitalist system. Industrialisation leads to the development of two classes of people: the bourgeoisie, or the owners of the means of production (e.g., factories, farms, businesses) and the proletariat, or the workers who earn wages. The division of society into two broad classes of people— the "haves" and the "have-nots", is beneficial to the owners of the means of production. The workers, who earn only subsistence wages, are denied access to many resources available to the wealthy owners. According to Marx, the bourgeoisie use their power to control the institutions of society to their advantage.

The conflict perspective, which originated primarily out of Marx's writings on class struggles, presents society in a different light than do the other perspectives. While these focus on the positive aspects of society that contribute to its stability, the conflict perspective focuses on the conflicting and ever-changing nature of society. Unlike functionalists who defend the status quo, avoid social change and believe people cooperate to effect social order; conflict theorists challenge the status quo and encourage social change, even when this means social revolution.

Today, conflict theorists find social conflict between any groups in which the potential for inequality exists: race, gender, religious, political, economic and so on. Conflict theorists note that unequal groups usually have conflicting values and agendas, causing them to compete against one another. This constant competition between groups forms the basis for the ever-changing nature of society. When applied to the Indian sanitation system, the conflict perspective explains the causes of exploitation and subjugation of certain sections of people for generations, creating social inequality and exclusion.

3. Symbolic Interactionist Perspective

Both the functionalist and the conflict perspectives are concerned with larger or broader aspects of society such as institutions and large social groups that influence the social world. This other level of sociological analysis is concerned with the social psychological dynamics of individuals interacting in small groups. This perspective, generally known as symbolic interactionist perspective, directs sociologists to consider the symbols and details of everyday life, what these symbols mean and how people interact with each other. Although symbolic interactionism traces its origins to Max Weber's assertion that individuals act according to their interpretation of the meaning of their world, American philosopher George H. Mead introduced this perspective in sociology.

Symbolic interactionism was largely influenced by the works of early thinkers such as George Simmel, Charles Cooley, G.H. Mead, Herbert Blumer and Erving Goffman. Symbolic interactionism emphasises that human behaviour is influenced by definitions and meanings that are created and maintained through symbolic interaction with others. Sociologist W.I. Thomas emphasised the importance of definitions and meanings in social behaviour and its consequences. He suggested that humans respond to their definition of a situation rather than to the objective situation itself. Hence, Thomas noted that situations that we define as real become real in their consequences.

Symbolic interactionism suggests that our identity or self is shaped by social interaction. According to the symbolic interactionist perspective, people attach meanings to symbols, and then act according to their subjective interpretation of these symbols. This subjective interpretation is made evident in verbal conversations, in which spoken words serve as the predominant symbols. The words have a certain meaning for the sender, and, during effective communication, they hopefully have the same meaning for the receiver. Therefore, words are not static things; they require intention and interpretation. Conversation is an interaction of symbols between individuals who constantly interpret the world around them. Anything can serve as a symbol as long as it refers to something beyond itself. Thus, symbolic interactionists give serious thought to how people act, and then seek to determine what meanings individuals assign to their own actions and symbols, as well as to those of others.

Besides these, there are other types of theories that reflect the particular aspect of the individual in society. For example, the anomie theory of R.K. Merton and differential association theory of Edwin H. Sutherland focus on the causes of deviant behaviour. Labelling theory, phenomenological and conflict theory deal with the meanings of the particular behaviour and the impact of these meanings on people's behaviour. The interactionist perspective is relevant in understanding sanitation concept and the related processes; most important, the whole world of sanitation is socially constructed. This idea is elaborated elsewhere in this volume.

Approaches to Public Health

The approaches to public health are relevant in understanding sanitation. Park and Park discuss approaches to public health:

1. Regulatory Approach

The regulatory approach or legal approach seeks to protect the health of the public through the enforcement of laws and regulations, e.g. Epidemic Diseases Act, 1897 and The Prevention of Food Adulteration Act, 1954. Although there are sufficient legal measures, the implementation is very poor; they remain only on paper. They are only used in emergency situations or on specific occasions like fairs, festivals or outbreak of epidemics. In areas involving personal choice, for example, giving up smoking, family planning, etc., laws have no place in a democratic society. The legal approach also has the disadvantage that it requires vast administrative machinery to enforce laws and also involves considerable expenditure.

2. Service Approach

The service or administrative approach aims at providing all health facilities needed by the community in the hope that people will use them to improve their own health. The service approach proved a failure as it was not based on the felt needs of the people. For example, when water seal latrines were provided free of cost in some villages in India under the Community Development Programme, people did not use them. This serves to illustrate that we may provide free service to the people, but there is no guarantee that the service will be used by them.

3. Educational Approach

The educational approach is a major means today for achieving change in health practices and the recognition of health needs. It involves motivation, communication and decision-making. The result, although slow, is permanent and enduring. Sufficient time should be allowed to have the desired change brought about. There are certain problems which can be solved only through education, for example, nutritional problems, infant and child care, personal hygiene and family planning. The educational approach is used widely today for solution of community health problems. It is consistent with democratic philosophy which does not order the individual. The educational approaches may be classified as:

a. Individual and family approach;
b. small group approach; and
c. mass approach.

Since individuals vary significantly in their socio-economic conditions, traditions, attitudes, beliefs and level of knowledge, a single educational approach may not be suitable. A combination of approaches must be evolved depending upon local circumstances. These public health approaches are quite relevant in the context of sanitation awareness. The desired results may be brought about through systematic service and educational planning with the support of a regulatory system.

Social Perspectives on the Sanitation Challenge (Milet, et al 2010), presents a collection of social scientific perspectives of science and technology studies, environmental sociology and urban studies dealing with innovative sanitation issues and concepts, perceptions and decision-making support. They comprise a valuable resource for political scientists, environmental engineers, urban planners involved in the study, design and implementation of sanitation projects worldwide and whose work relates to meeting the ambitious MDG on sanitation. If the goal is to reach people without sustainable access to safe drinking water and basic sanitation, we need new technologies and innovative sanitation concepts, new tools for decision-making and an understanding of diverse stakeholder perspectives along the sanitation chain.

In developed countries, the sanitation challenge is to initiate a transition from strongly centralised, water-based infrastructure regimes towards more sustainable, source-separation oriented sanitation regimes. This calls for social scientific research and demonstration on different levels and scales, including concept development, institutional learning and governance building. In the developing world, the sanitation challenge is to provide sanitation services to the poor and the very poor, without compromising on sustainability. In this context, the compendium presents new configurations that employ the best practices of sanitation technology and management for rural and urban contexts. *Social Perspectives on the Sanitation Challenge* is unique in its presentation of social scientific research findings from urban planners, sociologists, economists, political scientists and environmental engineers who are involved in international sanitation research and implementation (Ibid).

Misra and Goldar (2008) have undertaken a study to gain an understanding of the baseline water supply and sewerage services in Delhi and assess consumer coping strategies and associated costs, their preferences for service improvements, willingness to pay and affordability for the preferred options. The survey results bring out the deficiencies in services, and the significant coping costs the consumers are bearing. The survey data reveals that the consumers are willing to pay, and can afford the extra cost that service improvement will entail. The data indicates that for poor households in informal settlements, substantial improvements in water supply can be made by introducing or implementing paid group connections.

The study on consumer coping costs, water treatment plant and affordability shows that domestic and non-domestic consumers in Delhi are bearing a huge cost to cope with the inadequacies of current water supply and sewerage services. Nearly one-fifth of households in authorised colonies are making use of additional water sources, such as their own bore wells, housing society bore wells or bottled water. Domestic consumers face considerable difficulties due to limited hours of water supply, low pressure and water quality problems. These problems have compelled consumers to invest in storage, booster pumps and filters. The study demonstrates that significant social gains are expected by improving efficiency of the water supply and sanitation delivery system.

Solid waste management (SWM), typically a straightforward public health service to be provided by the local administration, is a complex, multi-layered issue. At one level, efficiency and efficacy of service provision have significant implications for public health and sustainability of operations, and recent years have seen private sector participation being explored as a means of enhancing service provision. The private sector participation in SWM is a difficult and contentious issue.

The public sector, on its own, has not been able to respond effectively to the SWM challenge. On the other hand, private and civil society participation also poses several challenges, especially in terms of equity and accountability. Further, the nature and efficiency of civil society responses to SWM problems is shaped by a host of local conditions and variables, quality of volunteers and leadership, and especially the response of the Urban Local Bodies. In addition, while ecological considerations are slowly gaining ascendance in SWM policy, certain sections of people continue to remain missing from the large SWM discourse. These are the conservancy workers, people who work on the dumpsites and on the streets, and the urban poor for whom SWM is a luxury that they cannot afford to spend time, effort or money on. There is a need for an inclusive policy that addresses these concerns as well (Srinivasan 2006).

Decentralisation in delivery of water supply leads to better quality of services. The participation of local government in distribution of water supply and household contribution to operation and maintenance appear to have a positive impact on quality. Quality of piped water has been observed to be better in villages where the local government participates in operation and maintenance. Division of responsibility according to the comparative advantage of local government and the Public Health Engineering Department has yielded the best result. Household contribution for maintenance also has been found to have a positive impact on quality of water supply services. Overall, the studies suggest that decentralisation has a positive impact on quality of water supply (as quoted in Nagla 2015).

One of the major challenges in India is providing sustainable sanitation and hygiene to its vast, diverse and growing population. The Government of India has declared its commitment to achieving the MDG goals and universal sanitation coverage in the country by the year 2022, but with the current rural sanitation coverage, this is a challenging task. The Ministry of Drinking Water and Sanitation has already risen to the occasion with renewed strategies and approaches. The Total Sanitation Campaign has been revamped and renamed the Nirmal Bharat Abhiyan (NBA) in April 2012 by adopting community-led and people-centred strategies with a saturation approach backed by post-achievement incentives.

One of the major shifts in the approach under the NBA has been to adopt a more holistic approach in addressing issues related to sanitation. Apart from addressing the issues of building individual household toilets, community toilets and constructing toilets in anganwadi centres and schools, the government has placed a lot of emphasis on providing the much-needed flexibility to households to choose the sanitation technology they prefer from a variety of options based on socio-cultural aspects, hydro geographical conditions and economic status. The government has also streamlined steps to make available sanitation material and equipment within the reach of the common people by providing incentives for the setting up of production centres and Rural Sanitary Marts in rural areas. These Marts ensure that a variety of pans, soakages, compost pits, vermin composting processes and washing platforms are made available at nominal cost to the general public (Nagla 2015).

Solid and Liquid Waste Management (SLWM), which is essential for promoting a hygienic and healthy environment, has been accorded prime importance. Under the SLWM component, the government is promoting innovative and adaptable initiatives like compost pits, vermin composting, common and individual biogas plants, and low-cost drainage, apart from collection, segregation and disposal of household waste at the village level.

These initiatives will be successful if the general public is educated about the benefits of incorporating safe sanitary practices and if they are made aware of the various facilities and incentives being provided by the government. A comprehensive Sanitation and Hygiene Advocacy and Communication Strategy Framework has been launched by the Ministry with the objective of rolling out a number of communication activities in a phased manner to sensitise the general public about various aspects of sanitation. An intensive audio visual and radio campaign has been launched at the national level while the states and the gram panchayats (GPs) have been urged to also include interpersonal communication and direct media activities. The need to broaden communication on rural sanitation and its various facets has been accepted and is being initiated with vigour.

Quite a few GPs across the length and breadth of the country have been awarded Nirmal Gram Puraskars, as an acknowledgment of the significant sanitation initiatives taken up in their areas. Many of these GPs are shining examples of how to overcome extraordinary odds to achieve this status (Nagla 2015). The success stories documented can be lessons of great inspiration and serve as models for various GPS, districts and states across India in overcoming hurdles and obstacles in various fields as diverse as community participation, sustainability, resource mobilisation, SLWM, programme implementation, information, education and communication (IEC) practices and institutional reforms. The services of community members, grassroot sanitation workers, Panchayati Raj Institutions (PRIs) and government officials have been documented for the wonderful work and sincere efforts they have put in to provide a clean and healthy environment and it is hoped that they will continue to be role models for the NBA programme (Jain 2014).

Social Development Perspectives

A social development perspective supports integrated approaches to water supply and sanitation (WS&S) approach. This approach understands and involves users and responds flexibly towards their concerns. Social development objectives in WS&S include ensuring dialogue and interventions. They are responsive to demand; reach poor or disadvantaged populations and socially excluded groups, promote empowerment, local voices and ownership, and recognise the different needs and contributions of both women and men. A social development perspective is supported by social analysis and by incorporating social issues and participatory approaches into development planning.

The response to WS&S which evolved during the 1980s was the basic services approach. It identified lack of access to basic services which are the basic rights, such as water, healthcare and education, as both a cause and a symptom of poverty (Jarman 1997). In his introduction to social development issues in an urban context, Jarman examines the relationship between poverty and water supply and sanitation in the city, providing best practice examples of interventions.

Gender Perspective on Water Resources and Sanitation

It has been observed that there is a difference between the perspective on sanitation of women and that of men. For women, it especially meant keeping themselves, their houses and their children clean. Understanding of sanitation was closely related to open defecation and the need for toilets, especially in crowded urban settlements. In fact, an open defecation-free environment and use of toilets were identified with sanitation across all countries (Water Aid 2011).

The global commitments made in the areas of water and sanitation do not specifically address the equitable division of power, work, access to and control of resources between women and men. It will be critical to mainstream gender perspectives into the planning process to ensure that the specific needs and concerns of women and men from all social groups are taken into account in development, use and management of water resources and sanitation. In most cultures, women are primarily responsible for the use and management of water resources, sanitation and health at the household level. Over the years, women have accumulated an impressive store of environmental wisdom, being the ones to find water, to educate children in hygiene matters and to understand the impact of poor sanitation on health. At the same time, women and girls are often obliged to walk many hours every day fetching water, while men are rarely expected to perform such tasks (Nagla 2015). The importance of involving both women and men in the management of water and sanitation has been recognised at the global level.

Sanitation Organisations

WASH is an acronym that stands for "water, sanitation and hygiene". Affordable and sustainable access to WASH is a key public health issue within international development and is the focus of Sustainable Development Goal (SDG) 6. Several international development agencies assert that attention to WASH can also improve health, life expectancy, student learning, gender equality and other important issues of international development. Access to WASH includes safe water, adequate sanitation and hygiene education. This can reduce illness and death, and also reduce poverty and improve socio-economic development.

Lack of sanitation contributes to child deaths due to diarrhoea, mainly in developing countries. Chronic diarrhoea can have long-term negative effects on children, in terms of both physical and cognitive development. In addition, lack of WASH facilities can prevent students from attending school, impose an unusual burden on women and reduce work productivity.

The MDGs included improvement of WASH services in Target 7.C. This has been replaced by the SDGS, where Goal 6 aims to ensure availability and sustainable management of water and sanitation for all. Access to WASH, in particular safe water, adequate sanitation and proper hygiene education, can reduce illness and death, and also affect poverty reduction and socio-economic development. The UN's International Year of Sanitation in 2008 helped to increase attention for funding of sanitation in WASH programmes of many donors.

UNICEF's WASH team works in over 100 countries worldwide to improve water and sanitation services, as well as basic hygiene practices. In times of crisis, children are particularly vulnerable; UNICEF responds and provides emergency relief to those in need. The WASH programme supports national and state governments in developing and implementing a range of replicable intervention models for sanitation, hygiene and water supply.

The youth can lend a hand to promote better health. For example, Ador, a 12-year-old boy living in the Philippines, knows that the solution to better health can be found right in the palm of his hand. Ador has been attending training in sanitation and hygiene. That is why he is committed to educating his peers on how the simple task of hand washing can go a long way to improve the health of the entire community. The use of clean water and sanitation techniques can help prevent the transmission of waterborne diseases and serious illnesses, particularly for children. Therefore, a plan has been formulated to stop preventable deaths by establishing sustainable, community-led water and sanitation systems for villages in the Philippines; children like Ador are catalysts for positive change.

With an aim to achieve a cleaner India, the religious and spiritual heads of different faiths have joined hands to fight global climate change and clean up the Ganges along with other rivers. The initiative was taken up under the leadership of inter-faith leader Swami Chidanand Saraswati (co-founder of the Global Interfaith WASH Alliance). This focuses on achieving peace and environmental protection and starting a sanitation revolution. On World Toilet Day, a huge crowd including youth and many leaders from different communities, pledged to create a clean environment and proper sanitation. Swami Saraswati said, "It's time that we should move from building temples to more and more toilets." For Saraswati, the Ganga is not a religious topic but a lifeline for millions of people in the country.

Swami Saraswati said, "India faces a big challenge in terms of water, sanitation and hygiene. People in rural areas have toilets but they do not use them. It is because of orthodox mindset and unawareness. This is what we are fighting against." Religious leaders can help to fight the toilet crisis and open defecation in rural areas. People have to be made aware of the serious effects it can have on their health. Each person needs to be told about and shown with the help of microscopes, the germs that find way into their food and body. Open defecation is one of the major reasons for contamination of sources of water.

Swami Saraswati and his team have received support from the religious leaders of Shia and Sunni Muslim communities, the Akal Takht, the supreme temporal body of the Sikhs and others. Swami Saraswati states that religious practices, such as idol immersion in the rivers, add to water pollution. There is certainly a lack of awareness and creating awareness is imperative for bringing about a change in the mindset and behaviour. For this, education is a prerequisite and then comes cinema, posters and so on.

Sulabh Movement

Sulabh international, through the efforts of Dr Bindeshwar Pathak, stands out as a revolutionary campaign in the field of sanitation. Sociologist, social activist and founder of the Sulabh Sanitation and Social Reform Movement, Dr Pathak believes that the toilet is a tool for social change. He has received a great deal of national and international recognition for his work, including the Stockholm Water Prize in 2009 and the Padma Bhushan in 1991, and is considered a pioneer in social reform.

The Sulabh International Social Service Organisation, a non-profit voluntary social organisation, is dedicated to the Gandhian ideology of emancipation of scavengers. Sulabh has been working for the removal of untouchability and social discrimination against scavengers, a section of Indian society condemned to clean and carry human excreta manually. Sulabh is noted for achieving success in the field of cost-effective sanitation, liberation of scavengers, social transformation of society, prevention of environmental pollution and development of non-conventional sources of energy.

Sulabh popularised Sulabh Shauchalaya, an environment friendly two-pit, pour-flush compost toilet that is socially acceptable, economically affordable and technologically appropriate. It does not require scavengers to clean the pits and has helped liberate over a million scavengers. Construction and maintenance of public toilets at public places and in slums on pay-and-use basis is a hallmark of Sulabh in the field of sanitation. So far, it has constructed and is maintaining over 8,000 such public toilets in India and has constructed 200 biogas plants all over the country. Production of biogas from public toilets and recycling and reuse of effluent through a simple and convenient method is a major breakthrough in the field of sanitation and community health. The Sulabh International Social Service Organisation was formed in March 1970. Today, over five decades later, the organisation is one of the best-known NGOs working in the sanitation sector, both nationally and internationally.

Today, it is not merely an NGO, but a movement. Sulabh has also been invited to help out in neighbouring countries like Nepal, Bhutan, Afghanistan and Bangladesh. It has also taken up many programmes in collaboration with the United Nations Centre for Human Settlements, Nairobi, and the International Water and Sanitation Centre, Loughborough University of Technology, UK, through the Water Engineering and Development Centre.

Sulabh has also been closely working in collaboration with national agencies like the NBO, CBRI, HUDCO, and the ministries of Housing and Urban Poverty Alleviation, Social Justice and Empowerment and Rural Development of the Government of India and also with the All India Institute of Hygiene and Public Health, Kolkata. Sulabh's two-pit, pour-flush toilet technology, innovatively designed and modified over the years, has been evaluated by many international agencies like UNDP, World Bank, UNICEF and WHO and recommended for global replication, especially in developing countries. In addition, agencies like the ODA (Overseas Development Agency of the British Government), BORDA, SIDA (the

Danish International Development Agency) and EEC (European Economic Community) have collaborated with Sulabh.

Sulabh's achievements are noteworthy: it has been able to restore human rights and dignity to more than a million scavengers, set up about 11 lakh household toilets and 7,500 community toilet blocks, constructed over 190 human excreta-based biogas plants and made 640 towns scavenging-free. The sanitation facilities created by Sulabh are used by over 10 million people every day.

Chapter 3

HISTORY OF SANITATION IN INDIA

Sanitation is the biggest concern in India. Various strategies and programmes have been implemented to improve the sanitation conditions in India, both rural and urban. Despite progress, access to improved sanitation remains far lower in India compared to many other countries. An estimated 55 per cent of all Indians, or close to 600 million people, still do not have access to any kind of toilet. Among them, Indians who live in urban slums and rural environment are affected the most (Sengupta 2018).

Almost 74 per cent of the rural population still defecates in the open. The idea of building a facility for defecation in rural areas may not seem natural as the cash income is very low. Where such facilities exist, they are also often inadequate. In fact, this is not an issue of income; it should be the responsibility of the GPs to provide such facilities in villages. The sanitation landscape in India is still littered with 13 million unsanitary bucket latrines which require scavengers to conduct house-to-house collection. Over 7,00,000 Indians still make their living this way (United Nations 2008).

The situation in urban areas is not so critical but the sanitation problems in crowded slum environments are equally serious. In these areas, the main challenge is to ensure safe environmental sanitation. Even in areas where households have toilets, the contents of bucket latrines and pits, even of sewers, are often emptied without any environmental and health considerations. Sewerage systems, if they are available, commonly suffer from poor maintenance which leads to overflow of raw sewage. Today, in megacities such as Kolkata, Mumbai and New Delhi, the antiquated sewerage systems simply cannot handle the increased load.

History of Sanitation

The earliest evidence of urban sanitation was seen in Harappa, Mohenjo-Daro and the recently discovered Rakhigarhi of the Indus Valley Civilisation. Their urban plan included the world's first urban sanitation systems. Within the city, individual homes or groups of homes obtained water from wells. From a room that appears to have been set aside for bathing, wastewater was directed to covered drains, which lined the major streets. Roman cities and Roman villas had elements of sanitation systems, delivering water in the streets of towns such as Pompeii, and building stone and wooden drains to collect and remove wastewater from populated areas. But there is little record of other sanitation system in most of Europe until the High Middle Ages. Unsanitary conditions and overcrowding were widespread throughout Europe and Asia during the Middle Ages, resulting periodically in cataclysmic pandemics such as the Plague of Justinian (541–42) and the Black Death (1347–51), which killed tens of millions of people and radically altered societies (Cipolla 1980). Medieval towns had people to clear away the rubbish. However, the vast majority of people did not live in towns; they lived in the country where rubbish could just be buried or burnt or turned into compost or eaten by pigs. It wouldn't have been such a problem.

Bathing was less common than it is now; as few people had indoor plumbing. When one has to fetch water by hand, fill a tub and empty it afterwards, bathing is less attractive. But some wealthy people had bathrooms in their castles or palaces, and the rich had servants to fill and empty the baths and heat up the water. For example, King Henry III of England had a spectacular bath. The Westminster Chronicle of 1225 writes that he took delivery that year of a French-made bath carved in stone in the shape of a peacock "covered all over with eyes like a real peacock, made of precious stones, pearls, silver and sapphires" (as quoted in Nagla 2015).

Squires would be expected to help the lords they served bathe, among their other duties, largely depending on their status. Places such as the Latin East and Spain where such things as public baths, with associated barbers/ surgeons were maintained or rebuilt, continued to be used by the people of the area, of varying social levels and hygiene. For the common people, bathing at home would mean a wooden tub or barrel, which would have to be filled with water by hand. The common people in towns enjoyed going to the public baths. Queen Matilda, wife of King Henry I of England, built the first public baths and public lavatories in London. Monasteries often had piped water, and had bathhouse and lavers (stone troughs) used for washing before and after meals.

Cassen (1978) argues that Indian levels of personal hygiene were probably well above those of medieval Europe. Information is available of people being more unsanitary in urban areas than rural areas and for having worse housing and diet. Mortality rates were probably higher in urban areas, despite their having a population concentrated in the productive age groups (Davis 1951). But differences between the urban and rural areas are nearly as high as those between urban slums and rural slums; the latter can be as unsanitary as urban ones (Jeffery 1988:40).

Some of the important developments in sanitation and hygiene in different periods of history are listed by Nagla (2015) in his *Sociology of Sanitation*:

- 2000 BCE: Ancient Indo-Aryan water purification. In this period, water was purified by boiling and filtering.
- 460-377 BCE: The birth of hygiene. During the time of Greek physician Hippocrates, hygiene became known as the branch of medicine dedicated to health (as distinct from therapeutics, the treatment of disease).
- 300 BCE–CE 4000: The system of aqueducts built in ancient Rome provided inhabitants with fresh running water, which was piped directly to the homes of the wealthy, and to public fountains and baths. This greatly improved domestic sanitation and adequate disposal of sewage.
- 1600s–1700s: Human contact with waste was minimised in Japanese cities because it was collected for use as crop fertiliser. Sewage was not discharged into rivers so, pollution of waterways was minimised.
- 1800s: England's population increased rapidly but its number of toilets did not. Most human waste made its way into rivers, polluting the water and giving rise to foul odours.
- In 1842, public health reformer Sir Edwin Chadwick said in his sanitary Health Report: "only two or three public privies…for the great bulk of inhabitants"; "the whole area of the cellars of both

houses was full of night soil (human excrement)"; "a square court… occupied entirely as a dung receptacle of the most disgusting kind"; "a dunghill in one street… is never removed… the malarious oozes through the wall, and runs over the pavement."

- As a result of Sir Edwin Chadwick's report, the 1848 Public Health Act was instituted, followed by the 1866 Sanitary Act, making local authorities responsible for sanitary regulation including sewage disposal, water supply, and housing density and occupancy, and introducing penalties for persons suffering from dangerous infectious diseases who endangered others in public places.
- 1854: Dr John Snow showed that cholera was spread though water.
- 1860: The first septic tank was invented by Louis Moureas and used by communities to remove solids from waste before the liquid was discharged into a body of water. This design was improved by use of trickling sand filtration from 1893.
- 1865: In New York, domestic garbage and filth of every kind is thrown into the streets. In winter, the filth and garbage accumulate in the streets to a depth sometimes of two or three feet.
- 1800s–1900s: Sewer systems were constructed in many European and US cities, initially discharging untreated sewage into water-bodies. When discharge of untreated sewerage became increasingly unacceptable, experimentation towards improved treatment methods resulted in sewage farming, chemical precipitation, filtration, sedimentation, chemical treatment and activated sludge treatment using aerobic microorganisms.
- 1900: The plague was brought to the Rocks area of Sydney by rats on ships. This led to one of the first major clean ups of Sydney; slums were demolished and streets were lime-washed; 1,423 dead animals were removed from Sydney Harbour, 44,548 rats destroyed, more than 28,455 tons of garbage taken out to sea and another 25,430 tons of garbage burned.
- 1960s: Garbage compactors. The first patents for garbage compactors were filed in the US.
- 2004: The National Health and Medical Research Council (Australia) published the Australian Drinking Water Guidelines, providing guidance on what constitutes good quality drinking water. Australia's drinking water is currently sourced from dams, rainwater, bore water

> and desalination plants, whilst increasingly; treated grey water is being reused for irrigation and for selected household uses.

Analysing from a historical perspective, the situation of sanitation has not been so bad in India. Archaeological excavations in India have revealed the Harappan Model of urban sanitation. Mahatma Gandhi on sanitation is yet another stand post. In the modern period, the world witnessed yet another economical and most effective Sulabh International Model of Sanitation, introduced by Bindeshwar Pathak. But even then, the coverage of sanitation is far lower than what is required on the developmental scale. Till now, access to proper sanitation has remained the privilege of only a small section of society in India.

It is very important for modern social developers to look into the past of sanitation in ancient society for better understanding of sanitation as a problem. However, history presents very little information regarding the means employed in very early times for sanitation and for the protection of health. During these times, the measures enforced in dealing with outbreaks of infectious disease depended chiefly upon the various theories of those in charge of this area of public service. Plague and cholera were common diseases through which thousands of people died in Europe and in other countries.

In spite of the meagre information, historians are of the opinion that sanitation facilities existed in ancient society. If we go to the ancient history of the world, the use of toilets and sewage systems can be observed and the construction of bathrooms and swimming pools are so established that they were used for hundreds of years. In the words of Dr Pathak, unlike body functions like dance, drama and songs, defecation is considered very low. As a result, very few scholars have documented precisely the toilet habits of our predecessors. Nobel Prize winner for Medicine (1913) Charles Richet attributes this silence to the disgust that arises from the noxiousness and lack of usefulness of human waste. The more developed the society, the more sanitised it became and vice versa (Narayanan 2013).

Indus Valley Civilisation, from Mohenjo-Daro and Harappa

As long as man did not have an established abode, he did not have a toilet. He defecated wherever he felt like doing so. When he learnt to have a fixed house, he moved his toilet to the courtyard and then within his home. Once this was done, it became a challenge to deal with the smell and the need was felt to have a toilet which could intake human wastes and dispose them out of the house instantly and thus help maintain cleanliness. Man tried various ways to do so; methods like chamber pots, which were cleaned manually by the servants or slaves; toilets protruding out of the top floor of the house or the castle with disposal of wastes in the river below; or common toilets with holes on the top and a flowing river or stream underneath; or just entering the river or stream and disposing of the waste of the human body. While the rich used luxurious toilet chairs or close stools, the poor defecated on the roads, in the jungle or straight into the river (Pathak 2015).

In the ancient world, people were capable of designing quite sophisticated toilets. Stone Age farmers lived in a village at Skara Brae in the Orkney Islands; some of their stone huts had drains built under them and some houses had cubicles over the drains. By 2800 BCE, private bathrooms, located on the ground floor, were found in many houses of the Harappa civilisation. Western Style toilets were also made from bricks and wooden toilet seats on top (Pais 2015).

In ancient Egypt, rich people had proper bathrooms and toilets in their homes. Toilet seats were made of limestone. Poor people used a wooden stool with a hole in it. Underneath was a container filled with sand, which had to be emptied by hand. Throughout most part of history, sanitation practices were practically nonexistent. Yet the history of sanitation dates back at least 7,000 years, to the Babylonians, Egyptians, Greeks and Romans; 7,000 years ago the Babylonians discovered that contaminated water could cause disease. They brought in fresh water every day. And 2,000 years ago, physician Hippocrates discovered that cleansing could prevent infection. In the Indus Valley Civilisation (2600–1900 BCE) streets were built on a grid pattern and networks of sewers were dug under them. Toilets were flushed with water.

The ancient Indus Valley Civilisation of northwest South Asia, including Pakistan and parts of India, was prominent in hydraulic engineering, and had many water supply and sanitation devices that were the first of their kind. In ancient and medieval times there were public toilets. They looked like a bench with a hole in it, and a deep pit at the bottom of the hole where all the human waste would collect, occasionally being shovelled out by unfortunate peasants or servants. They also had the world's earliest known system of flush toilets. These existed in many homes, and were connected to a common sewerage drain. Most houses also had private wells. The sewage was then led into cesspools, built at the intersection of two drains, which had stairs leading to them for periodic cleaning. Plumbing was done using earthenware plumbing pipes with broad flanges for easy joining with asphalt to stop leaks. Harappa, Lothal and Mohenjo Daro are three of the extensive archaeological excavations in the region of the Indus Valley Civilisation. They are noted for sophisticated public works that included sewage drainage systems, public wells, and private and public baths (Kadence 2018).

Sanitation in ancient Rome was a complex system similar in many ways to modern sanitation systems. A system of 13 Roman aqueducts provided the inhabitants of Rome with water of varying quality; the best being reserved for potable supplies. Poorer quality water was used in public baths and in latrines, which were an early form of toilets. Latrine systems have been found in many places, such as, in Housesteads, a Roman fort on Hadrian's Wall, in Pompeii, Herculaneum, and elsewhere that flushed waste away with a stream of water. Romans used sea sponges on a stick, dipped in vinegar, after defecation.

The Romans had a complex system of sewers covered by stones, much like modern sewers. Waste flushed from the latrines flowed through a central channel into the main sewage system and then into a nearby river or stream. It is estimated that the first sewers of ancient Rome were built between 800 and 735 BCE. Drainage systems evolved slowly, and began primarily as a means to drain marshes and storm runoff. Around CE 100, direct connections of homes to sewers began, and the Romans completed most of the sewer system infrastructure. Sewers were laid throughout the city, serving public and some private latrines, and also served as dumping grounds for homes not directly connected to a sewer. It was mostly the wealthy whose homes were connected to the sewers, through outlets that ran under an extension of the latrine. In general, the poor used pots that they were supposed to empty into the sewer, or visit public latrines. Public latrines date back to the 2nd century BCE. Whether intentionally or not, they became places of socialisation. Long bench-like seats with keyhole shaped openings cut in rows offered little privacy (Tebyan 2010).

The Romans recycled public bath wastewater by using it as part of the flow that flushed the latrines. Terra cotta piping was used in the plumbing that carried wastewater from homes. The Romans were the first to seal pipes with concrete to resist the high water pressures developed in siphons and elsewhere.

The system in Rome was copied in all provincial towns and cities of the Roman Empire, and in villas that could afford the plumbing. Roman citizens came to expect high standards of hygiene, and the army was also well provided with latrines and bath houses. Aqueducts were used everywhere in the empire not just to supply drinking water to private houses but also to supply other needs such as irrigation and public fountains. Indeed, many of the provincial aqueducts survive in working order to the present day, although modernised and updated.

After the fall of the Western Roman Empire in the 5th century CE, sophisticated plumbing disappeared from Europe for centuries. In Saxon times, toilets were simply pits in the ground with wooden seats over them. However, in the middle ages, monks built stone or wooden lavatories over rivers. At Port Chester Castle in the 12th century, monks built stone chutes leading to the sea. When the tide went in and out it would flush away the sewage. Medieval cities, castles and monasteries had their own wells, fountains or cisterns. Usually towns built a few modest latrines for the inhabitants, but these were mostly inadequate for the size of the population. The lack of proper sanitation increased the effects of epidemics in medieval towns in Europe.

Personal cleanliness in medieval times was hampered by a lack of access to fresh water supplies and frequent problems with sewage disposal in towns. During medieval times, it was widely believed that bad smells were the cause of disease and so if the smell could be combated, the threat of disease was lessened. Town authorities across Europe made attempts to get rid of their rubbish and sewage, even if the link between waste and disease wasn't fully understood. In the late 13th century, the Great Conduit of London supplied the city with clean water and in other towns, rivers were often used to carry away waste, to the detriment of those downstream.

Another problem was the lack of separation between industrial and domestic living areas. Many industries such as butchery, dyeing and tanning were carried out in or alongside living accommodation, meaning that dirt and strong foul smells were part of everyday life. Waste from these industries often made its way back into the local water supply, further endangering health. The widespread practice of covering floors with a rush matting was another potential health hazard. Unless the floor covering was changed frequently (as done in wealthy households), animal droppings and particles of food would rot within the rushes, spreading germs and diseases.

Therefore, medieval times were truly the Dark Ages as far as sanitation was concerned. Towns were dirty and crowded, and disease and epidemics spread unchecked because of the lack of sanitation. Water was contaminated, and personal hygiene was virtually unknown. Tuberculosis, cholera, diphtheria, smallpox, yellow fever, all were rampant. It is not surprising that health during the Middle Ages was poor and the mortality rates following illnesses were high. This was the period of the Crusades and battles for power. Siege, warfare and constant battle were the norm in the Middle Age. Knights and soldiers suffered from various health problems such as wounds, abscesses and fractures. These were treated in unsanitary environments, making the condition worse. The only cure for toothache was having the tooth pulled without anaesthetics. Dreadful amputations were performed by surgeons.

Sanitation and Society during the Colonial Period

The fall of the Roman Empire also marked the end of this early sanitation culture. Due to lack of development, flush toilets and sewage systems did not exist in medieval Europe. Faeces were simply poured into the gutters. This situation didn't change until the end of the 16th century, when the English poet, Sir John Harington, invented the first modern water closet, an undertaking assigned to him by his famous aunt, Queen Elizabeth I. Though Harington drew up a precise construction manual, the first water closet of our modern age fell into oblivion. In spite of Harington's invention of a flushing lavatory with a cistern, the idea failed to catch on. People continued to use chamber pots or cess pits, which were cleaned by men called gong farmers. In 1775, Alexander Cummings reinvented the water closet and introduced the first strap to keep sewer odours from escaping. In 1885 Thomas Twyford revolutionises toilet design by replacing the metal and wood contraptions with an all-porcelain design. In 1870, John Randall Mann patented a three-pipe water closet, developing a method to utilise the suction force of a siphon to aid the flush (Plumbing 1994).

The first modern public lavatory with flush toilets opened in London in 1852. Meanwhile, Joseph Gayetty invented toilet paper in 1857. At first toilet paper was sold in sheets. It was first sold in rolls in the US in 1890 and in Europe in 1928. Soft toilet paper went on sale in 1942. However, after it was invented in the West, toilet paper was a luxury. In the early 20th century, many families used newspaper (Toilet Paper History 2018).

However, flush toilets were a luxury at first and they did not become common till the late 19th century. In the early 19th century, working class homes often did not have their own toilet and households had to share. Sometimes one had to queue to use it. In the 19th century, toilet pans were made of porcelain. They were usually decorated, embossed or painted with attractive colours. Seats were of wood, and cisterns were often emptied by pulling a chain. At first toilet bowls were boxed in, but the first pedestal toilet bowl was made in 1884. Meanwhile the vacant/engaged bolt for public toilets was patented in 1883. Also popular in the 19th century were earth closets. An earth closet was a box of granulated clay over a pan. When one pulled a lever, clay covered the contents of the pan. In rural areas, flush lavatories did not replace earth closets until the early 20th century.

However, inside toilets were luxurious in the 19th century. Working class homes had outside lavatories. About the 1900s, some houses were built for skilled workers with bathrooms and inside toilets. However, it was decades before inside toilets became universal. In the 19th century in New York City, living conditions were nearly as filthy as in the Middle Ages, and yearly epidemics swept through populations, killing many. The average life span was less than 40 years of age. But during the mid-1800s, the link between germs and diseases was proven. Soaps, disinfectants and pharmaceuticals began to be developed, and it was first recognised that diseases could be controlled.

Here began the Sanitation Revolution, and public health practices such as garbage collection, water treatment, public health departments and regulations, as well as personal bathing, became part of the culture. The death rate among children dropped, and the average life span increased over the years, up to age 74. In the second half of the 19th century, scientists such as Louis Pasteur began to recognise the relationship between disease and hygiene; as a result, the demand for more hygiene became increasingly louder. At a very early stage, ceramics specialist Villeroy and Boch saw the market potential of the sanitaryware sector with its bathtubs, sinks, toilets and tiles. By 1870, Villeroy and Boch was already equipping public swimming baths, private bathrooms and hospitals with easy care tiles. As early as the mid-1870s, the company was offering a small range of urinals and toilets. Developments made in the area of production methods and materials soon facilitated industrial production. Since Villeroy and Boch was able to produce sanitaryware in such large quantities, these items became affordable for the broad strata of society by 1899.

Present day Sanitation

In the present context, people in rich countries take toilets for granted yet in poor countries, millions of people do not have hygienic toilets. The word toilet is derived from the French word toilette, which means little cloth. In the 17th century, it was a cloth cover for a dressing table, called a toilet table. If a woman was at her toilet it meant she was dressing and preparing her appearance. By the 19th century, toilet room or toilet was a euphemism for a certain room. The word lavatory comes from the Latin "lavare" meaning to wash. In the 17th century a lavatory was a place for washing. Later it became a euphemism for a certain room. Now, the word "restroom" is used for toilets in developed countries (Lambert 2018).

The word "restroom" originated in the US. Some Americans prefer restroom over bathroom because public restrooms rarely have bathtubs. The word washroom is often used in the US for a laundry room or utility room. On board a ship, the toilets are called the heads. Originally they were just wooden boards with holes cut in them hanging over the sides of the ships. They were placed at the head of the ship. On land there are many euphemisms for toilets. One is "the smallest room in the house". An old euphemism for going to the toilet was "going to spend a penny" because public lavatories used to cost one penny to use. In the modern world, sanitation has assumed importance for health and the dignity aspects of human life. At present, sanitation has evolved into luxurious comfort; in earlier days it was only for the purpose of defecating, but at present it also has gained importance for dignity. The concept of the toilet has changed with its structure, design and other facilities. Modern toilets are more attractive than bedrooms. People decorate their toilets and add fragrance. Some people use costly material for construction of toilets.

A wide selection of toilets can be found today, in a great variety of shapes and colours and offering additional comfort. They can be floor standing or wall-mounted; a combination of toilet and cistern, or with prewall installation systems; wash out toilets with ceramic ledges, or wash down toilets with direct access into the trap water. There is even more; in recent years a whole series of innovations have been developed particularly in the area of sanitation. In view of increasing scarcity of water resources, now companies offer modern, environment-friendly flushing systems, such as Omnia Green Gain or Aquareduct, which function with as little as 3.5 litres to 4.5 litres of water per flush. Extremely convincing qualities are also displayed by the ceramic surface finish, Ceramic Plus. Its easycare properties help reduce the amount of water and cleaning agents needed. The Pure Air WC opens up a totally new dimension in WC comfort (Aquarooms 2013).

Without sanitation, life would be nightmarish. Human and animal waste would be annoying on the streets along with garbage and food scraps, producing a stench so foul that it would need one to keep the windows closed even in the sweltering heat of summer. The offensive odour and accumulating muck would be the least of your worries. Preventable diseases such as cholera and yellow fever would be rampant, life expectancy would be extremely short, and infant mortality rates would be staggeringly high.

Sanitation Initiatives in India

Swachh Bharat Mission (SBM)

The World Bank supports the Government of India in implementing the rural component of the Swachh Bharat Mission (SBM), or the Clean India Mission. The Mission is the country's largest-ever, drive to improve sanitation. It was launched by the Government of India in 2014 with the aim of ending open defecation by 2 October 2019, Mahatma Gandhi's 150th birth anniversary. The programme also seeks to ensure that communities sustain their open defecation-free status, and improve the management of liquid and solid wastes. World Bank support will help accelerate results in India's states by giving them performance-based incentives.

Improving sanitation in the villages has proved to be one of India's greatest development challenges. Three out of five people in rural India suffer the indignity of defecating in the open. Girls and women have to venture out before dawn or after dark, leaving them vulnerable to harassment. One in every ten deaths in India is linked to poor sanitation. And nearly 44 million children under five remain stunted, deprived of the chance to achieve their full potential. It is said the country loses the equivalent of 6 per cent of GDP due to inadequate sanitation (World Bank 2016).

Past efforts to address this problem have had some success. Although toilets were built, without adequate motivation to use them, villagers often continued to adhere to age-old practices, and abandoned the new toilets or put them to alternative uses. Building on lessons learnt from past experience, the new Mission will use trained facilitators to motivate people to use toilets by addressing the cultural and behavioural patterns that have prevented them from doing so. Once the desire to use toilets is established, villages will be placed in charge of drawing up their own plans to end open defecation. The facilitators will help villagers choose where to build the new toilets and masons will be trained to construct the kind of toilets that are best suited to the local terrain.

While budgetary resources and technical assistance are being made available from the Central Government, states will have the flexibility to adopt the messages and methods that resonate most with the social and cultural sensibilities of their people. Implementation on the ground will be monitored. A national sample-survey of rural sanitation will be conducted every year by independent third-party agencies. Sanitation improvements will be measured in terms of the number of rural people who have stopped open defecation, whether villages have sustained their open defecation-free status, and the improvements they have made in SLWM.

Based on the national sample survey findings, the World Bank will release funds every year to the Government of India. The central government will in turn pass on these funds to the states, where the grant money will flow through district and block levels to successful villages. These incentives will be in addition to the budgetary support provided by the Central Government to the states for funding programme investments; they will therefore be additional grants based on states' performance (Ibid).

By promoting and sustaining changed behaviours, the programme will help accelerate progress towards an open defecation free India as well as the achievement of other goals under the Clean India Mission. The World Bank will also help strengthen the institutional capacities of the national Ministry of Drinking Water Supply and Sanitation, as well as of selected states, particularly those which face the greatest challenges in sanitation.

Water and Sanitation

A direct relationship exists between water, sanitation, health, nutrition and human well-being. Consumption of contaminated drinking water, improper disposal of human excreta, lack of personal and food hygiene and improper disposal of solid and liquid waste have been the major causes of many diseases in developing countries like India.

Water supply and sanitation were added to the national agenda during the country's first Five Year Plan (1951-56). It was only in the early 1980s, with the thrust of the International Water and Sanitation Decade, that India's first nationwide programme for rural sanitation, the Central Rural Sanitation Programme (CRSP), was launched in 1986 by the Ministry of Rural Development with the objective of improving the quality of life of rural people and to provide privacy and dignity to women. The programme provided a large subsidy for construction of sanitary latrines for below the poverty line (BPL) households. It was supply-driven, highly subsidised, and laid emphasis on a single construction model. Based on the recommendations of the National Seminar on Rural Sanitation in September 1992, the programme was revised. The revised programme aimed at an integrated approach to rural sanitation.

Mahatma Gandhi was the first person who wanted to end the practice of open defecation and manual scavenging. He appealed to people to keep India clean and restore the human rights and dignity of the untouchables. Gandhiji advocated the use of the trench latrine which he himself used while he was in Phoenix Ashram in Durban, South Africa. He asked his followers and freedom fighters to use trench latrines in their homes as far as possible and also suggested the use of '*tatti par mitti*' or covering human excreta with soil so that flies could not sit on excreta.

The celebrated novelist, E. M. Forster, the author of *A Passage to India* wrote the preface to the book, *Untouchable* by Mulk Raj Anand in 1935. He writes: "No God is needed to rescue the untouchables, no vows in self-sacrifice and abnegation on the part of more fortunate Indians but simply and solely, the flush system. Introduce water closets and main drainage throughout India, and all the wicked rubbish about untouchability will disappear" (Forster 2001). Sulabh has experimented in this direction with proven results.

Sanitation Policies and Programmes

Before the 1860s, sanitary arrangements for the public were hardly discussed. By 1823, the Governor-General allowed the surplus from town taxes to be spent on urban improvements; but in Dacca, at least, most efforts went into widening roads, draining marshes and clearing land for a racecourse. There was more concern for the health of the army; medical officers were encouraged to submit details of the climate, geography and medical statistics. One measure of civilian preventive medicine was vaccination against smallpox which was supported intermittently.

Preventive health measures in India are usually dated from the Royal Commission appointed to inquire into the sanitary state of the army in India, which submitted its report in 1863. This Commission was established because of the deaths of British soldiers from disease during the mutiny caused by injuries in fighting. It reported that the health of the army could not be separated from the sanitary condition of the native population close by, and that good measure of water supply, drainage, paving, cleansing and general constitution in these towns would be attended to with most beneficial results for the health of the troops quartered near them.

The priority for sanitary work was based on military arguments, and it retained this basis for the rest of the 19th century. The Government of India implemented the proposal of the Commission's 1863 report as sanitary commissions in each presidency with advisory but less executive powers. These sanitary commissions were replaced two years later by a single sanitary commissioner each, and by 1868, one for each of the provinces. For 20 years, not much was achieved, partly because sanitary officers were subordinated to medical officers and partly because sanitary concerns were restricted to official circles. Technical disputes about the relationship between sanitary measures and medical science hindered the implementation of policy, especially with respect to the role of clean water in preventing cholera.

The Indian system of medicine was not convinced of the need to separate sanitary from medical work. Indian authorities had no training in epidemiology. In 1866, an international sanitary conference in Constantinople concluded that India was the source of cholera epidemics, and that the Indian Government had failed to control them. Indians were inferior, and one sign of their inferiority was their relentless attachment to superstition, which made it impossible to tamper with religious customs, especially pilgrimages, widely agreed to be a major route of cholera transmission. The surplus water probably formed stagnant pools, ideal breeding grounds for mosquitoes, thus increasing the spread of malaria, though deaths due to dysentery, cholera and diarrhoea probably declined.

In the late 1880s, Florence Nightingale pressed the Indian Government to improve sanitary arrangements in the villages which had been almost totally ignored. Training in hygiene and sanitation was expanded and over the next years, graduates were brought into sanitary work. Activity was severely restricted by the shortage of funds available, the limitations of policymakers and by the ignorance, prejudices, callousness and superstitions of the people.

Yet medical administrators appreciated the links between providing sanitation and the population's health, especially in urban areas where collective arrangements for waste disposal, water supply and drainage were major concerns. The other impetus to urban renewal came from plague epidemics. Plague was probably common in India before the British arrived and its association with rats was known.

Water sanitation is the most powerful preventive medicine and investment in sanitation and water is an effective mechanism in reducing risks and deaths due to killer diseases like child diarrhoea, immunisation proved in reduction of measles, meaning that preventive care can eliminate many diseases.

The governments, state as well as central, have initiated several steps and implemented effective programmes in relation to sanitation. Although this volume covers details of these programmes in the subsequent chapters, I would like to present here a brief account of these programmes.

The environmental hygiene committee (1948–49) appointed by the Central Government, was the first agency charged with an overall assessment of the country regarding problems in the entire field of environmental hygiene. The Committee recommended a comprehensive plan to provide safe water supply and adequate sanitation services to 90 per cent of the population within a period of 40 years. However, sanitation was never perceived as a priority, especially in rural areas.

At the Central Government level, there are some schemes and policies that focus specifically on water and sanitation in urban settings. Services to the urban poor include access to water supply and sanitation, which largely improves the sanitation facilities in the urban areas.

The National Urban Sanitation Policy of 2008 aims to transform urban India into healthy and liveable cities and towns that will have universal sanitation coverage. It has an ambitious plan, focussing on the urban poor and women, to have all cities and towns become totally sanitised, healthy and liveable. The main goals of the policy are: awareness generation and behavioural change; open defecation-free cities; integrated city-wide sanitation; sanitary and safe disposal; and proper operation and maintenance of all sanitary installations.

All states are encouraged to prepare state sanitation strategies taking into account their historical legacy with reference to sanitation, climate and physiographic factors, economic, social and political parameters and institutional variables. It has been suggested that state governments should monitor the performance of cities using instruments such as citizens' report cards, citizen monitoring committees, self-assessment systems and intercity computations. States will also sensitise people to adopt a holistic approach to improve sanitation and hygiene for a clean environment while accelerating overall development in the state. This was done under the Central Government's NBA sanitation drive.

Liberation and Rehabilitation of Scavengers

Dr Bindeshwar Pathak has been working for the liberation of scavengers through the Sulabh movement, a mixed package of technology, extensive training and social reforms, which is different from other social reform movements in that it combines technology with idealism. Much has changed in the status of scavengers in these years. The Sulabh concept and technology have been accepted as an alternative to the high-cost city sewerage system, and a large number of scavengers have been liberated and resettled in other professions.

The Parliament has to resolve to eliminate the practice of manual scavenging because the Prohibition of Employment as Manual Scavengers and their Rehabilitation Act,1993, has failed to achieve its desired goal. According to the bill, the district magistrate has to ensure that no person within his jurisdiction is engaged as a manual scavenger or constructs an insanitary latrine, and manual scavengers are rehabilitated. It makes it mandatory for municipalities, cantonment boards and railway authorities to construct adequate number of sanitary community latrines within three years of the Act coming into force.

Sanitation Programmes in India

Historically, Indian society has often given high priority to sanitation. Excavations at Harappa and Mohenjo daro reveal ingenious solutions to facilitate wastewater conveyance through underground drainage systems. Sanitary engineering, as far back as 5,000 years ago, was at a developed stage. Such visions on improved sanitary practices continued across the reign of various dynasties, like the Mauryas, Guptas or the southern kingdom of Vijayanagara that ruled the subcontinent. Even from an ideological point of view, various social reformers of India propagated the importance of sanitation. From Patanjali's philosophy to the writings of Vivekananda and the Gandhian concept of sanitation, the emphasis on sanitation was integral to India's cultural foundation.

It was in 1986 that the government launched the Central Rural Sanitation Programme (CRSP), the first nationwide sanitation programme. It was restructured in 1999, with a shift from a high subsidy to a low subsidy model. The supply-driven approach was altered to a demand-driven model with increased emphasis on public participation. In 2001, the same programme was overhauled with the introduction of the Total Sanitation Campaign (TSC), which carried forward the demand-driven approach focusing on awareness building. As a fillip to the TSC, the Nirmal Gram Puraskar (NGP) was launched, to recognise the achievements and efforts of GPs towards full sanitation coverage. In 2007, TSC was renamed Nirmal Bharat Abhiyan (NBA). It was not until the inception of the National Urban Sanitation Policy (NUSP) in 2008 that urban sanitation was allotted focused attention at the national level. In 2014, NBA was transformed into Swachh Bharat Mission (SBM).

Central Rural Sanitation Programme, 1986

In realisation of the importance of sanitation for improving the quality of life and its impact on productivity, the Ministry of Rural Development has been making concerted efforts to ensure total sanitation coverage. The CRSP aims at improving the quality of life of the rural poor and to provide privacy and dignity to women in rural areas. This was intended to supplement the efforts of the states. The programme provided for 100 per cent subsidy for construction of sanitary latrines for Scheduled Castes, Scheduled Tribes and landless labourers and subsidy as per the rate prevailing in the states for the general public.

Based on the feedback received on implementation of the programme from the states, UNICEF and voluntary organisations, the programme was revised by the Government of India in March 1991. For the construction of individual sanitary latrines, there was liberal subsidy at the rate of 95 per cent for Scheduled Castes/Scheduled Tribes and people below the poverty line. The programme also provided for construction of village complexes with bathing facilities, hand pumps, latrines, drainage facilities and washing platforms. Up to 5 per cent of the outlay could be utilised towards administrative cost and another 10 per cent for training of masons, awareness and health education. The contribution by the states' funds was limited to one-third of the assistance received from the Central Government.

The programme has since been further revised in September 1992, and the strategy outlined in the Eighth Five Year Plan. The revised programme aimed at generation of felt need and people's participation. The subsidy pattern has been changed, limiting it to 80 per cent for persons below the poverty line for individual household latrines. For exclusive sanitary complexes for women, the subsidy is limited to 70 per cent with the balance 30 per cent being the contribution by the panchayats/beneficiaries. For other sanitation facilities in the village, the subsidy is 50 per cent the balance cost being met by the panchayats. The revised programme aims at an integrated approach of rural sanitation. The concept of sanitary marts for supply of materials required for construction of sanitary latrines and involvement of voluntary organisations in publicity campaign and execution of the programme are also new elements. At least 10 per cent of the total funds are to be channelled through voluntary organisations. The subsidy is shared equally by the Central and the state governments.

Another salient feature of the revised programme was to develop at least one model village covering facilities like sanitary latrines, conversion of dry latrine, garbage pits, soakage pits, drainage and pavement of lanes. Sanitary latrines in village institutions, clean surrounding around ponds, tanks, hand pumps and other drinking water sources. The Central Rural Sanitation Programme was restructured in 1999, exhibiting a paradigm shift in approach and the TSC was introduced.

Total Sanitation Campaign, 1999

The CRSP was a supply-driven, high-subsidy and infrastructure-oriented programme. As a result of these deficiencies and low financial allocations, it had little impact on the gigantic sanitation problem. The experience of community-driven, awareness generating campaign-based programmes in some states and the results of evaluation of CRSP led to the formulation of the TSC approach in 1999.

The main objectives of the TSC include:

- Bringing about an improvement in the general quality of life in the rural areas;
- generating felt demand for sanitation facilities through awareness creation and health education;
- promoting hygiene education and sanitary habits among students;
- eliminating open defecation to minimise risk of contamination of drinking water sources and food; and
- converting dry latrines to pour-flush latrines, and eliminating manual scavenging, wherever in existence in rural areas.

The strategy is to make the programme "community-led" and "people-centred". A demand-driven approach is adopted with increased emphasis on awareness creation and demand generation for sanitary facilities in houses and schools and for a cleaner environment. Alternative delivery mechanisms are adopted to meet the community needs. Subsidy for individual household latrine units has been replaced by incentives for the poorest of the poor households. Rural school sanitation is a major component and an entry point for wider acceptance of sanitation by the rural people. Technology improvisations to meet the customer preferences and location-specific intensive campaign involving PRIs, cooperatives, women's groups, self-help groups and NGOs are also important components of the strategy. The strategy addresses all sections of the rural population to bring about the relevant behavioural changes for improved sanitation and hygiene practices and meet their sanitary hardware requirements in an affordable and accessible manner by offering a wide range of technological choices.

Implementation of TSC was proposed in project mode and was implemented with the district as the unit. The TSC project cycle in the project districts was expected to take about four years or less for implementation. In 2013, the programme evaluation organisation of the Planning Commission was entrusted to conduct an independent evaluation of the TSC programme in order to assess its socio-economic impact. The study tried to assess the impact in terms of reduction in open defecation and build-up of toilet facilities at the household level. In spite of 14 years of implementation of the programme, it was surprising to see the existence of open defecation in rural India to the extent of 72.63 per cent.

The study further showed that the role of rural sanitary marts/production centres as alternative delivery mechanism to encourage cost effective and appropriate technologies for ecologically safe and sustainable sanitation is insignificant. Further, it appeared that the Rural Sanitary Marts/Production Centres mechanism has been adopted in letter but not in spirit in most states, with many states not even opting for this mechanism.

The study finds that policy variables such as TSC awareness and awareness of waterborne diseases due to squalid sanitary practices emerge as significant factors impacting household level open defecation and toilet availability. With greater awareness, households are likely to exhibit improved sanitary and hygienic behaviour, construct toilets and reduce open defecation. The effect of incentive on households' toilet availability is also found to be positive and significant. Moreover, well designed, functional toilet facilities are also a step ahead in reducing open defecation, which is a very straightforward and expected outcome. Other variables like water availability and education are important determinants of availability of household toilet provision and open defecation. The study also finds that educational attainment is an important determinant of sanitation practices and hygienic behaviour. Families with better levels of educational attainment are more likely to refrain from open defecation. Adequacy of water in the area where the toilet is to be constructed is also a prerequisite for effecting reduced open defecation.

Nirmal Gram Puraskar, 2003

The Government of India has been promoting sanitation coverage in campaign mode to ensure better health and quality of life for people in rural India. To add vigour to its implementation, the Government of India launched an award based incentive scheme for fully sanitised and open defecation free GPs, blocks, districts and states called "Nirmal Gram Puraskar" (NGP) in October 2003 and gave away the first awards in 2005 as a component of its flagship scheme, TSC. NGP, till 2011, was given by the Ministry of Drinking Water and Sanitation at all levels of PRIs, that is, GP, block panchayat and district panchayat. It was decided that with the transition to NBA, selection of GPs to award Nirmal Gram Puraskar from the year 2012 would be taken up by the states, while selection of the blocks and district panchayats shall continue to be with the Centre.

National Urban Sanitation Policy, 2008

The Ministry of Urban Development, Government of India, developed the "National Urban Sanitation Policy" in 2008. The vision of the policy is that all Indian cities and towns become totally sanitised, healthy and livable and ensure and sustain good public health and environmental outcomes for all their citizens with special focus on hygienic and affordable sanitation facilities for the urban poor and women. The focus of the policy is on awareness generation and behavioural change by generating awareness about sanitation and its linkages with public and environmental health amongst communities and institutions and also promoting mechanisms to bring about and sustain behavioural changes aimed at adoption of healthy sanitation practices.

The overall goal of this policy is to transform urban India into community-driven, totally sanitised, healthy and liveable cities and towns. The specific goals are:

a. Awareness Generation and Behaviour Change.
b. Achieving Open Defecation-Free Cities.
c. Integrated City-Wide Sanitation.

The National Urban Sanitation Policy takes into account all the elements of environmental sanitation, including solid waste management; generation of industrial and other specialised/hazardous wastes; drainage; as also the management of drinking water supply, generating awareness of the benefits of a hygienic and clean environment and thereafter brings about behaviour change, elimination of open defecation, integrated citywide sanitation, safe disposal and proper operation and maintenance of all sanitary installations are some of the goals of the project. Special focus has been given to hygienic and affordable sanitation facilities for the urban poor particularly for the urban poor and women and will ensure improved cleanliness in cities and towns. The NUSP envisages transforming all the towns and cities of India into 100 per cent sanitised, healthy and livable spaces, ensuring sustained public health and improved environmental outcomes for all its citizens.

Nirmal Bharat Abhiyan, 2012

The Nirmal Bharat Abhiyan (NBA) is a comprehensive programme to ensure sanitation facilities in rural areas with a broader goal to eradicate the practice of open defecation. In fact, the Total Sanitation Campaign started in 1999 was renamed Nirmal Bharat Abhiyan in April 2012. The objective is to accelerate sanitation coverage in rural areas so as to comprehensively cover the rural community through renewed strategies and saturation approach. The revised approach emphasised more on IEC, human resource development, capacity development activities to increase awareness among rural people and generation of demand for facilities for rural sanitation.

Swachh Bharat Abhiyan, 2014

Swachh Bharat Abhiyan was launched on 2 October 2014 (Gandhi Jayanti). This campaign aims to accomplish the vision of 'Clean India' by 2 October 2019, the 150th birth anniversary of Mahatma Gandhi. The Ministry of Drinking Water and Sanitation will implement the programme in rural areas while the Ministry of Urban Development will do the same in urban areas. The Nirmal Bharat Abhiyan will be restructured into the Swachh Bharat Mission with two sub-missions: Swachh Bharat Mission (rural) and Swachh Bharat Mission (urban). Budgetary provisions for the two sub-missions will be provided separately in the demands for grants of both ministries.

The programme includes elimination of open defecation, conversion of insanitary toilets to pour-flush toilets, eradication of manual scavenging, municipal solid waste management, bringing about a behavioural change in people regarding healthy sanitation practices; generating awareness among citizens about sanitation and its linkages with public health; strengthening of urban local bodies to design, execute and operate systems to fulfil these objectives; and creating and enabling an environment for private sector participation in capital expenditure and operational expenditure. The urban component of the programme consists of providing individual household toilets, community and public toilets and municipal solid waste management in all 4,041 statutory towns.

Lapses in Sanitation Programmes in India

The sanitation promoting programmes in India (CRSP, TSP and the initiative taken under National Rural Health Mission) fail to build strategies to develop sanitation standards in India at large. There are visible sanitation deficits in policy formulation, implementation and technology appropriation within sanitation promoting programmes and also in the larger development strategy followed in India. The important sanitation lapses are:

- Sanitation standards are undefined in India. An open defecation-free environment is not a measureable standard or indicator. Many other standards need to be defined.
- Sanitation is yet to become a core thrust of the public health facilities and primary healthcare.
- There is no defined sanitation standard for industries, factories, urban spaces, municipalities, housing colonies or even neighbourhoods.
- Associating sanitation only with open defecation by the household is lending a very narrow meaning to sanitation.
- Sanitation infrastructure and its technological base are highly inadequate in India.
- Sanitation is neither seen as a right nor a duty. There is no punishment for violators.
- There is no binding sanitation policy at national or even state level.
- The religiously, culturally or even socially approved insanitary works are not banned.
- No effort has been made to understand the open defecation behaviour of people. It has been assumed that provision or availability of toilets and latrines will change the behaviour automatically or awareness generation will help in changing the behaviour. This is the biggest strategic lapse.

Chapter 4

SANITATION AND CULTURE

Society consists of people who live in groups such as in family or form social relationships like friendship. Study of social institutions in relation to sanitation enables the researcher to understand the base of the problem of sanitation. Various institutions like family, caste, religion, education and village community have their own problems of sanitation. Now, more and more people come to live in towns and cities, and face the problem of accommodation. As a result, some of them end up living in slums. Slums generally face the problem of disposal of waste, toilets and drinking water. Since sanitation is a serious problem in slums, we need to consider the relationship between slums and sanitation.

Sanitation practices are also related to culture. The methods of managing sanitation needs are culturally designed and supported and hence we need to study the interplay between sanitation and culture. Culture is a very broad term that includes all aspects like walks of life, modes of behaviour, philosophies, morals, manners, customs and traditions, religious, political, economic and other activities. It includes all that man has acquired in his individual and social life. Culture distinguishes human beings from animals. Most of the behaviours of animals are instinctual whereas the behaviour of human beings is learnt behaviour. Human beings alone are able to communicate through language, have norms and other rules of society and are able to acquire and transmit knowledge. Man alone creates culture and lives by the dictate of culture.

According to E.B. Taylor, "Culture is that complex whole which includes knowledge, belief, art, morals, law, custom and any other capabilities and habits acquired by man as a member of society." Graham Wallas defines culture as, "An accumulation of thoughts, values and objects, it is the social heritage acquired by us from the preceding generations through learning."

Culture is not inherited biologically but learnt socially by man through the process of socialisation. It is social in the sense it originates and develops through social interaction and is shared by the members of society. It is transmitted from one generation to the next through the vehicle of language. Bierstadt calls culture "the memory of human race" because culture is cumulative. In its cumulative capacity culture becomes richer and richer. Different parts of culture are interconnected. Though sometimes there may be conflict in some elements of culture, soon the conflict will be resolved and there will be integration. Though culture is relatively stable, it is subject to slow but constant change. Culture is satisfying for individuals and groups belonging to a particular culture because it provides opportunities and means for the satisfaction of our needs and desires.

Culture is a complex process, and includes some important elements. According to Harry M. Johnson, cognitive elements, beliefs, norms, values, signs and symbols are important elements of culture. Cognitive elements refer to the knowledge of man as a member of society. Cultures of all societies include a vast amount of knowledge about the physical and social world. Secondly, people have beliefs in their cultures. Tested empirical knowledge and untested beliefs are elements of culture which go hand in hand. Norms are shared standards of behaviour. Norms include customs, traditions, laws, legislation, rules, etc. Values are higher order norms. Values may be said to be the measure of goodness and desirability. A sign includes the existence of a thing, event or condition in the past, present and future. Symbols are important in communication and expression. In all cultures, language is a symbol.

Cultural Diversity in India

India is a land of myriad cultures. People have been living in India for thousands of years. The cultural origins of the Indian subcontinent can be traced back to the Indus Valley Civilisation. Since earliest times, people started migrating to India. From the 12th century, India came under the Mughal rule. Since the late 16th century, India was under the influence of European powers till 1947 when India gained Independence. All people who came to India became one with Indian culture. From this has evolved the composite Indian culture. This diversity has enriched our social life.

People of India are divided on the basis of region, religion, values, language, food habits, dress, patterns and behaviour. Hindus, Muslims, Buddhists, Sikhs, Christians, Jains, Parsis and those belonging to different religions, live in India. We find diversity in the clothing and food habits of Indians. Clothing depends upon the climate, physical features and traditions of the respective regions. There is diversity in our food habits too, due to climatic conditions, crops and other geographical factors.

The relationship between culture and sanitation in the Indian context is very close. Understanding the social habits of people is essential for the study of sanitation. Sanitation is an essential part of every person's life. It is an activity which every individual or group of people follows in one way or another, in their daily live, in different forms. For example, a person who is born in a city washes his hands in the wash basin while a person born in the village washes his hands outside the house. In the study of the culture of sanitation, we understand the relationship between culture and sanitation. Some of the components of the culture of sanitation are associated with manual scavenging, the attitudes of people of different castes and beliefs towards dirt and the problem of manual scavenging, and solutions for ending it. India is a nation of ancient and firmly entrenched traditions and culture. For thousands of years, religion, geography and the necessities of a rural agrarian society have sculpted a complex caste system based on status, hierarchy and, above all, a strict division of labour.

Nearly half of India's population have no toilet at home. The situation is worse in the villages, where two-thirds of the homes don't have toilets. Open defecation is widespread, and remains a major impediment in achieving the MDGs which include reducing by half, the proportion of people without access to basic sanitation. The lack of toilets and preference for open defecation is a cultural issue in a society where the habit actually perpetuates social oppression, and there is reduced but continued existence of human scavengers and sweepers.

Mahatma Gandhi once inspected toilets in the city of Rajkot in Gujarat. He reported that they were dark and stinking and reeking with filth and worms in the homes of the wealthy and in a Hindu temple. The homes of the untouchables simply had no toilets. India's enduring shame is clearly rooted in cultural attitudes. More than half a century after Independence, many Indians continue to relieve themselves in the open and litter unhesitatingly, but keep their homes spotlessly clean. The State has failed to extend sanitation facilities, but people must also take the blame.

Social Construction of Sanitation, Dirt and Hygiene

Idea about dirt and hygiene vary from culture to culture and has changed from century to century. What is dirty in one place is clean in another. What was seen as clean by our forebears is unacceptably dirty in the late 20th century. The explanation offered by anthropology for dirt is that it is matter out of its proper place. As each society has rules that create order, violations of that order constitute a threat to society. As physical objects which are in the wrong place, or hard to classify, are labelled as dirty, so the label "dirty" is given to marginal behaviour and social categories which provide a threat to the social order (Douglas 1966). To combat the dangers of dirt, there is hygiene, which serves to preserve order, to eliminate dirt and to preserve health.

Dirt is multifaceted in nature and ubiquitous, and a corollary to hygiene. Rules about hygiene are to be found throughout every society. Hygiene is not only the private practice of individuals, it is a requirement of each society. Hygiene provides a barrier to the transmission of disease, and also provides a barrier to disorder, chaos and social collapse. Simply providing public services, whether it be water supply, sanitation, curative services or health education, does not in itself guarantee improvement in health status. Just because a service is there does not guarantee that it will be used, or that it is used to the best possible health advantage. Some households contrive to preserve health even without these services. A framework that goes beyond the provision of services, beyond the standard public health perspective, is needed, for a more effective way of working.

Berman, et al. (1994) offer a solution and suggest that at the household level, external conditions and internal processes come together to produce health. They propose that households combine their own knowledge, resources and behavioural patterns with available technologies, services, information and support from outside the home, to produce desired outcomes, one of which is good health. Similarly, in relation to the public and domestic domains of disease transmission, Cairncross (1996) points out that the endemic disease that is responsible for the vast majority of the toll of death and illness in developing countries is largely transmitted within households.

What image comes to mind when one thinks of hygiene varies according to our upbringing. Hygiene means different things to different people. Hygiene is a social phenomenon in the context of the social reality. Boot and Cairncross (1993) provide a useful definition of hygiene: "The practice of keeping oneself and one's surrounding clean, especially in order to prevent illness or the spread of infection." The idea of hygiene thus comprises two concerns: the avoidance of dirt, and the prevention of disease. Hence, ideas about hygiene are not absolute. They vary from culture to culture and also through history.

According to McLaughlin (1971) "Dirt is the evidence of the imperfection in life". He suggests that there is no such thing as absolute dirt: soup on a plate before we eat it is food; the leftovers on the plate are dirty. Secretions pus, vomit, urine and faeces are inescapably dirty. Anthropologist Mary Douglas (1966) was one of the first to realise that dirt was the reflection of the culture which defined it. Dirt is a by-product of a systematic ordering and classification of matter. That which does not fit within the system is rejected and labelled as dirt.

Douglas says that hygiene is not a matter of mere health, but is a construct that can only be understood in relation to other fundamental social values such as cleanliness, order, purity, sacredness, veneration and their corollaries: dirt, disorder, pollution, profanity and defilement. To elicit the actual view of hygiene in any society we have to go to the rationalist surface, to find out the cultural and psychological foundation of hygiene. Hygiene springs from the need of an individual for social order; order creates harmony and health. Religion, natural philosophy and science have arranged to offer satisfactory post-rationalisation for what is a fundamental need for order.

Hygiene and pollution rules are found in every society and are to be understood in the social framework of ideologies, underpinning forces and rationality behind them. In India, the religious conception of the pure/impure dichotomy subtends the whole hierarchical order of society. In his classic work, *Homo Hierarchicus*, Dumont (1980) states that the fundamental institution in India is caste. Caste is based on a hierarchical opposition of the pure and the impure, the superior and inferior. If the ritual and purity of the Brahmins helped to set them apart from society, this would have also contributed to the legitimisation of the Brahmins' position at the top of the hierarchy.

Eventually, Brahmin religion became dominant throughout India among Hindus justified by hierarchical ordering of society based on degrees of purity. Scriptural prescriptions about pollution and purity help to keep each group in their allotted rank in the social hierarchy. The relationship of one group to another is defined by their ritual purity with Brahmins at the top of the purity scale and "untouchables", who traditionally have the polluting professions (leather work, garbage and night soil collection) at the bottom of the scale (Dumont 1980). Social sanctions, which work all the way up the edifice of caste, keep the system in place (Curtis 1998). In other countries, secular morality often plays a similar role. For example, elaborate cleanliness, fresh clothes and perfumes are not only more available to the rich, but serve to reinforce the distinction between the rich and the poor and thus perpetuate inequality. If poverty and oppression can be justified on the grounds of a lack of hygiene, then we are dealing with a potentially explosive concept. If hygiene is intimately related with power, rank and caste, then no effort to promote hygiene can afford to be dealing with a purely scientific issue.

Hygiene keeps society in order because of the threat of disease. But for this order, society has to believe in it. Society provides two categories of explanation of natural phenomena such as birth, growth, the changing of the seasons, cause of disease, calamity and death. The first is the agency of some external force still deriving its power from religion, magic or symbolism. The second is the agency of properties that are intrinsic to the natural world and designated as naturalistic or scientific. While it is commonly thought that societies have evolved away from mystical explanation and towards the scientific, the two categories cannot be separated so easily.

Disease is one consequence of offences against the natural order. Burkert (1992) suggests that to try to separate the divine from the earthly in early societies is wasted effort: "In archaic societies the social and physical ills were not clearly differentiated... the administration of justice and healing can be seen to fuse... An offence is the source of illness, illness is the result of an offence, be it in the personal, the social or the religious sphere. Even the Greek word 'Nosos' embraces both the physical and the social ailments and disturbances."

Throughout history, people have been advised, exhorted and ordered to conform to certain rules of hygiene behaviour. The explanations offered have included factors such as public and private morality, religious purity and the preservation of health. As the scientific understanding of disease transmission has advanced, so the case for hygiene for health reasons has come to dominate in our supposedly scientific societies. However, motivations for domestic hygiene lie not in the avoidance of specific diseases, but in subtle social forces. On the other hand, health scientists ignore the social forces in the path of disease transmission (Nagla 2015).

Meaning of Sanitation

We have already discussed sanitation at length in Chapter 2. Broadly, sanitation is the hygienic means of promoting health through prevention of human contact with the hazards of wastes as well as the treatment and proper disposal of wastes. The importance of the isolation of waste lies in an effort to prevent disease, which can be transmitted through human waste, which afflicts both developed countries as well as developing countries to differing degrees. It is estimated that up to 5 million people die each year from preventable waterborne diseases (Gleick 2002).

Sanitation is a necessity for a healthy life. There are two schools of thought: the "miasmatists" who regarded miasmas as being responsible for disease; and the "contagionists" who believed that disease came from bodily contact, sharing of substances such as food and water, or proximity. Edwin Chadwick (as cited in Nagla 2015), the great sanitary reformer, explained that epidemic fevers were due to miasmas arising from decaying animals and vegetable matter. In the wake of industrialisation and urbanisation came the concern that urban population concentrations were the breeding ground for filth, epidemic and vice, all of which threatened the social order. But the stated concern of sanitarians was that "epidemic disease was the product of dirt and decomposing matter". The elite used new theories about disease to explain their fear of the threat of the poor; the poor saw their disease as a consequence of their poverty.

Social Structure

Social structure determines the nature of individuals which reflects cultural beliefs and practices, beliefs about sanitation and disease, and attitudes towards hygiene. These function as forces of change and in response to these forces, we can analyse the change. Therefore, social and cultural considerations are important to understand the institutional functioning of sanitation.

Consideration should be given to institutions of a political, economic and social nature that are operating at the national and/or local level such as government, the civil service, religious institutions, schools and colleges, the family, and to the forms of leadership and authority that are generally accepted by the majority of the people. It is also important to consider the various roles and patterns of behaviour of individuals and social groups, and to determine who is traditionally responsible for such areas as water supplies, environmental hygiene, family health and children's defecation habits. For example, caste sanctions and strictures still govern all social, religious and economic activities of an average Indian in the villages and, to a decreasing extent, the towns and cities. Hence, socio-cultural considerations based on caste, marriage, family and other social institutions establish the beliefs and practices which determine the nature of sanitation.

Cultural Beliefs and Practices

Group and community identity, gender roles, the relative importance attached to different forms of authority and the ways in which it is exercised are all influenced by culture, which is everything that is passed down by human society including language, laws, customs, beliefs and moral standards. Culture shapes human behaviour in many different ways, including the status attached to different roles and what is deemed to be acceptable personal and social behaviour. In many cultures, the elderly command traditional authority and influence within the family and community.

With regard to sanitation behaviour, defecation is often a private matter which people are unwilling to discuss openly, while the burying of faeces is widely practised to ward off evil spirits. Contact with faecal matter is unacceptable to certain individuals in societies where it is the responsibility of low-income or low-caste groups, while taboos may dictate that separate facilities should be provided for particular social groups. A particular cultural practice to be considered, which has direct technical consequences, is the method of anal cleansing used by the community; whether use of water, stones, corn cobs or thick pieces of paper will affect the design of the sanitation system. Culture also influences how people interpret and evaluate the environment in which they live. Investments in sanitation seek to improve health by providing a clean physical environment for households.

The sanitation behaviour of individuals usually has a rational basis, and people are often aware of the environmental causes of ill-health. Many societies have detailed knowledge of the physical environment as a provider of resources for curative and preventive medicine and also as a cause of illness. They also have an understanding of the environment, not only in its physical sense, but also in relation to social and spiritual factors. This holistic view of the environment permeates many of the cultural beliefs and customs that impinge on both water use patterns and sanitation behaviour.

Although communities may lack knowledge of modern medical explanations of disease, they often have concepts of what is pure and polluting. Of the water resources available to particular households for domestic purposes, running water may be most acceptable for drinking because it is exposed to sunlight; it is considered to be "alive" and therefore "pure", while water in shallow wells, which does not have these attributes, is deemed suitable only for washing and cooking. Communities have been observed to use the environmental resources available to them, such as bamboo, to bring fast-flowing river water to their villages in preference to more convenient well water that is unacceptable in taste, colour and smell.

Concepts of clean and dirty, pure and polluting, are well developed in major world religions, and have a ritual and spiritual significance as well as referring to a physical state. When people are told that new sanitation facilities will make their environment cleaner, it is their own interpretation of this concept that will be used. Clean may have quite different meanings to project promoters and the recipients. Thus, "It is essential to look into traditional categories of cleanliness and dirtiness, purity and pollution before embarking on a campaign to motivate people to accept a project in improved...sanitation or to change their behaviour to comply with new standards of cleanliness (Bourne 1984).

Attitude towards Sanitation Facilities

Evidence of the value attached by communities to cleanliness and environmental sanitation is found in studies related to diarrhoea. People's perceptions of the causes of diarrhoea may be divided into three categories: physical, social and spiritual. In many cases, physical causes are identified with the faecal oral transmission routes of diarrhoea. Households associate diarrhoea with a polluted environment including uncovered food, dirty water and flies. As on-site sanitation involves improving the physical environment, it may be accepted as one of the means by which to reduce the incidence of disease. Equally, social and spiritual causes are perceived to be important. But these three apparently unrelated causes of diarrhoea should not be interpreted as mutually exclusive or divergent approaches to disease. They are often closely interrelated in practice, within a holistic interpretation of the environment.

Efforts should be made to determine how a community's beliefs, knowledge and control over the environment can be connected in a positive way. Careful judgement is required to distinguish between those beliefs and ritual behaviour that are conducive to good sanitation practice and those that need to be changed. Access to education may increase awareness of the health benefits of improved sanitation technology, while income will influence the capacity of a household to acquire particular facilities. Community organisations and influential leaders can assist in marketing the concept by emphasising factors valued locally. These may include the status attached to possessing a facility, or its functional value in terms of comfort.

Households vary widely in the resources of money, labour and time available to them and have their own priorities. For those with limited resources, the costs of a sanitation system in the short term may be too great when set against their need for food, shelter and clothing. In terms of capital investment, latrines may be very costly for households if they take a long time to clean, are difficult to use or involve radical changes in social habits (Pacey 1980). The demographic composition, economic characteristics and attitudes to sanitation of individual households change over time. Experience shows that once people start to improve their houses their interest in latrines is likely to be aroused. Some households may be encouraged to install a latrine as one aspect of the modernisation process.

Caste, Religion and Sanitation

The institutions of caste and religion, the two important components of Indian culture, are essentially related to sanitation. It is in the caste system that a person is born, brought up and dies. Caste also determines one's choice of occupation. Caste largely determines the differences in modes of domestic and social life. The contribution of the caste system to the problem of sanitation is significant in present society. Studies have shown that there are differences among castes regarding sanitation. SCs and STs, the most disadvantaged groups in India, have poor household sanitation and drainage.

Religion is a major concern of man. It is concerned with rituals, beliefs and practices. Religion guides and influences people's behaviour. There are differences with regard to sanitation among different religions. India is the origin of important world religions like Hinduism, Buddhism, Jainism and Sikhism. Throughout India's history, religion has been an important part of the country's culture. Hindu practices include daily rituals such as puja (worship) and recitations, annual festivals and occasional pilgrimages.

On the other hand, the social, religious, political, economic and cultural life of Indians is influenced by the caste system. Though the caste system is an aspect of Hindu society, it is also found among members of other religions. Much has been said about the security afforded by the caste system to each of the castes. According to Hutton, an individual's membership in a caste canalises his choice in marriage, acts as his trade union, his friendly or benefit society, his status club and his orphanage; it takes the place for him of health insurance and if need be, provides for his funeral. Mencher (1974) is of the view that the security afforded by caste is only to the man at the top or perhaps in the middle rungs. From the point of view of people at the bottom, caste has functioned and continues to function as a very effective system of economic exploitation.

Each caste had its own occupation. These occupations were hereditary. With the hereditary occupations of caste it became obligatory monopolies of families belonging to a particular caste. It is not merely a right to perform such occupations but it is the duty imposed by birth. Wiser analysed the *jajmani* system to explain the mutual services rendered by different castes. Dumont (1980) conceded that this system was based on religious values rather than economic logic.

The concepts of purity and pollution are closely related to caste hierarchy. The higher the rank of a Hindu, the higher the level of purity; the lower the rank, the more impure he is. Dumont holds the notion of purity and pollution interlinked with the caste system and untouchability. Purity restrictions are prevalent regarding marriage, drink, food, touch and occupation. Purity is associated with ritual cleanliness such as daily bathing in flowing water, dressing in properly laundered clothes of approved materials, eating only the foods appropriate for one's caste, refraining from physical contact with people of lower rank and avoiding involvement with ritually impure substances. The pollution includes body wastes and excretions, especially those of another adult person. Contact with the products of death or violence are typically polluting and threatening to ritual purity.

As people are graded on the basis of purity and pollution, occupations are also graded. The occupations of the Brahmins are pure whereas the occupations of the untouchables are impure. Occupations like handling of leather or a dead cow, the removal of human waste, working at the cremation ground, sweeping the streets, etc., are considered lowest and impure. The prohibition against touching a dead cow was extended to the playing of a cowhide drum. In northern India, leather workers are known as Chamars. Traditionally, the scavenging caste was known as Bhangi but now they prefer to be called Valmikis. Other occupations such as washerman, fisherman and toddy tapper connote untouchability in some areas.

Singh and Ziyauddin (2000) felt that caste-based occupational groups in India, like that of manual scavengers, constitute one group which is socially, economically, psychologically and politically marginalised section of society. Although manual scavenging was banned twice (1952 and 1993), this practice still continues in various pockets of the country under different names. The evil of manual scavenging is directly related to the lack of availability of sanitation facilities.

Manual scavenging is a caste-based occupation carried out by Dalits. These communities are invariably placed at the bottom of the caste hierarchy as well as Dalit subcaste hierarchy. Manual scavengers are exposed to the most virulent forms of viral and bacterial infections that affect their skin, eyes, limbs, respiratory and gastro-intestinal systems; tuberculosis is widespread.

Untouchability and Sanitation

Though the origin of the caste system in India goes back more than 3000 years, untouchability is of later origin. Till about the 2nd century CE certain castes like the Ayogava, Paulkasas and Nishads were despised, but were not considered untouchables. The notion of purity and pollution, as Dumont observed, is integrally linked with the practice of untouchability. Gradually, this notion of purity and pollution freed itself from its specific and original task of separating the untouchables from others but began to be operative at different phases of the caste system. Imputed with maximum degree of ritual and social impurity, the occupations of these castes were held to be the lowest in the hierarchy. With the emergence of castes there also arose many subcastes among the untouchables.

The untouchables were involved in occupations which were usually considered to be polluting or defiling. Swine herding is defiling because swine defiles. Leather defiles and consequently the making and repairing of shoes became an occupation of the untouchables. Occupations like scavenging, removing carcasses from the village and the like became the occupations of the untouchables. Though they were related to other castes through the *jajmani* relations, they were not eligible to receive several services from the upper castes.

Traditionally, the untouchables were assigned occupations which were ritually polluting like fishing, killing or disposing of dead cattle or working with their hides for a living. Also, pursuing activities that brought them into contact with matters emitted from the human body, such as faeces, urine, sweat and spittle, a category that included such occupational groups like sweepers and washermen. They also conveyed news of deaths, collected wood for funerals and work as agricultural labourers. Later, the occupations of the untouchables were stigmatised and were done by only by them. With the passage of time, the untouchables and lower caste people were not allowed to do any other jobs where they could attain the social status of people of other castes. So, their social mobility was restricted. With the development of towns and cities, there arose the need for scavenging. As other castes were not ready to do these jobs, municipalities had to bring in untouchables from the rural areas. In many towns and cities they are housed in colonies and work as sweepers, cleaners of sewage lines and as railway sweepers.

The untouchables lived on the periphery of society and suffered from social segregation and restrictions, in addition to being poor. They were not allowed to worship in temples with others, nor draw water from the same wells as others. These handicaps are most pronounced with regard to access to water and sanitation. The Dalits or SCs still face multiple types of deprivation and discrimination with regard to access to natural resources, especially water.

In India, more than 20 per cent of Dalits do not have access to safe drinking water; 48.4 per cent of Dalit villages are denied access to a water source. Only 10 per cent of Dalit households have access to sanitation as compared to 27 per cent for non-Dalit households, and the vast majority of Dalits depends on the goodwill of upper caste community members for access to water from public wells. Dalit women stand in separate queues near the bore well to fetch water and wait till the non-Dalits finish taking water. Dalits are not allowed to use taps and wells located in non-Dalit areas (Purohit 2015); 27 per cent Dalit households have water sources within the premises as compared to 45 per cent for the general population. Further, 23.7 per cent of Dalit households have access to a latrine facility as compared to 42.3 per cent for general households (Pais 2015).

Dalits and Manual Scavenging

Though we have progressed, there are still towns and cities where scavenging is done manually. It is estimated that every day, 13 lakh people in India, of which more than 80 per cent are Dalit women, are forced to clean human excrement with their bare hands for little to no wages. Of the 7,70,338 manual scavengers and their dependants across India, so far, only 4,27,870 persons have been assisted under the National Scheme of Liberation and Rehabilitation of Scavengers (NSLRS) and the remaining number yet to be rehabilitated is 3,42,468 (Pais 2015). Access to sanitation is non-existent for these people as they have to do these menial jobs with their bare hands and they have a higher risk of occupational illness and health hazards.

Dalit women are the worst affected by the lack of access to water and sanitation. Their connection with water resources is very intricate. A Dalit woman has all the burden of household work in the family and she is the one who is responsible for bringing water for the family and, therefore, she is the one who faces discrimination at the water source. Even young girls from the family are assigned to do this job and they also face similar conditions. They even drop out of school as collecting water from faraway sources becomes their primary responsibility and they thereby lose any chance of being educated and earn money for the family. They are the ones who face verbal and physical abuse from the dominant castes and they are under constant threat while collecting water from public wells and taps. Sometimes, dominant caste women don't allow Dalit women to touch the public source of water and they pour water into the pots of Dalit women. As a result, how much water they take back home also depends on the whims and fancies of dominant caste women. The concept of purity and pollution still dominates the thinking of people even after untouchability is abolished legally. Availability and distribution of water too has a strong relationship with the social structure. The control of water and other natural resources by dominant caste women makes Dalit women even more helpless.

Lack of access to water directly affects the health of Dalit women and children. Lack of access to drinking water and good sanitation facilities leads to poor health; making children drop out of school. Dalit women and girls spend half their calorie intake in fetching water. Poor-quality water and sanitation facilities are also the main source of communicable and other waterborne diseases. Hence, Dalits face further discrimination and marginalisation while accessing health facilities and this vicious circle goes on.

Social Components in Scavenging and Cleanliness

Caste System

The caste system can be considered one of the important components of scavenging. Caste system not only gives status to an individual, it also allots an occupation. The individual is supposed to take up the occupation of his parents. The caste system also gives status to the occupation of the individual. The occupations are graded; those performed by upper castes are accorded higher status and the occupation taken up by lower castes are despised and given low status.

One of the many disabilities of the lower caste people is that they have no right to choose their own occupation. They were not allowed to engage in occupations which were reserved for the members of higher castes and were compelled to stick to their traditional occupations like scavenging, carrying dead animals from the streets, sweeping, cleaning, leather work, herding swine, collecting wood for funerals, carrying news and messages regarding dead people, basket making and so on. Though manual scavenging was abolished in 2013, it still continues in parts of India. It is thought to be most prevalent in Gujarat, Madhya Pradesh, Uttar Pradesh and Rajasthan. Some municipalities in India still run public dry toilets (Pais 2015).

Further, the inferiority associated with their occupation holds them back in gaining social mobility. In all the town and city municipalities and city corporations, persons involved in sweeping the streets and carrying dirts to dumping yards are all Dalits. Though, in many places, the dirt is carried by trucks, those who fill the trucks and drive them are Dalits. No person of the upper caste ventures into these jobs.

Culture

Culture is another component of scavenging. Cultural values in the past dictated that lower caste people were subservient to upper caste people. The lower caste people in the past had to take care of the upper caste people by obeying their orders and doing menial jobs like washing their clothes, cleaning their houses, working in their fields, cleaning their faeces, cleaning animal waste and so one. The culture of the upper caste people was to stay at home wearing nice clothes and ornaments. Thus, the culture consisted of upper caste or class people having toilets and bathroom facilities in the house or on the premises while the lower caste people had to go in the open for defecation. This culture in the past has continued to the present, in towns and cities.

Education and Awareness

In ancient times education was the monopoly of the upper castes. Since Independence, the government has made provisions for education of all by through reservation system, providing books, uniforms and other facilities. In spite of these, most SCs are not able to get the benefits of these provisions. Legally, manual scavenging is abolished, yet it continues. Only proper education and awareness about this evil practice can end scavenging.

Social Domination and Social Deprivation

The upper castes had always dominated the lower castes. The upper castes have been able to select ritually pure occupations and higher paying jobs for themselves and leave menial and less paying jobs to the lower castes. Hence, impure jobs are allotted to the impure castes. Further, being socially deprived, they lack basic freedom due to their low socio-economic status. Since their wages are very low, they are economically deprived and low social status is accorded to them. This has further resulted in indiscriminate humiliation and exploitation.

Concepts of Karma and Dharma

The concepts of karma and dharma are intimately related to Hinduism and the caste system. Dharma signifies behaviour that is considered to be in accordance with the order that makes life and the universe possible. The concept of dharma includes duties, rights, laws, conduct, virtues and 'right way of living'. So, it allots a duty to an untouchable or Dalit to perform the duties of his/her caste. According to the karma doctrine, the course of life of every living being here and hereafter is determined by his karma or his deeds. A pious life leads to comfort, contentment and general well-being in the present life and rebirth in higher and better forms of existence. It also implies that a Dalit's life in the present world is the result of his past actions. So, these two concepts hold him back from changing his occupation. In addition to these concepts, there are concepts of '*papa*' and '*punya*'. *Papa* refers to punishment for bad deeds and *punya* refers to reward for good deeds. The scavengers' ideology is that since they do their dharma, the duty of their caste, they will get *punya*.

Culture and Dirt Attitudes

The attitudes towards sanitation and dirt depend on the culture. It may vary depending upon the geographical factors, availability of water, and types of people on the basis of caste and religion. In a place where there is shortage of water, the attitude towards dirt may be different than where there is availability of water. The attitudes may also be different between Hindus and Muslims. Similarly, it is different in Brahmins as compared to scavengers who belong to the lowest caste.

Water is synonymous with life and, therefore, it is the most integral and inevitable part of each individual. Though water is required for drinking and cooking it is also essential for cleaning. In this connection, the SCs have handicaps regarding access to water and sanitation. In rural India, there is discrimination with regard to access to public water bodies and structures.

Attitudes towards human waste are somewhat akin to attitudes towards dirt. The mental disposition towards both is the result of cultural norms. And one of the dominant influences of social disposition is religion. Islam also holds the concept of purity. It is believed that human excreta is wastage and is a restricted and polluted type. There are certain explanations in Islamic preaching about the use of toilets. Purification of the human body with water except in some situations is important. Muslim doctrine prescribes strict procedures regarding contact with faecal material. Only the left hand can be used for cleansing after elimination; the right is used for eating. A Muslim is obligated to use water to cleanse parts of the body through which impurities pass. This obligation has direct implications for planning toilet facilities. Having a toilet attached to the home is not prescribed by Islam. In fact, it is considered a sin to have a toilet attached. But in urban areas, people are forced to avoid such an attitude. They use separate footwear for the toilet and they consider it to be the place of shaitan or the demon. There are instances of Muslims using waterless toilets. In Yemen and Zanzibar, where waterless systems have been traditional, the users wash themselves away from the toilet opening. Since this has not posed a problem for traditional waterless systems, it might be an acceptable solution in other countries (as cited in Pais 2015).

The *Atharva Veda* specifies the use of water for sanitation. It has been observed that Hindus carry a brass vessel filled with water to a secluded spot away from running water, public roads or temples. After defecation, the anal region is cleansed with water. As followers of the *Atharva Veda*, primarily upper caste Hindus use more water for sanitary purposes than lower caste Hindus, especially the untouchables, who traditionally carried night soil. India's lowest caste and people belonging to lower classes defecate openly in public. The right hand is considered pure and the left hand dirty because of its use. The Ganges is considered a holy river even though it is full of effluents from humans and industries. People bathe, wash clothes and bathe animals in this river. Sometimes half-burnt corpses float with the current. It is the case with other holy rivers of India also. In Hindu culture, anything that leaves or is detached from the body is considered "dirty"'. If you were to carry out an act that secretes matter from your body, you must wash afterwards. This is not only related to defecation, but also nose-picking, cutting nails and getting a haircut.

The toilet, therefore, is considered a dirty place and people who have a toilet in villages would not have it close to their house; others would just go somewhere in the fields. In cities, people are forced, more or less to have a bathroom with a toilet in the house, but it is still considered a dirty place. In many places, people keep a separate pair of slippers to wear inside the bathroom. As a consequence, cleaning toilets is considered a dirty task.

Most municipalities in India are not equipped with the latest machines to clean the sewage system and sewage workers are employed under compulsion to enter the underground sewerage lines through the manholes, and clean them wherever the lines are clogged for whatever reason. The job of the sewer worker is to inspect and maintain the underground network pipes that make up the sewerage system. Sewage workers have to remove solid wastes which block the flow of fluid waste in the sewage system. For this reason, sewage workers regularly enter manholes which contain poisonous gases.

The working conditions of sewage workers are very dangerous; they are provided with a rope and bucket to clean the manhole manually. While working like this, they have to inhale various poisonous gases that are harmful for their health and sometimes for their lives. Sewage workers usually have cuts, injuries, irritation of the eyes, skin rashes and related health problems. The existing protective equipment is neither adequate nor up to standard. Also, most of the sewage workers are not educated on how to use protective equipment and are recruited on contract basis and on daily wages. A large number of sewer workers die before retirement. Further, while working on busy roads, there is always the risk of traffic accidents.

Beliefs about ritual purity and impurity form some of the most pervasive themes in Hindu culture. These concepts are applied to matters of personal conduct, health and justice, and are fundamental to the concept of untouchability. In fact, purity has little to do with cleanliness and hygiene; similarly, impurity has little to do with dirt. The concepts of purity and pollution are central to the notion of caste in India.

In Hindu ideology, ritual purity or impurity constitutes the criterion generally accepted for justifying and explaining the rank of a caste in the caste hierarchy. The Brahmins at the top of the caste were considered pure. However, they could be polluted if they came in contact with an untouchable or if they were to accept food or gifts from them. By any chance, if a Brahmin came into physical contact with an untouchable, he would consider himself the polluted and would take a ritual bath and sometimes even wash his clothes to remove the pollution. Other castes do their best to stay away from the untouchables.

The concept of purity and impurity is the key to the many apparent enigmas of the caste system and Ketkar (1990) regards it as the chief principle on which the caste system depends. According to Ketkar, the Brahmin is at the top of society because he is more pure and sacred than other castes, while the Mahar and Paraiyan are at the bottom because they are impure. Thus, purity is the pivot on which the entire system is positioned. Rank, social position and economic condition have no direct effect on the gradation from the standpoint of caste.

For Dumont (1980), the opposition of pure and impure is the basis of understanding caste, caste hierarchy and caste occupation. People whose traditional occupations put them in contact with leather, dead animals, toilets and sewers, and sweeping are usually associated with the lower castes or untouchables. At the other social extreme are Brahmins, who never have contact with such substances and, ideally, deal only with learning, books or temple rituals and are considered pure. Middle castes, which sometimes have contact with polluting substances in their traditional work, have an intermediate purity status. Barbers, who have contact with bodily substances as they cut people's hair, are seen as lower caste, though not untouchable.

Purity and impurity regarding sanitation is quite difficult to understand in a general perspective. Purity is referred to as the absence of impurity, and impurity is the absence of purity. The purity concept can be referred to in different aspects of social life. If purity is referred to only in cleanliness then it can be referred to as sanitation among humans. But purity and impurity in society is wider in nature. Though ritual purity has little to do with cleanliness and hygiene and, ritual impurity has little to do with dirt, in sanitation, both ritual and physical impurity are present. Similarly, those involved in sanitation such as sweepers and scavengers are impure, both ritually and physically, because they live in unhygienic conditions. However, in recent years, because of the economic and social advancement made by some members of SCs, they have become physically pure.

In Hindu ideology and culture, not only people were considered pure or impure, even occupations were considered pure and impure. Occupations such as learning and offering sacrifices were considered pure and were performed by the Brahmins whereas occupations like sweeping and scavenging were considered impure and were performed by the untouchables. Not only people and occupations were considered pure or impure, also the food they ate.

In addition, ingredients varied from caste to caste in their cooking, and the concept of purity remained fundamental to Hindu cooking. Strict rules were followed in order to retain maximum purity. The idea of keeping all pollutants away can be seen by the location of the kitchen in Indian houses. The kitchen is normally a separate room located at a slight distance from the main house with shoes or any other leather items not being allowed near this space. Anything that was potentially a pollutant was to be kept away. Even low caste people were to be kept away from the food of higher castes for the low caste person could pollute the food simply by touching. Only Brahmin cooking was acceptable to all, by high and low castes.

A woman is seen as a pollutant and contagious with pollution during her menstrual period. During a woman's monthly period, she would be banned from cooking or serving food because her impurity was very contagious during that time. Not only what one did to keep the impurities away, but also what one ate to maintain a pure diet was important. Ritual purity has been the cause of evil in society in the sense that "pure" people started discriminating against people of the lower castes. They were not allowed to enter temples, public places, and draw water from wells and ponds. They were forced to do menial and scavenging jobs and were exploited by the upper castes.

Family and Kinship

Family is the base for all social relationships and all social actions. The family can be the reason for social problems and it can also be the solution to problems. If a home is in good condition, it will result in the good condition of society. The sanitation measures which are adopted in a family can bring about a clean and healthy environment for the family and also for society. Cleanliness and hygiene should begin from the family. However, most families in present-day India lack proper sanitation facilities.

The family performs certain universal functions. Sociology of sanitation is mainly concerned with the educational and social function of the family. The family has to take care of the sanitation of an individual right from childhood. Education begins from home and the family can be one of the solutions for sanitation. By providing education in sanitation, the family can develop awareness in a child.

Through the dimension of family sanitation we can understand how a family can take care of the sanitation issue.. The sanitation of the family begins from the kitchen and goes on to washing of clothes, cleaning of the house, disposal of household waste, disposal of human and animal waste and safe storage of water. The kitchen is the place where the family cooks food for its members. Members of the family should take care of the kitchen sanitation for better health of the family. Disposal of kitchen waste and kitchen water should be done properly. Similarly, the water after washing clothes should be properly disposed of. In the same way, the waste of the house, after cleaning, should be disposed of in a hygienic way.

Human waste should be properly disposed of. The toilets should be connected to the sewage system provided by the municipality. Where there is no such arrangement, toilet waste can be connected to the septic tank. In villages, toilets should be built and the waste should be directed to the septic tank. In such cases, the septic tank should be constructed 150 ft away from the drinking water source. In rural areas, animal or human waste should not be exposed to the environment and it can be used for other purposes like biogas and fertilisers. While digging wells and building water tanks, precautions should be taken that they are away from the drains.

In India, urban families are not too worried about sanitation as government agencies take care of it. The urban agencies collect the waste from the houses or from the public dump and dispose it of in designated areas. Human waste is removed by connecting the toilets to the drains. Urban families have to dispose of waste in the way prescribed by the Corporations or nagar panchayats. Sometimes the drain pipes get blocked with people disposing of unwanted things through the drains causing serious damage to public health. Moreover, sanitation is a serious problem in slum areas. In the slum areas, families should ensure that their areas are clean and both human and animal wastes are properly disposed of.

Families in rural places have to be responsible for better sanitation. Often, since people in rural areas have to earn for survival, they forget the importance of sanitation. Hence, they get exposed to different kinds of diseases. Since there are less or no toilet facilities, people defecate in the open. They may not even dispose of wastewater from the kitchen or other areas properly. It is a common scene in rural areas for people to bathe, wash clothes and bathe domestic animals in the same ponds from where they fetch water for household use. In such conditions there is a need to educate rural families about sanitation.

In its general sense, education is a form of learning in which the knowledge, skills and habits of a group of people are transferred from one generation to the next. Education frequently takes place under the guidance of others, but may also be autodidactic (learnt by self). The processes of education and sanitation are closely related. Educational institutions are the primary contributors to awareness about sanitation in human life and society. The education acquired from pre-primary level to graduation level is supposed to bring about awareness in sanitation. But it is the duty of the teachers at the pre-primary and primary levels to teach children about health and hygiene. In school, it is the responsibility of the school management to take care of the issues regarding sanitation. At college level, the students and the institution can educate the youth about the importance of sanitation and also the students or the youth can create awareness about sanitation by conducting camps. Medical colleges can be the most responsible kind of institutions in the matter of sanitation. Therefore, sociology of sanitation can lead educational institutions to a better future where there will not be any sanitation issue. Sociology of sanitation can find out the problems of sanitation in the education sector, raise questions and generate answers to the problems.

School authorities should ensure a healthy environment. The waste of the school should be taken out of the school, at least 100 metres away. Children should be provided safe and adequate drinking water. There should be adequate latrine or toilet facilities for the children andseparate toilets for boys and girls. School authorities should also ensure that these toilets are regularly cleaned. Government records show that two-thirds of schools lack adequate sanitation facilities. The few that do have mostly been rendered non-functional with no water supply, dilapidated soak pits, and no soap and other materials. Children are the best change agents as they absorb and popularise new ideas and concepts of sanitation not only in their schools but also in their families and neighbourhood. Schools are learning laboratories where habits of good sanitation practices, and personal health and hygiene are inculcated. Besides, presence of school toilets, safe drinking water, clean surroundings and basic information on hygiene improves the learning abilities of children, improves their health and improves attendance, especially of the girl child, with far-reaching consequences on the health of the community.

Sociology of sanitation gives a detailed structure for schools and their sanitation for a better understanding of sanitation at school. It is based on the belief that children are far more receptive to new ideas and are at an age when they can be influenced to cultivate the habits of good personal hygiene. The school sanitation programme aims to make a visible impact on the health and hygiene of children through improvement in health and hygiene practices of children, their families and communities. The promotion of personal hygiene and environmental sanitation within schools can help children to adopt good habits during their formative years.

We can observe that sanitation is a problem across all sections of Indian society. And it has been more so in villages and among the ethnic groups of India. The general health of the rural masses is poor and as a result their death rate is higher. Due to the rural set-up, birth rate is also high. Lack of facilities such as pure drinking water, latrines, drainage, health centres, clinics, medicines and hospitals affect the general health of rural people. Villagers depend on a few sources of drinking water such as wells, rivulets and ponds. In summer, most villages have acute shortage of drinking water. Due to lack of nutritious food and poor food habits, villagers are becoming victims of various diseases. They are not aware of preventive medicines through which they can prevent diseases. Generally, rural people neglect cleanliness and live in unhygienic environment.

There are some important reasons for sanitation problems faced by village communities (Pais 2015):

1. Poverty: This is the major reason for lack of sanitation in rural societies. The families or households may not be able to bear the expense of establishing sanitation conditions. Thus, families are forced to defecate in open spaces.
2. Lack of Education: Villagers are comparatively less educated. They do not know the importance of sanitation or good health conditions. Lack of knowledge about sanitation makes them victims of an unhygienic environment.
3. Lack of Water Resources: Villagers have less water resources for their needs. They use the water from ponds or wells for domestic purposes and they wash their clothes and animals in the same water sources which lead to health problems.
4. Lack of Awareness about Health Related Diseases: Villagers do not worry until they get afflicted with diseases due to lack of sanitation. They are not concerned about a healthy environment; they prefer to go to the hospital only when they have health problems. Further, the practice of manual scavenging still exists very much in our country.

Gender Issues Related to Sanitation

There are many gender issues in sanitation which need to be taken into account to improve development efforts. Many scholars who deal with the different tasks of men and women have observed that all tasks related to sanitation are duties assigned to women.

The following are the gender issues related to sanitation:

1. Women are responsible for water in the house: Women and men usually have very different roles in water and sanitation activities and these differences are particularly pronounced in rural areas. Women are most often the users, providers and managers of water in rural households and are the guardians of household hygiene. If the water system breaks down, women are likely to be most affected, for they may have to travel farther for water or use other means to meet the household's water and sanitation needs. In case of drought or flood, women remain responsible for sourcing water and have to go even farther to find it, or compromise by using less and less clean water, which influences the hygiene situation of the household.
2. Women are responsible for hygiene at home: Women of households and also of villages are seen as the cleaners of the yard, the house, the kitchen, the bathroom and the toilet facilities. Both the cleaning and the fetching of water take a lot of time. Women are responsible for their own hygiene, their children and menfolk; they have to do the work for all of them and women suffer when they themselves have a negative influence of bad hygiene, by getting ailments and diseases. Also, if their children are ill, it amounts to extra work for them. When their menfolk and parents are ill, that gives them extra work, and more water to carry. So women are at the centre of hygiene for all.
3. Women are responsible for the health of the family, especially of children: Women, who are aware of the connection between the dirtiness and illness of family members, will put in extra effort to keep the house, the kitchen, the food and the sanitary facilities clean. When somebody is ill, women usually have the responsibility of taking care of them.

4. Women are responsible for the sick and the elderly: Hygiene becomes doubly important when there are sick family members who could infect others. Extra water is needed, and a lot of extra work needs to be done. Gender ideology prescribes that women do all this and at the same time take care of the elderlies in the family, with the difference that sick people in the house should be an exceptional situation.
5. Women menstruate, get pregnant and give birth: Women, while menstruating, are generally seen as unclean. They should clean their blood themselves, and that is one of the reasons that women always have to clean everything. During pregnancy, giving birth and breast feeding, the risk of getting infections is high. All women need to avoid that by giving lots of attention and spending extra energy on hygiene. The direct relation with the quality and quantity of water available during that time, and the fact that she will not always be able to get it, makes her very vulnerable. Maternal mortality is directly related to hygiene, and hygiene to sanitary facilities and their cleanliness.
6. Gender issues of toilets: In both rural and urban areas, women without toilets go out to relieve themselves only in the dark, because their gender ideology tells them that they cannot take the risk of being seen. They often face risks such snakebites, scorpion stings, or attack by other creatures, and also from men. There are endless stories of women getting harassed and even raped when going out in the dark. For men and children this is no problem, they can go anywhere and at any time. Women who go out in the daylight are seen as fallen women who ask for trouble. Furthermore, to wait till dark, results in constipation and adapted diet and drinking habits, leading to serious health problems.

Proper sanitation facilities are essential for women for fewer infections, less sexual harassment security and physical dignity; good sanitation will empower women. There is an economic benefit of having water close to home so that the saved time can be used to generate some income. Securing good sanitary facilities to meet family needs has a direct bearing on not only women's health but also on their access to education and employment. In rural areas, fetching water takes more time which keeps girls out of school and limits the economic productivity of women. Girls who reach menstrual age are discouraged from further schooling due inadequate sanitation in schools and in public places. Measures like providing schools with water and latrines, and promoting hygiene education in the classroom can enable them in getting education.

Improved sanitation facilities with regular and safe water supply, and good latrine facilities enhance not only the health of women but of the entire family. The time saved in fetching water can be used to maintain the health of the family members. Access to adequate sanitary latrines is a matter of security, privacy and human dignity, particularly for women. Access to adequate and clean, nearby water is a matter of women's health, their access to education, employment, livelihood and their empowerment.

Poor sanitation is something that not only affects the health of the people of the country; it also affects the development of the nation. In fact, women are most affected by the hazards of lack of proper sanitation. In India, majority of girls drop out of school because of lack of toilets. Only 22 per cent of them manage to even complete Class X. Women and marginalised populations are mostly affected by lack of water and sanitation in rural India (Ahmed 2005; Coles and Wallace 2005). School sanitation and girls' school sanitation facilities across the country remain woefully inadequate. Commercial sanitary towels are too expensive for young girls to buy each month. During menstruation, girls have no alternative than to use bundles of cloth, usually stripped from old clothing. In some areas, it is ash or sand wrapped in leaves or newspaper. Due to lack of facilities at school for girls to wash, dry and change clothes, many are too embarrassed to attend lessons while menstruating.

Sanitation and Environmental Sanitation

Environmental sanitation refers to the sanitation in the environment in which we live. It is aimed at improving or maintaining the standard of basic environmental conditions affecting the well-being of people. It is the environment in which an individual lives, interacts with others and satisfies his basic physical and social needs. So, the responsibility of environmental sanitation begins from the individual. The environment in which the individual lives, i.e., where the group or the community lives is important. Since man is an integral part of the group or society, the individual is as responsible as the group for the environment.

Environmental sanitation is a set of actions geared towards improving the quality of the environment and reducing the incidence of disease. By doing so, we hope that living conditions will improve and health problems will decrease. The management of water, solid waste and industrial waste, as well as the topics of pollution of various types come under the umbrella of environmental sanitation. It is said that environmental sanitation is very vital for any nation. So, in order to live in a world free from diseases, we must embark on the task of cleaning our houses, neighbourhoods and public places. According to WHO, there are four areas that must be reviewed for environmental sanitation to be effective: planning, water supply, sanitation and hygiene education.

Environmental sanitation involves both household and environmental sanitation. Household sanitation also involves household food safety, and the maintenance of clean living conditions which do not promote the spread of disease. This includes general cleaning in the places where we keep food. Due to lack of environmental sanitation, many become sick and die. Improper disposal of human excreta could give people different illnesses such as hepatitis A, and other gastrointestinal tract diseases. Faeces or human waste harbours lots of harmful microorganisms that could definitely cause illness. Water drainage, if not properly maintained and cleaned, could be a possible cradle for vectors and disease-causing insects.

It is important that different beliefs and practices be altered for a better environment. Personal hygiene is the first step in ensuring environmental cleanliness. Self-discipline is the key to sanitation of the environment. Next is household cleanliness. Cleanliness must be maintained all the time inside the house, especially in damp areas such as the bathroom and the kitchen because it is in these places that harmful microorganisms are often found. Different disease-causing organisms live in food and various bathroom surfaces; therefore, it is necessary that proper sanitation is practiced.

Having a clean community would be the next step. Proper waste disposal and maintaining cleanliness throughout the community, particularly in the streets and on sidewalks, are essential for a healthier community. Environmental sanitation depends on social and cultural practices and beliefs, and these have to be considered in planning interventions.

Sanitation in Public Places

Lack of sanitation in public places may cause environmental pollution which leads to diseases. The responsibility for the provision of sanitation facilities in public places is not always obvious, especially where these are informal gathering places.

There are several basic rules for sanitation in public places:

1. Sufficient toilet facilities for the maximum number of people using the area during the day. The toilet facilities should be arranged in separate blocks for men and women.
2. Toilet facilities should not be connected directly to kitchens. This reduces the number of flies entering the kitchen and odours reaching the kitchen. People using the toilet facilities may not pass directly through the kitchen.
3. A hand washing basin with clean water and soap close to the toilet facilities. There should be separate similar facilities near the kitchen or where food is handled.
4. Clean and reliable water supply for hand washing, personal hygiene and flushing of toilet facilities.
5. Refuse must be disposed of properly and not allowed to build up, as it will attract flies and vermin.

Waste Management

Environmental experts have indicated that environmental conditions in a given area may be affected by waste management, the process used to dispose of garbage. How waste is disposed of varies based on living conditions and the accepted standard of living in a geographical area. While some communities provide wastewater treatment and trash collection, others do not, which reduces the ability to control the well-being of the environment and its people. When waste is not removed and treated properly, pollution may lead to the spread of disease; when proper disposal and treatment methods are followed, disease and pollution can usually be reduced. Environmental sanitation is not limited to the pollution of water and the improper disposal of household waste. When factories or businesses dispose of chemical and physical waste in ways that directly affect the environment, it is often referred to as industrial pollution.

Problems of Environmental Sanitation in India

The sanitary conditions in India are appalling and need a great awakening. Improvement in sanitation requires newer strategies and targeted interventions with follow-up evaluation. The need of the hour is to identify the existing system of environmental sanitation with respect to its structure and functioning and to prioritise the control strategies according to the need of the country.

Environmental sanitation comprises both a change in behaviour and facilities to form a hygienic environment. The following are some of the important causes for lack of environmental sanitation in India:

1. Lack of Social Responsibility: There is an absence of social responsibility among the people. It has been observed that in general, permanent residents of a locality are concerned about environmental sanitation, but the migrant group of people are not that worried about this because they may not be in that area after a few years.
2. Lack of Social Awareness about Sanitation: People lack knowledge of environmental sanitation. Though a child is supposed to learn from the family about sanitation, often the parents themselves do not have proper knowledge of sanitation. Knowledge about sanitation and awareness of their social responsibility may help people to keep their immediate environment clean.
3. Lack of Education: Education often enhances the desire for a better life. Knowledge of sanitation is acquired in the process of education. If at all society wants people to keep the environment clean, then it should be implemented through education.
4. Over-Crowded Population: Environmental sanitation is a bigger challenge where there is a large population settled in a particular area without proper sanitation facilities. In urban areas or in slums, the problem of environmental sanitation arises. Migrants settle in places which are already congested. Lack of toilet facilities forces them to defecate in the open, which pollutes the environment and generates disease.

A number of innovative approaches to improve water supply and sanitation have been tested in India, in particular, in the early 2000s. The Total Sanitation Campaign gives strong emphasis on IEC, capacity building and hygiene education for effective behaviour change with the involvement of PRIs, community-based organisations (CBOs) and NGOs (Kumar, et al 2011). The key intervention areas are: individual household latrines, school sanitation and hygiene education, community sanitary complexes and anganwadi centre toilets supported by rural sanitary marts and production centres.

In spite of these efforts, India faces certain challenges with regard to environmental sanitation:

1. Prevention of contamination of water in distribution systems;
2. growing water scarcity and the potential for water reuse and conservation;
3. implementing innovative low-cost sanitation systems;
4. providing sustainable water supplies and sanitation for urban and semi-urban areas;
5. reducing disparities within regions in the country; and
6. sustainability of water and sanitation services.

In the absence of proper sanitation, people suffer from high levels of infectious, contagious, water borne, airborne and vectorborne diseases, leading to high incidence of morbidity and mortality. Although there have been several initiatives at the national level to increase sanitation coverage in India, a substantial part of the urban population, especially in slums, has no adequate sanitation facilities made available to them by the government or public machinery.

Community toilets not only provide a sanitation facility but at the same time have a demonstrative effect as well. People using these become habitual users of toilets, and in turn realise the need for individual household toilets. Community toilets, thus, are the tools for bringing behavioural change amongst the public residing in slum areas as well as in generating a demand for the use of individual toilets.

The community toilets in municipal areas are maintained by the corporations through their health departments. Some community toilets have been constructed and are being maintained by Sulabh International on a pay-and-use basis. The upkeep of the community toilets constructed by municipal corporations has been dismal, with the conditions turning so unsanitary that people prefer open defecation to using the community toilets. Many community toilets have also become non-functional on account of a variety of reasons ranging from non-availability of water to lack of maintenance.

The possible reasons for non-use of community toilets are (Pais 2015):

- Faulty construction, not conforming to norms of availability of sustainable water supply, ventilation, natural lighting, etc.
- lacking in special provision for children and differently-abled persons;
- lacking in safety and security for women;
- lack of operation and maintenance and financial issues;
- insufficient funds for running the system;
- non-availability of funds for augmentation, rectification and upgradation of facilities;
- no consultations with the community on design and location of community toilets;
- lack of motivation and non-generation of felt need towards sanitation;
- lack of public health and hygiene education among poorer sections of the society; and
- lack of sensitisation on gender issues.

Use of the community toilets also depends on the availability of infrastructure facilities such as water, bathing facility and effluent disposal in sewer line or in septic tank. Availability of water has not been ensured in all the community toilets. Their limited use is also explained by lesser availability and accessibility, apart from poor maintenance in terms of irregular or no water supply, bad sanitary conditions and lack of proper drainage. Involving user groups in maintenance is another measure tried successfully in the southern part of the country. The chances of success of these groups are more when women are actively involved.

Sanitation is an issue that starts from the individual and spreads to the community. Therefore, interpersonal communication measures with strong interactive mode will facilitate effective communication to bring desired behavioural change. This will include enhancing knowledge regarding hygiene and sanitation and encouraging conversion of the knowledge into practice.

Social scientists have observed different reasons for poor sanitation in slums.

1. *Lack of Education and Awareness*: Due to lack of education and awareness, people defecate in the open which harms the social life of slum dwellers. Further, people are not responsible for proper maintenance of sanitation facilities.
2. *Poverty among Slum Dwellers*: Those living in slums are economically poor. When people can hardly afford a house they cannot afford a toilet. So, they use the public toilet which is always stuck with drainage problems and is unclean, or they defecate in the open.
3. *Inadequate Water Supply*: Water is an essential requirement; and the slums not getting adequate supply of water is a serious problem. Inadequate water supply in slums will lead to unclean toilets and also create problems for drinking, bathing and washing clothes.
4. *Unplanned Slums*: The government and the city planners are very busy in the planning of towns and cities but they ignore the poor. This results in poor people settling in very congested areas, where they do not get sufficient sanitation facilities.

Sanitation among ethnic groups is considered to be a serious problem. The problem of ill-health is one of serious problems among the tribal people. Tribal population suffer from various diseases like forest fever, yellow fever, typhoid, malaria, small pox, venereal diseases and skin diseases. The intensity of these diseases is serious due to the absence of proper treatment and medical assistance. Like teachers, doctors are also not showing any interest to work in tribal areas.

Tribal people live in huts, with small openings which prevent sunlight entering and free flow of fresh air. They use wood as fuel for cooking which creates a lot of smoke. As a result, they suffer from TB, eye problems and other diseases. Some tribal keep their cattle very close to their houses. Sanitation among ethnic groups is deplorable. One of the important causes is inadequate water facilities. Tribal people hardly have water sources for survival. Secondly, tribal or ethnic people are poor. They may not be able to construct a toilet when it is hard for them to earn money for daily survival. They also lack education; as a result they are not aware of the principles of sanitation. The cultural attitude of tribal people sometimes becomes a problem in establishing sanitation facilities. Even though the government provides sanitation facilities, they do not wish to use the sanitation facilities like toilets inside their living area.

Corporate Social Responsibility

The corporate sector has some responsibility for the community or society and it is known as Corporate Social Responsibility (CSR). The concept of CSR became prominent in the US in the 1960s. It is a process with the aim of embracing responsibility for the company's actions and encouraging a positive impact through its activities on the environment, consumers, employees, communities, stakeholders and all other members of the public sphere who may also be considered stakeholders.

CSR is a management concept whereby companies integrate social and environmental concerns in their business operations and interactions with their stakeholders. Secondly, companies have a lot of power in the community and in the national economy. They control a lot of assets, and may have budgets at their disposal for socially conscious investments and programmes.

Corporate houses have understood the importance of social responsibility and as a result are involved in developmental work right from the village to large urban centres. In fact, the corporate sector is well suited to the service of the poor because of their knowledge and understanding of the needs of the communities. At the rural level, corporates are involved in rural development projects like education, construction of roads, health and sanitation projects. In cities, they are involved in the improvement of slums and other poor areas.

Problems of environmental sanitation in India are common both in rural and urban areas. Park and Park (1977:94) highlight the problem of rural environmental sanitation in India, especially in relation to disposal of human excreta, disposal of waste, water supply and housing. Besides, another concern of environmental sanitation is public toilets.

The most important problem in rural sanitation in India today is the disposal of human excreta. Surveys in different parts of the country have revealed that many people still defecate in the open. A popular belief among the village folk is that the excreta of children are harmless. Children are permitted to defecate in the backyards close to the houses. Adults go to the fields for defecation. Sociologists have found several reasons why an average Indian villager does not accept a latrine: a latrine close to the house is considered unhygienic because of the bad smell; latrines are meant for city dwellers, where no field for defecation is available; the houses are small, and there is no space to locate a latrine; latrines are only meant for females and invalids; ignorance that faeces lead to infections—it is considered as only something that is impure. Thus the problem of excreta disposal is bound up with numerous customs and beliefs. The health hazards associated with improper excreta disposal are soil pollution, water pollution and transmission of diseases by flies, unclean hands and polluted food.

The wastewater from the houses is permitted to collect in ditches and overflow into the streets, as there is usually no drainage system in the countryside. The average villager is not aware that mosquitoes breed in collections of dirty water. Household refuse is invariably thrown in front of the house and permitted to accumulate and decompose. Periodically, it is removed to the fields and used as manure. The animal dung (cow/buffalo dung) is allowed to accumulate and when a sufficient quantity is reached, it is pressed into cakes, sun dried and used as fuel. These heaps of dung cakes are sources of fly-breeding.

Wells, ponds and rivers occupy a pivotal place in the cultural environment of a village. These are places where people not only draw water, but also bathe and wash their clothes. These are also places where the animals are bathed and given a drink. Tanks and ponds are used for washing, bathing, ablution and sometimes even as a source of drinking water. Some rivers are considered holy. People go on pilgrimage to have a dip in the holy rivers. They not only bathe and wash their clothes in the river, but also drink the raw water, which they consider sacred. Samples of holy water are bottled and carried over long distances for distribution among friends and relatives. These cause epidemics of cholera and gastro-enteritis.

Rural houses are practically the same all over the country. They are usually kutcha and damp, ill-lighted and ill-ventilated. For reasons of security, no windows are provided, and if one is provided, it is merely a small hole. Absence of a separate kitchen, latrine, bathroom and drainage are characteristic features of an average rural house. Animal keeping is very common in villages. Infrequently, human beings and animals live under one roof. India is still lagging far behind many countries in the field of environmental sanitation. Most cities and towns in India are characterised by overcrowding, congestion, inadequate water supply and inadequate facilities of disposal of human excreta, wastewater and solid wastes. Most of the problems in the country are due to a defective environment, which in turn robs people of their health, destroy their livelihoods, and undermines their overall development potential (Pandve 2008).

A public toilet is a public facility. Public toilets may be standalone buildings or contained within buildings such as railway stations, schools, bars, restaurants, nightclubs or filling stations. Public toilets can also be found on some public transport vehicles, for use by passengers. Public toilets are usually fixed facilities, but can also refer to smaller portable toilets, or larger portable toilets constructed as portable buildings. Public toilets are commonly separated as male and female facilities, although some can be unisex, particularly the smaller or single occupancy types. Both male and female toilets may incorporate toilet cubicles, while many male toilets also feature urinals. Public toilets incorporate accessible toilets and features to cater for people with disabilities. Public toilets may be unattended or be staffed by an attendant, provided by the local authority or the owner of the larger building.

Environmental and Soil Sanitation

Environmental sanitation is a more comprehensive term than soil sanitation; soil sanitation is mostly limited to water supplies and disposal of human and animal wastes. All sources of water are related to soil, as rainwater must fall and flow on, or percolate into some soils, and in polluted soils, it gets heavily contaminated with materials and sources of infection. Similarly, all human and animal wastes including excreta and decomposable rubbish are deposited on soils, which in turn contaminate surface water supplies or soak into subsoil water sources. Prevention of soil pollution is a major issue of soil sanitation, and clean soils in addition to hygienic houses and neighbourhoods, as well as prevention of atmospheric pollution, by and large, comprises environmental sanitation. Environmental and soil sanitation is of primary importance, and so is the first line of defence for primary prevention, as it helps in turn secondary and tertiary preventive methods.

The more the soil pollution, the greater the chances of accumulated decomposing organic matter which collects on the surface, and soaks into superficial layers of soil, pollutes water supplies, breeds insects, vermin and rodents which are either direct sources of disease, or indirect vectors or act as reservoir hosts. Diseases which relate to soil pollution are waterborne infections and protozoal, helminthic and insectborne, as well as bacterial, and viral infections which are incidental to polluted water and soils. (Dakshinamurty 1962:198-202).

Ecological approach to sanitation seeks to contain, treat and reuse excreta where possible thus, minimising contamination and making optimum use of resources. The key issue here is that each community, region or country needs to work out what is the most sensible and cost-effective way of thinking about sanitation in the short- and long-terms and then act accordingly. Ecological sanitation is sometimes presented as a radical alternative to conventional sanitation systems. It is based on composting or vermin-composting toilets where an extra separation of urine and faeces at the source for sanitisation and recycling has been done. It thus eliminates the creation of black water and eliminates faecal pathogens. If ecological sanitation is practiced, municipal wastewater consists only of grey water, which can be recycled for gardening. However, in most cases, grey water continues to be discharged into sewers.

The UN states that wherever humans gather, their waste also accumulates. Progress in sanitation and improved hygiene has greatly improved health, but many people still have no adequate means of disposing their waste. This is a growing nuisance for heavily populated areas, carrying the risk of infectious diseases, particularly for vulnerable groups such as the very young, elderly and people suffering from diseases that lower their resistance. Poorly controlled waste also means daily exposure to an unpleasant environment. The build of faecal contamination in rivers and other waters is not just a human risk; other species are also affected, threatening the ecological balance of the environment. The discharge of untreated wastewater and excreta into the environment affects human health through several routes such as by polluting drinking water; entry into the food chain, for example via fruits, vegetables or fish and shellfish; bathing, recreational and other contact with contaminated water; and by providing breeding sites for flies and insects that spread diseases.

Many diseases are spread from person to person by germs in faeces. Some experts believe illness from poor sanitation can be prevented only if people change their personal habits, or " "behaviours", about staying clean. But this idea often leads to failure because it does not consider the barriers that people face in their daily lives, such as poverty or lack of access to clean water. Then when behaviour does not change, people are blamed for their own poor health. Other experts look for technical solutions, such as modern toilets that flush water. Technical solutions often come from outside a community and may not fit the traditions or conditions of the community. Sometimes they create more problems than they solve. The disease caused by germs from poor hygiene and sanitation will not be prevented if people are blamed for their own poor health, or if only technical solutions are promoted (Conant 2005).

Every year more than 200 million tonnes of human waste, and vast quantities of wastewater and solid waste go uncollected and untreated around the world, fouling the environment and exposing millions of children, women and the public at large to disease and squalor. Improved sanitation leads to less environmental degradation, increased sustainability of environmental resources and a more secure future for not only women and children but also to the whole society.

Chapter 5

SOCIAL UPLIFT OF MANUAL SCAVENGERS

"It drips on her head most days, says Champaben, but in the monsoon season it's worse. In rain, worms multiply. Every day, nonetheless, she gets up and walks to her owners' house, and there she picks up their excrement with her bare hands or a piece of tin, scrapes it into a basket, puts the basket on her head or shoulders, and carries it to the nearest waste dump. She has no mask, no gloves and no protection. She is paid a pittance if she is paid at all. She regularly gets dysentery, giardia and brain fever. She does this because a 3000 year old social hierarchy says she has to."

—Rose George.

A scavenger is generally understood as a person who collects the waste and does the needful as the given society permits or suggests. However, in the Indian context, the scavenger is reduced to mean a "manual scavenger". Therefore, a scavenger is one who is partially or wholly engaged in the obnoxious task of manually removing night soil and filth. The dependent of a scavenger is one who is a member of his family or is dependent on him, irrespective of whether he is partially or wholly engaged in the said occupation. The scavenger community is distributed all over the country; that is, different castes are engaged in this job in different parts of the country.

The scavengers in Haryana are called Valmiki/Balmiki, Chuhra, Bhangi, Lalbegi and Khakrobe. Chaudhary and Jamadar are two titles commonly used for this community; the latter is normally used for the working class. Locally, they are called Chuhra, because they claim to be the descendants of

Valmiki or Balmiki. One of the Chuhra gurus (teacher) is another name for Bal Mik, who is believed to have written the epic, *Ramayana*. Their other guru is Lalbeg and it is after this guru that they are also called Lalbegi; and they still call their priests Lalgurus (Ibbetson 1974:294).

Risley, the Commissioner for the 1901 Census, classified castes—the scavenger castes—on the basis of the Census data, into seven main categories according to their social standing and ranked the Jatis in the local hierarchy. The scavenging castes were known by different names in different states. Bhangi, Balmiki, Chuhra, Mehtar, Mazhabi, Lalbegi and Halalkhor in northern India; Har, Hadi, Hela, Dom and Sanei in eastern India; Mukhiyar, Thoti, Chachati, Pakay and Relli in southern India; and Mehtar, Bhangias, Halalkhor, Ghasi, Olgana, Zadmalli, Barvashia, Metariya, Jamphoda and Mela in western and central India. They made an effort to unite and have a common name. In the 1911 Census, some of them started reporting as Adi Dharmi, Adi Dravida, Adi Karnataka and Adi Andhran (Srivastava 1997:178). Ibbetson (1974) included Chuhra, Dhanak and Khatik in the scavenger castes. These castes are numerically and economically one of the most significant in the province.

Socially they are the lowest of the low, and as a rule can hardly be said to stand even at the foot of the social ladder, though some sections of the clan have moved up the first one or two steps. Their hereditary occupation is scavenging, sweeping the houses and streets, carrying to the fields and distributing manure. In city and village houses, women are strictly secluded for removing night soil. After them, the so-called impure animals are pigs and fowls. They eat the flesh of animals that have died of disease or by natural death. They are the hereditary workers in grass and reeds, from which they make winnowing pans and other articles used in agriculture. They eat the meat of jackals, lizards, tortoises and pigs. Many of them have abandoned scavenging and taken to leatherwork and to weaving, and by doing so have climbed one or two steps in the social grades (Nagla 2015).

The term Bhangi is derived from the Sanskrit word bhangi meaning hemp; it may be due to their drinking habits. The Bhangi was described as a representative of the chandala of Manu, who is said to have descended from the union of a Sudra man and a Brahmin woman. The Bhangis were traditionally associated with scavenging, sweeping and basket making. In the colonial period, they were brought into urban areas for scavenging and sweeping and became an urban community. With the widespread use of septic latrines and other modes of public conveniences, in recent years the practice of carrying head loads of night soil has perceptibly declined in many parts of India. The National Scheme for Liberation and Rehabilitation of Scavengers and their Dependents (1991–92) seeks to liberate them from their existing "hereditary obnoxious and inhuman occupations of manually removing night soil and filth" and to provide for and engage them in "alternative and dignified occupations". Today, the Bhangis have taken to other occupations as well.

The Churas are the sweeper and scavenger of the united Punjab and the present-day Haryana, found throughout the province. They are also called Churha, Chruhe, Bhangi and Khakrobe. The major occupation of the Churhas is the removal of dead animals and night soil and scavenging. In recent years, some of them have acquired land and taken to agriculture. A few of them are engaged in sharecropping. Traditionally, the Chuhras are linked with other communities through economic relationships. They used to receive polluted clothes at the time of birth or death and on ceremonial or ritual occasions like the solar and lunar eclipse. They are also given leftover food while seeking alms. They accept both kachha (raw) and pucca (cooked) food from other communities, but no other community accepts any food from them (Nagla 2015).

Lalbegi is a class of Mohammedan sweepers supposed to have come from the northern parts of India; some with sepoy regiments, others as wanderers in search of work. Though styled Mohammedans, they neither practise circumcision nor abstain from pork. The Lalbegi are employed as sweepers in European households, and are always addressed as "jamadar" by the other servants. They eat the leavings of Europeans and drink any sort of wine or spirits. They do not eat with the Raut. The Raut abstain from food that has come from a European table and do not touch a dead body. The religious rites of the Lalbegi are partly Hindu, partly Mohammadan.

A few of the Lalbegi keep the fast of Ramadan, although they dare not enter a public mosque. Their funeral ceremonies are peculiar. The dead may not be buried in a Muslim cemetery, but are consigned to the ground in some waste and jungly spot. Thus, the word Lalbegi is derived from lalbeg, "the eponymous ancestor of the tribe" (Risley 1891). Their surnames are Begi and Balmiki. They are found in Bihar, Uttar Pradesh, Arunachal Pradesh, Delhi, Meghalaya and Mizoram. The Lalbegi are landless. Most men, women and grown-up children work in municipalities as sweepers. Their oral traditions recall that they were earlier Balmiki, but after taking initiation from Saint Kabir, have become Lalbegis. They also claim that their original homeland was Rajasthan.

The scavengers earn their livelihood by scavenging in the fields and at the construction sites. They are also engaged in animal husbandry, poultry and piggery. A few of them have land. Their traditional primary occupation is scavenging, including removal of night soil from houses and offices. Their secondary occupations include manual work, playing in bands, petty trade, hawking, vending of fruit and vegetables, selling of meat and eggs. Some also own small tea stalls and restaurants. They depend on the local market for their day-to-day needs. In towns and cities they carry out business in cash, but in villages, there is the barter system. However, today in the villages of Haryana, there is a decline in scavenging work. Some families engage in scavenging work for the care of animals. In small towns, the Brahmins, Baniyas or Punjabis employ some persons for scavenging work. In some areas of the cities, pit latrines still exist in houses where scavengers are employed by paying ₹20 per month for cleaning the latrine from the pit. They carry human excreta on their heads and throw it at the garbage dump from where the corporation carries it away.

Scavengers are mostly landless; hence they work as labourers in agriculture, plantation and industries. Many of them still make a living from the traditional low-yielding occupations such as leather work, flaying dead cattle, scavenging, weaving, dyeing, bamboo craft, fishery, wild herbs and fruit gathering. These occupations, being in the unorganised sector, require more labour, a full day's work and the total employment of the family with low returns. Their social status is considered low because of the involvement in so-called unclean work. Children below the age of 15 years also do the scavenging work; they get their payment in cash or in kind.

Working hours of scavengers vary in formal and informal organisations. They work eight hours in formal organisations like municipal committees, hospitals, schools, colleges, universities, banks and in government jobs. Generally, females do scavenging on roads and males clean gutters, as assigned by the municipalities. They visit 30–40 houses daily for cleaning the flush and doing sweeping work in the household. Their tools of scavenging are brooms (small and big), mops (duster on a long stick), a bamboo basket, shallow pan, shovel and ash. There is no problem in getting jobs for scavengers. 95 per cent of scavengers are in either private or public jobs. There is no competition for their work from other communities. Traditionally, this occupation is meant for them because of the Hindu social order. It there is something wrong in the sewerage, it is repaired by the scavengers. Therefore, they always have private earnings. Moreover, all the members of the family are engaged in work. Nevertheless, they compete with their own community members to claim such work in households.

Women take the help of daughters in scavenging because ultimately daughters have to do the same work. Earlier, women scavengers used to do only scavenging in a household. Now they do other work like cleaning the utensils and washing clothes. They do not have any type of leave; they work even when they are ill as they fear losing their work if they are not regular.

Women have a role in agricultural operations, scavenging and in social, religious and political spheres. Their traditional occupation is scavenging. They are also engaged in labour work like animal husbandry, poultry, piggery, playing musical instruments in a concert and the like. In recent years, a few entrepreneurs, scholars or creative artists or administrators have come up in this community. Some members of the community work as teachers, engineers and doctors while some have taken up white-collar jobs. There are instances of members serving in defence, police and railway services; political leadership has also emerged at the village level.

Scavengers through the Ages

The recovery of materials from waste to be reused or recycled has been carried out for millennia, and probably throughout the whole of human history. Wastes result from the production and consumption processes by which society satisfies its needs. Wood, ceramics, metals, glass, paper, textiles and food wastes represent some of the most commonly discarded materials. When these materials are no longer needed, they are discarded and become part of the waste stream. Yet, such materials may be useful and are considered a resource by others. Scavengers, those individuals who informally recover items from waste for the purpose of reuse or recycling, play an important role in transforming objects of discard into objects of value. In this role, scavengers are mediators in the relationship between societies and their environment (Downs and Medina 2000).

In contemporary societies, scavenging activities reduce the amount of wastes that need to be collected, transported and disposed of, and extend the life of dumps and landfills. Reuse and recycling also render environmental benefits; they reduce water and energy use and lower pollution of solid, liquid and gaseous byproducts, compared with the manufacture of products from fresh resources. Thus, scavenging reduces society's exploitation of natural resources, a necessary step towards minimising the impact of human society on the environment, and towards sustainable development.

Despite the clear environmental benefits of scavenging, it is an activity that has received very little attention from scholars. While the impact of scavenging may once have been limited to the immediate physical and cultural environment of villages or towns, today it constitutes an activity that has significant implications for the economy and environment, particularly in developing countries. Scavenging remains a poorly understood social and historical phenomenon. Scavengers have been portrayed as poor and marginal. Yet in both agrarian and industrialised societies, past and present, there is clear evidence that they are not always poor, and that they play an important role in supplying raw materials for agriculture, petty commodity production and industry (Ibid.). Scavenging and recycling activities are hardly new or recent. They have existed for millennia. Yet, throughout, it is clear that scavenging represents an adaptive response to scarcity.

Scavenging in Prehistory

Some of the earliest instances of coping with scarcity occur in hunting-gathering societies, where seasonal variations in the availability of plants and the risks associated with hunting, may have been compensated for by scavenging. In Africa, the early hominids scavenged in order to complement their diet, especially during the dry season, when plant foods were most scarce. Risks associated with hunting may have been avoided by the scavenging of meat from animals killed by predators, or dead from natural causes. Blumenschine and Cavallo (1992), indeed, argue that scavenging may have been more important to human survival and evolution than previously thought. Among contemporary societies in sub-Saharan Africa, human scavenging of meat from dead animals has been observed. Chimpanzees and baboons have also been observed scavenging the kills of cheetahs and leopards. Blumenschine and Cavallo (Ibid), in fact, hypothesise that 2 million years ago, scavenging may have been more common than hunting. They have found some evidence of early hominids' use of stone tools to extract bone marrow from carcasses of dead animals. Thus, scavenging might have played an important role in the survival of the human species.

Scavenging in Antiquity

When humans lived a nomadic existence, waste disposal was not a major concern, since wastes were usually dumped around people's foraging (open) areas. The wastes generated by hunter and gatherer groups were mostly organic in nature, such as bones, feathers, shells, the inedible portions of fruits and vegetables, as well as ash from fires and old stone items. With the advent of permanent settlements in the Neolithic era, waste disposal started to become an issue. It became apparent that some wastes could be reused or recycled since reuse or recycling involved less effort and time than obtaining fresh resources. Archaeological evidence suggests that metal scrap and metallic objects no longer useful may have been melted and recycled as early as 3000 BCE, the beginning of metallurgy. Pieces of broken pottery were also reused or recycled soon after pottery was invented. Plunderers along the Mediterranean coast are said to have dismantled the giant statue of the Colossus of Rhodes, felled 800 years earlier by an earthquake, and sold the bronze to weapons makers for melting (Downs and Medina 2000).

Ancient civilisations displayed different attitudes towards solid waste and towards the people who routinely came in contact with those wastes. In most cases, garbage presented considerable problems for ancient cities. For some, living amid refuse seemed not to be a serious consideration; for others it was simply a nuisance, while still others made every effort to maintain clean surroundings and to dispose of wastes in a way they considered proper. The inhabitants of ancient Troy, around the year 1200 BCE, simply left their wastes on the floors of their homes or threw them into the streets. Urban settlements inhabited from the Neolithic through the Bronze Age consisted of superimposed habitation levels. In various African cultures, similar habits prevailed and as a result, street levels rose and new homes had to be built on higher ground. This practice forms the basis of archaeological stratigraphy. The Minoan civilisation which flourished in Crete from about 2500–1500 BCE, collected its wastes and disposed of them in holes, covering the refuse with earth at alternating layers. The Minoans developed the basic idea of what later would become known as sanitary landfills. And in ancient Egypt, the later occupants of Amarna, the city founded by Akhenaton in 1400 BCE and later abandoned, excavated houses, searching for things the original occupants had left behind (Ibid).

The main centres of classical cultures in the Mediterranean, Athens and Rome, encountered major problems in the disposal of wastes generated by their inhabitants. Athens, with a population of 3,15,000 at its height, around 500 BCE, created the first "municipal dump" known in the Western world and city sewers provided fertiliser for nearby agricultural fields. The Council of Athens enacted an ordinance requiring scavengers to dispose of the wastes they collected at least one mile from the city walls. Some scavengers were also engaged in the collection of mixed wastes, and not only in the recovery of reusable and recyclable materials. Athens also enacted the first known edict against throwing refuse into the streets.

Ancient Rome, due to its large size, with about one million inhabitants during the reign of Augustus (31 BCE-19 CE), generated a large amount of wastes and undertook several measures to deal with them. Street cleaning is mentioned in many Roman laws, and in inscriptions in the eastern Mediterranean at cities such as Pergamum. Julius Caesar, for instance, required citizens to sweep clean the street in front of their homes. Much of the waste Rome generated was flushed out through sewers—particularly through the Cloaca Maxima, Rome's main sewer, installed in 500 BCE and then into the sea. The Tiber was the repository for all sorts of wastes, including dead animals, corpses that had been denied burial and stale grain. Several emperors dredged the river in order to remove the accumulated refuse. Augustus widened the bed of the river, cleaned it up and appointed supervisors of the riverbed and banks of the Tiber (*curatores alvei et riparum Tiberis). Trajan* (CE 100) incorporated the sewers into the jurisdictions of the attendants and Aurelian (CE 400) later followed Augustus' example (Ibid).

Contact with wastes in ancient Rome was considered shameful. Slaves collected and disposed of the waste produced by wealthy Romans. Trajan had convicts clean up the sewers of Rome. Cesspool cleaning was regarded as particularly demeaning, and the individuals who carried that out had one of the lowest status in Roman society. Sanitation in Rome was deficient and posed risks to human health and the environment. Rats were abundant since they had plentiful sources of food and they could move and breed easily in the sewers. As a result of inadequate sanitation and waste disposal, periodic epidemics affected Rome and other Mediterranean cities.

Despite the deficient sanitation and waste management, the Romans engaged in the reuse and recycling of various materials; in 1992, Italian archaeologists discovered a sunken ship in the Adriatic Sea containing parts and pieces of Roman bronze statues. The age of the bronze cargo ranged from the fourth century BCE to the third century CE and is believed to be the first tangible proof of commerce in the recycling of ancient bronzes. Such bronzes were probably going to be melted and recycled into new products. Pliny the Elder mentioned in his writings the reuse of scrap copper and the manufacture of bronze mirrors in Brindisi in the first century CE (Ibid).

Additional reuse and recycling activities in Rome were included. Peddlers were common in Rome, selling, among other things, used clothes. Older stone buildings were often dismantled and the stones reused to construct new buildings. The reuse of older monuments was undertaken not only for practical purposes, but also had an aesthetic element to it. Possibly the best known example is the Arch of Constantine, in Rome, in which the fragments of earlier monuments of Trajan and Marcus Aurelius appeared. Independent scavengers collected solid wastes and excrement, which they sold to farmers as fertiliser. In the city, the "manure merchants" collected human excrement from the trenches that served as sewers and sold it to farmers. Urine was collected and used in the dyeing of fabrics and by fullers to cleanse clothing. Emperor Vespasian (CE 69-79) had urinals installed in public places and imposed a urine tax on their operators, who reportedly made a good business by selling the collected urine. Fullers placed jars outside their establishments for people to urinate in them, obtaining the urine for free. Fullers also collected the soft fluff produced by their combing of clothing, which was used to stuff cushions and pillows. While the Romans made great use of stone, bronze and wooden tablets to announce notable events, they also used reusable tablets on which wax could be erased or corrected, a practice that had a more benign effect on the environment (Carcopino 1941; Friedelander 1968; Cowell 1961; Anon 1941; Bilitewski and Marck 1994).

In China, records of the 2nd century BCE indicate the existence of a "sanitary police" force which was in charge of removing human and animal carcasses and of a "traffic police" that supervised street sweeping in the major cities. Researchers have found in China samples of paper made from linen rags dating to 65–66 BCE, probably collected by scavengers. For centuries, Chinese farmers have collected human excrement from roadside public latrines and used it as fertiliser in their fields. Farmers also acquired excrement from scavengers who collected it in urban areas. Excrement was so valued by Chinese farmers that they referred to the containers used to store it as "honey pots" (Rosen 1958; Furedy 1990; Furedy 1984).

Religion played an important role in the development of sanitary practices in the ancient world. One of the most remarkable examples concerns is the Jewish laws of cleanliness. Around the year 1600 BCE, a code attributed to Moses included sanitary laws that required every Jew to remove their own waste and bury it far from their homes. These laws have been preserved and expanded over the centuries. In India, the untouchables have historically been responsible for collecting the wastes generated by all castes. Islam also considers the handling of wastes an impure activity. Consequently, non-Muslims performed that task in Islamic countries. Shinto religion influenced the Japanese concept of cleanliness and their avoidance of things dirty. As a result, Japanese outcasts were in charge of removing corpses and dead animals from the streets, and performed tasks considered dirty by the general population (Hanley 1997).

The Maya (pre-Columbian culture of Mesoamerica) engaged in the reuse of various items, such as broken pottery, ground stones and stones taken from old buildings, in temples or other buildings. They saved resources by using used or broken jewellery, pottery and tools in burials. The Mayans also substituted less valuable, imitation for original art. Many of these reuse and recycling activities are apparent after the year 1200 in the Late Postclassic Period, and were perhaps an adaptation to economic decline. Other cultures reused and recycled pottery as well. Reuse of pottery was carried out by putting together pieces of broken objects and holding them with metal. Several cultures recycled pottery as well, collecting broken pieces of pottery, grounding and using them as temper in the manufacture of new pottery (Rathje and Murphy 1993; Sharer 1994).

Aztec scavengers were popularly known as pepenilia. The Aztecs engaged in intensive recycling in their capital, Tenochtitlan (present-day Mexico City). Scavengers collected human excrement from public latrines and used it as fertiliser, as well as in the tanning of hides. The excrement was so valued by farmers that it was bought and sold in Tlatelolco, the city's largest market. Each household had containers to store urine, which the Aztecs used as mordant in the dyeing of fabrics. Organic waste, in addition to being used as fertiliser, was fed to fatten the edible dog as izcuintli. The Aztecs had a high sense of order and cleanliness. Under Moctezuma

II's rule, littering and dumping of garbage was banned and penalised, and there were officials in charge of street sweeping. The Aztecs emphasised the productive use of their wastes and they also enacted harsh laws to protect the environment; the Chichimec Code prescribed the death penalty for cutting down a living tree (Bray 1968).

Scavenging in the Middle Ages, Renaissance and Early Modern Period

In medieval Europe, skinners, glove makers and curriers often located their operations downstream from dyers in order to take advantage of the alum flushed in the river. Human excrement provided fertiliser for backyard gardens and much of the household garbage was fed to pigs. Artisans collected urine and dog excrement for industrial purposes and used them to make saltpetre. In the 14th century, scrap dealers in Florence enrolled in the same guild as copper engravers (Barringer 1954; Reid 1991).

In Samarkand, Baghdad, Cairo and Damascus, paper was made from rags in the 9th century. Rag collectors salvaged hemp ropes, fishing nets, footwear soles and robes to be sold to papermakers. Records show that during the 12th and 13th centuries, Bedouins and Arabs looted Egyptian graves in order to recover burial clothes, to be reused or sold for recycling to papermakers. Papermaking from rags was introduced to Europe, via Spain, by the Arabs in the 10th century and it extended throughout Europe and North Africa between the 11th and 13th centuries. During that period, rag collectors in Spain were known as *pannorum collectores or pannicolorum collectores* (collectors of rags and little rags, respectively). And post-consumer rags used in papermaking were called *resuris veterum pannorum* (shaved old rags) in the 12th century (Vails 1980; Munsell 1980).

For much of the period between the 13th and 18th centuries, a chronic scarcity of rags existed in Spain and most of Europe. Demand for paper kept increasing while the supply of rags did not, because clothes were used as long as possible and not discarded frequently. Further, most clothes during this period were made of wool, a material not suitable for making paper. Rag collectors kept recovering post-consumer rags during this period, and they were known in Spain as *traperos.* The recovery of post-consumer rags for papermaking during the 17th and 18th centuries was of such economic importance that it commanded royal attention. In Spain, Felipe IV issued a decree in 1641 banning the export of rags collected in Murcia and Castilla and ordered that they be sold exclusively to an individual named Juan Otonel. Also in Spain, another royal edict exempted Catalonian rag collectors, middlemen and papermakers from any taxes on the collection and transport of rags and paper. The shortage of rags was so acute in 1778 that Felipe II authorised the Reglamento de Libre Comercio de Indias (free trade law between the Spanish Crown and its territories in the Americas), which exempted the rags collected in the Spanish colonies in the Americas from the payment of taxes. Thus, this law attempted to encourage Mexican rag collectors, also known as *traperos*, to collect more rags, which would be shipped to Spain, transformed into paper, part of which would be sent back to New Spain (Weeks 1969; Lena 1990; Anon 1941; Vails 1980).

Poverty afflicted a large percentage of the European population for several centuries. In 18th century France, about half of the population was permanently destitute. Also, in 1815, about half the population in Sweden were either landless peasants or beggars. Having low income with little to spend on clothing, garments were valuable. Hospital regulations in Perugia in 1582 provided that the clothes of the deceased should be given to their lawful inheritors. As a result of widespread poverty, people discarded old clothing infrequently and in small quantities. It has been estimated that French scavengers in 1760 collected at the most 2 kilograms of white linen a day. White linen constituted the most suitable raw material to make paper (Ponting 1991; Munsell 1980).

Conditions in New Spain (colonial Mexico) were no different from Europe regarding poverty and scarcity of rags. Anecdotal evidence shows that in the late 17th and early 18th centuries, scavengers recovered rags from Mexico City's waste. Mexican *traperos* sold the linen, cotton, hemp and other types of rags either to middlemen or directly to the paper mills. By the end of the 18th century, the supply of paper in New Spain was so insufficient that prices doubled. The high prices paid for paper encouraged the plundering of offices and archives. In this way, documents and books, in some cases more than one hundred years old, were stolen and mutilated. Vendors bought the stolen paper, and used it to wrap merchandise, as well as to make fireworks. As a result of the scarcity and high paper prices, official documents were reduced in size, and government employees were urged to shorten the size of the letters in their handwriting and to write on the margins of existing documents (Sanchez 1993).

Thus, despite a strong demand for rags, both from domestic and Iberian paper mills, and despite a large number of poor people probably willing to scavenge, an active export market did not develop in colonial Mexico. No records exist of exports of rags from New Spain to Spain in spite of the royal efforts to stimulate them. The reason seems to have been the inelastic supply of rags: the Mexican population was so poor that, regardless of the high prices, scavengers probably could not get significant amounts of rags because people discarded old clothing infrequently and in small quantities. While the quantity available and the demand varied greatly across time and space, it is clear that scavengers played a crucial role in papermaking by supplying rags to the paper mills for nearly 1,000 years in the Middle East and throughout the Medieval, Renaissance and Early Modern periods in Europe and in the Americas (Downs and Medina 2000).

The scavenging of marble and stones from older buildings was common in medieval Rome. The Coliseum and other structures built during the Roman period served as quarries in late Antiquity and into the Middle Ages. Reuse and recycling of materials was also commonly practised in Japan. During the Middle Ages (1185–1600) as well as during the Tokugawa Period (1600–1867), farmers used agricultural waste such as straw and hulls, as filler for constructing walls and as cushioning for straw mats to lay on the floor (tatami) and for pillows. When the use of cotton became widespread, virtually all used clothing was reused as diapers, rags and other household items. By the mid-Tokugawa period, an abundance of second-hand clothing shops existed in Edo (present Tokyo), and a market for old clothing was held in the Tomizawa area every morning at dawn. Old clothing reached such high prices in the 1720s that people began stealing clothes in order to sell them at the markets. Japanese farmers used human excrement extensively. The steep price of excrement forced many poor farmers to steal it to fertilise their fields. In Osaka, landlords had property rights over excrement, while urine belonged to the tenants. The strong demand for excrement and the high prices caused disputes among groups of excrement/urine collectors over collection rights in certain areas, as well as between collectors and farmers' associations. Outcasts performed the collection of excrement and urine, since the Japanese considered contact with these materials undesirable and dirty (Frederic 1972; Dunn 1972; Rathje and Murphy 1993; Hanley 1997).

The Japanese traditions of using movable furniture and sitting on the floor saved resources compared to the lavish homes and lifestyles of

Western upper classes. During the Tokugawa period, due to their self-imposed isolation and lack of imports, as well as the densely populated territory, the Japanese developed a resource-efficient culture, in which a simple lifestyle was the norm. Factors such as a limited resource base, pragmatism and religious influence (Zen Buddhism) shaped the Japanese resource-conserving traditions during this period (Hanley 1997).

In the US, in the years after the Civil War, the country experienced rapid urban growth and scavengers picked over kitchen waste, dead cats and dogs, and all kinds of materials to make a living. In pre-industrial America, before municipal waste collection existed, scavengers collected and disposed of the wastes generated in many towns and villages (Thompson 1879).

Even though most reuse and recycling activities were carried out by scavengers, in most cases, migrants, the poor and uneducated and several noted individuals have been associated with these activities. In medieval England, Geoffrey Chaucer served as Clerk of the Works at Westminster Palace in the late 14th century. One of his duties consisted of the collection and inventory of scrap metal, and in his *Tales of Canterbury*, he described the scavenging of materials from waste in his time. Queen Mary of England was interested in salvage drives and reportedly did not hesitate to stop her car to retrieve bits of scrap along the road. Paul Revere, the New England patriot, was a foundry pioneer and scrap buyer. He recycled old metal scrap in his farm at Canton, Massachusetts. Benjamin Franklin supported scavenging activities and bought rags and discarded paper from scavengers to obtain paper to publish the *Pennsylvania Gazette*. Abraham Lincoln's father was a part-time peddler. When he decided to move to Indiana, he acquired a trunk full of objects to peddle along the way, at that time a common practice when travellers wished to offset the cost of a trip. Giovanni Toclonia, founder of the Italian family of merchants of that name, was a scavenger himself (rag and bone man). Maxim Gorky, the Russian writer, gathered waste materials when he was a boy. And Wendell Wilkie, the presidential candidate, swept and collected scrap in a factory in his hometown of Elwood, Indiana (Lipsett 1974; Barringer 1954).

Scavenging in the 19th Century

Scavenging flourished during the 19th century. Urbanisation and industrialisation played major roles in the development of scavenging and recycling activities. While in 1800, no more than 2.5 per cent of the world's population lived in cities, by 1900 the urban population had risen to about 10 per cent. Factories in the cities attracted the rural poor, particularly from areas where overpopulation, lack of land and work were major problems. The migration process was first apparent in Britain, which in 1851 constituted the most urbanised country in the world, with 40 per cent of its population living in cities (Honenberg and Lees 1985; Sutcliffe 1984; Ponting 1991).

Starting in the 14th century, the word scavenger referred to the collectors of tolls or duties on merchandise sold by non-resident merchants in London and other English towns. But during the 19th century, scavenging acquired the meaning of cleaning, street sweeping, cleansing rivers and refuse collection. Scavengers received licences from cities to act as refuse collectors and to recover waste materials. In Edinburgh, one of the filthiest cities in Europe in the 19th century, residents threw their garbage into the streets at night, hoping that the scavengers would pick it up in the morning. Other British cities had similar practices. Individuals who recovered materials form waste were known as rag and bone men, totters, and rag pickers (Furedy 1990; Furedy 1984; Sicular 1990; Weeks 1969; Reid 1991; Melosi 1981).

An intensive recycling system also existed in the rest of Europe and in the US during the 19th century: the so-called "peddlers" (US), *chiffonniers* (France) and *lumpensammler* (Germany) and their scavenging activities have been reported. The Paris *chiffonniers* rose in 1831 against the police because new regulations prevented them from recovering items from the waste dumped on the streets (Weeks 1969; Reid 1991; Munsell 1980).

In the US, recycling was particularly extensive in New England, where individuals exchanged tin ware for rags, rubber and metal scrap. During the 19th century, peddling flourished. Peddlers, first equipped with backpacks and then with horse wagons, collected rags, bones, scrap metal and other waste materials from city alleys and municipal dumps. Peddlers also bartered a wide array of merchandise, such as pots, pans, washbasins, trays, beeswax, eyeglasses, calico, medicines and so forth in exchange for rags, bones and scrap metal. Scrap metal was melted and recycled into new products, while bones were used to make glue, and rags to make paper (Barringer 1954; Lipsett 1974).

Enterprising Jewish immigrants from Eastern Europe as well as Italian immigrants founded the scrap recycling industry in the US. Some of them started collecting scrap in sacks or horse carts, prospered and eventually became dealers and owners of steel mini mills. There were a number of depots specialising in equipping those immigrants as peddlers along the Northeast, with the larger ones based in Brooklyn. In order to facilitate the entry of recent migrants into peddling, as late as the 1930s, collectors could hire horses and wagons for $1 a day, plus 500 per day for feed. A peddler having a horse wagon had obvious advantages, such as the ability to travel longer distances, to collect and transport more materials and as a consequence, to earn a higher income (Katzaman 1988; Melosi 1987).

Statistics compiled at the end of the 19th century demonstrate that scavengers performed the bulk of refuse collection in many US cities. In Boston in 1890, scavenging teams collected approximately 3,50,000 loads of household wastes, ashes and street sweepings. In Chicago, 225 scavenger teams collected about 2,000 cubic yards of refuse daily during the same year. And, at the turn of the century in Manhattan, scavengers collected an average of 612 tonnes of wastes daily. Also, in New York City, scavengers removed 15,000 dead horses, then widely used for transportation, from city streets in 1880. Until 1878, New York City paid the so-called "scow trimmers" for their recycling services, and allowed them to keep what they recovered. These individuals rummaged through mixed wastes on the dumping scows, the barges used to transport the wastes from the city to the disposal sites, searching for reusable and recyclable items. Scow trimmers used the salvaged items for their own consumption or for sale. From 1878 to 1882, the city eliminated the payments but allowed the scavengers to salvage any items from the waste. And, starting in 1882, the city charged a flat fee from scow trimmers for the privilege of scavenging the city's refuse. Most of the scow trimmers were Italian immigrants organised by local padrones (Anon 1891; Hering and Greely 1921; Melosi 1981).

At the turn of the century, collectors in the Midwest and the Southeast recovered mostly horseshoes, wagon wheels and metal scrap from agricultural implements. In the Southwest, individuals gathered bison, cattle and horse bones accumulated on the prairies of Kansas, Oklahoma and Texas, which they sold to glue-making companies. Scavengers could also obtain scrap rubber in large quantities from discarded boots, shoes, rubber rollers from old washing machines and other products. A method commonly used at the turn of the century was called reduction by which dead animals and organic wastes were cooked to produce grease, used in the manufacture of perfume, lubricants, glycerine, candles and soap, as well as a residue that served as fertiliser (Lipsett 1974).

Contemporary Scavenging

The trade in bones, bottles and fur diminished gradually during the 20th century as industrialisation took over; the manufacture of paper from wood pulp replaced the need for rags and more metal became available from domestic and foreign sources. Until the 1950s, scavengers in the US collected various types of materials for reuse or recycling from dumps, when, for sanitary considerations, as well as potential liability suits from scavengers, dump scavenging was banned. Street scavenging, on the other hand, continues to exist in the US. The poor and the homeless recover materials from waste for reuse or recycling. No reliable data exists on the number of individuals engaged in scavenging, but it has been found to be a common activity among the homeless and the poor. Scavengers recover food to eat from restaurant wastes, from dumpsters at grocery stores, discarded clothes for reuse, recyclables for sale and whatever items can be sold such as books and repairable appliances (Demko and Jackson 1995; Royse 1987). Today, aluminium cans constitute the most common material recovered by scavengers in the US and other industrialised countries. Over the last few years, the price of aluminium and paper has been so attractive that scavengers steal these materials from source-separated recycling bins (Downs and Medina 2000).

Recycling programmes in the US and other industrialised countries have been created in order to deal with increasing amounts of solid waste, declining landfill capacity, public opposition to the setting up of landfills and incinerators, and a favourable view of recycling. But setting up a recycling programme requires investments that must be recouped from the sale of recyclables. Therefore, scavenging reduces the revenues needed by the recycling programmes, and many municipalities have undertaken efforts to eliminate scavenging.

In developing countries, on the other hand, scavenging plays an important role in supplying raw materials to industry, and represents a common survival strategy for the poor. Since third world cities usually lack recycling programmes, the bulk of recycling activities are carried out informally by scavengers. It has been estimated that in Africa, Asia and Latin America, up to 2 per cent of the urban population makes a living by recovering materials from waste. This translates into a figure of up to 30 million people in the developing world who are scavengers today (Bartone 1988; Medina 1997).

Scavengers in developing countries usually specialise in one or a few categories of materials. Sometimes the right to scavenge in certain neighbourhoods is actually bought and sold. In some cases, such as in several Mexican, Colombian and Ecuadorian cities, municipal collection crews bid to their supervisors for being assigned to collect wastes in upper-income areas, where recyclables are more plentiful. And in Mexico City, Bogota and Manila, city collection crews often include a "volunteer" whose sole responsibility is the recovery of recyclables inside the refuse collection vehicles; the revenue obtained from the sale of the salvaged items is then distributed among the crew and the volunteer (Castillo 1990; Gonzalez et al, 1993).

Despite the stereotypical view of scavengers as marginal individuals living on the edges of mainstream economy and society, scavengers often form stable communities and constitute an important component in the recycling of wastes in developing countries. The estimated number of scavengers operating in Bogota is 10,000 individuals, 12,000 in Cairo, 13,000 in Mexico City and 20,000 in Kolkata. Despite the lack of data at the national level, various studies have highlighted the economic importance of scavenging activities. In Bangkok, Jakarta, Kanpur, Karachi and Manila, scavenging saves each city at least $23 million per year in lower imports of raw materials, and reduced the need for collection, transport and disposal equipment, personnel and facilities. Indonesian scavengers reduce by one-third the amount of garbage that needs to be collected, transported and disposed of. In the city of Nuevo Laredo, Mexico, the economic impact of scavenging activities has been estimated at nearly half a million dollars per month. In 1985, plastic manufacturers in Cairo saved 50 per cent in raw material costs by recycling plastic gathered by scavengers instead of buying fresh material (Medina 1993; Cointreau 1990; Furedy 1984).

Scavenging activities are sometimes highly organised with bosses, specialisation and division of labour, as is the case in Mexico City, Kolkata and Cairo. And in some cities, such as Manila and Caracas, scavenging resembles an industrial activity with three shifts of scavengers who recover materials 24 hours a day. Scavenging takes place in a wide variety of settings: source separation at homes and small businesses, collection crews sort materials inside collection vehicles, at communal storage sites, dumpsters, illegal dumps, litter on the streets, and at municipal open dumps, composting plants and landfills. Many studies report that scavenging populations are largely composed of poor, migrant individuals from rural areas, though in certain areas, such as in Beijing, Cairo and Nuevo Laredo, they derive an income of over three times the prevalent minimum wage (Abad 1991; Indorf 1994; Birdbeck 1978; Thome-Kozmiensky 1982; Vogler 1984).

Scavenging and War

The scarcity of resources brought about by war stimulates the recovery of materials for recycling. In the Classical era, after battles, the victors and nearby residents recovered clothing, weapons and other items of value from the deceased. In *Les Miserables,* Victor Hugo described the recovery of reusable and recyclable items from the dead in combat, after the Battle of Waterloo was over. During the American Revolution, the women of the colonies brought to the town square their spare lead, pewter, iron kettles and pots in order to be melted to make weapons. During the US Civil War, drives in the South produced water pipes, sash weights, bells and other metal items to be recycled and made into weapons. During World War II, the Germans seized church bells and other bells inside the country and in the occupied territories to recover the metal (Barringer 1954; Lipsett 1974).

In the US, salvage drives during World War II and the Korean War produced 9 million and 2.5 million tons of scrap, respectively. War also generates large amounts of metal that can be available to scavengers: even today, Vietnamese peasants dig in agricultural fields and the jungle, searching for metal scrap left from the Vietnam War; and in the aftermath of the Persian Gulf War, Iraqi individuals recovered metal scrap from armament and metal scrap left over from the war to obtain extra cash (Barringer 1954; Lipsett 1974).

Siege situations in particular, and the scarcity they bring about in the besieged population, encourage scavenging. During the siege of Sarajevo by the Bosnian Serbs, some of its inhabitants survived by scavenging for food in waste bins, dumpsters and dumps. Sarajevans also collected all kinds of wooden items to be used as firewood. And during the siege of Grozny by the Russians in their efforts to defeat the Chechen Independence Movement, scavenging emerged as a survival strategy.

Hence, historical records and literature show that humans have engaged in scavenging activities throughout history and these may have played an important role in the survival of early hominids. Cultures show varying attitudes towards the wastes they generate, as well as towards the individuals who handle those wastes. More often, scavengers have been associated with dirt and regarded as the lowest stratum in the social hierarchy. Poor, immigrant and uneducated individuals usually constitute the majority of scavenging populations, which reinforces and perpetuates social perceptions of scavengers.

Begun merely as a coping mechanism in conditions of scarcity and in order to survive, scavenging became an important source of raw materials for agriculture, artisans and, with increasing industrialisation, for industry. Despite the popular perception of scavengers as marginal, they played a crucial role in supplying rags for papermaking for nearly 1,000 years, and they are still very important for the paper industry in developing countries today. Urbanisation and industrialisation, in the 19th century in Europe and in the US, and still an ongoing process in developing countries, encouraged migration from rural areas to the cities and increased demand for inexpensive raw materials. By choice, or forced by their inability to secure employment, some migrants become scavengers. Even though scavenging renders environmental benefits to society, such as energy saving, lower consumption of water, reduction in water and in pollution in manufacturing compared to the use of virgin materials, the motivation for scavengers is fundamentally economic. In economic terms, the environmental benefits of scavenging are merely positive externalities of this activity. If the price paid for a particular material is high enough, scavengers will recover it, and, in some cases, will even resort to stealing it. Scavenging represents an adaptive response to scarcity caused by chronic poverty, war and economic crises. Since these causal factors are not likely to disappear in the foreseeable future, scavenging is likely to exist in industrialised and developing countries alike (Downs and Medina 2000).

Scavengers in India

Traditionally, most of the toilets built in the 20th century in India were dry latrines that did not use a water-fed flushing system. In the late 1960s and through the 1970s, toilet pans in India were made of ceramic. They were in short supply and not affordable for most of the population. Access to expensive flush systems for toilets was also limited. Scarcity of water in urban areas resulted in the lack of adoption of pour flush toilets that required 5 litres of water. This meant that much of India's population either defecated in the open (65 per cent) or used dry latrines or bucket toilets that required daily removal and transportation of human waste. Human waste removal was carried out by scavengers who also carried human waste from bucket toilets as head loads (Pathak 1996).

Between 2002 and 2003, the Ministry for Social Justice and Empowerment, Government of India, admitted the existence of 6,76,000 people who lifted human excrement for a living. They cleaned the 9.2 million dry latrines that were spread across 21 states and Union Territories. Women who were regarded as untouchables and placed on the lowest rung of India's class system were responsible for cleaning these toilets. However, many agencies believe that official figures are deliberately understated because scavenging is illegal, and there are many different estimates. According to Sulabh, four to five million people were working as scavengers in 2005 and were often employed by the local civil bodies to clean excrement in public places (Ibid). In total, an estimated 750 million people in the country defecated in the open or used toilets that had to be cleaned manually by scavengers. This lack of access, scarcity of water and low affordability of flush toilets formed a set of barriers to liberate scavengers.

Gandhi, who pioneered the sanitation movement in India, was one of the earliest social scientists that acknowledge that scavengers deserve equal treatment and alternative livelihoods. He learned that scavengers often had to clean the dry latrines before sunrise, because people of other (higher) castes did not even want to come into contact with a scavenger's shadow.

Efforts at Empowerment

Scavenging has been an occupation imposed upon certain categories of people by society, which later continued as a traditional occupation where a section of people among SCs was ordained to clean night soil and carry it on their heads. This class of people of India is known as manual scavengers. Manual scavenging exists primarily because of the absence of water use latrines or the presence of dry toilets. Using a broom, a tin plate and a drum, they clear and carry human excreta from toilets, most often on their heads, to dumping grounds and disposal sites. They are exposed to the most virulent forms of viral and bacterial infections that affect their skin, eyes, limbs, respiratory and gastrointestinal systems. Their children are also caught up in this. Under these circumstances, it is almost impossible for their children to become educated. Mostly, the women of the scavenger families are engaged in scavenging. Even though in modern times these people wish to leave the profession, their social, economic, educational and cultural constraints have made it difficult for them to find an alternative profession. The social stigma of untouchability continues to stick, in one form or the other, largely because of the unclean nature of their occupation. Over the decades, especially after Independence, several steps have been initiated to eradicate manual scavenging in India.

The conditions of the scavengers is not merely an economic issue, rather, it is a complex situation entangled with issues of health, and religious and social life. The Government of India and other voluntary organisations have made efforts from the beginning to lift this section of people out of their unfortunate situation.

Government Initiatives

In the past (before 1980), the main efforts of the government were concentrated on improving the working and living conditions of scavengers and not the core problem of converting dry latrines to pour-flush latrines in any systemic manner. In 1980–81, the Ministry of Home Affairs took up the Centrally sponsored Scheme for Liberation of Scavengers by way of conversion of existing dry latrines into low-cost pour-flush latrines and providing alternative employment to the unemployed scavengers as one of the measures for removal of untouchability and providing financial assistance in selected towns.

A Task Force constituted by the Planning Commission in July 1989 suggested a separate scheme for liberation and rehabilitation of scavengers. It also explored the bases for the enactment of certain legislation to ban construction and continuation of dry latrines and prohibit the practice of manual scavenging. In 1992, the scheme of "Liberation of Scavengers" was bifurcated. For conversion of dry latrines into water-use flush latrines, an Integrated Low Cost Sanitation Scheme (ILCS) was started. The NSLRS was started for providing alternative employment to the liberated scavengers and their dependents.

Taking into consideration the seriousness of the problem and the requests of the state governments, the Parliament enacted the Employment of Manual Scavengers and Construction of Dry Latrines (Prohibition) Act, 1993. The Act provides that no person shall:

- Engage in or employ for or permit to be engaged in or employed for any other person for manually carrying human excreta; or
- construct or maintain a dry latrine.

Self-Employment Scheme for Rehabilitation of Manual Scavengers (SRMS)

A successor scheme to the NSLRS was introduced in January 2007, as a scheme of national priority, with the objective to rehabilitate the remaining manual scavengers and their dependents in alternative occupations, in a time-bound manner. Eighteen states/UTs had reported 1,18,474 manual scavengers to be covered. All these states/UTs confirmed disbursement of loans for alternative occupations to all the 78,941 eligible and willing beneficiaries by June 2010.

Nevertheless, there were reports of existence of manual scavenging. The House-listing and Housing Census, 2011, reported that there were about 26 lakh insanitary latrines in the country. Accordingly, the Parliament passed the Prohibition of Employment as Manual Scavengers and their Rehabilitation Act, 2013 (MS Act, 2013) which came into effect from 6 December 2013. This Act intends to:

1. Eliminate insanitary latrines
2. Prohibit
    a. Employment as manual scavengers
    b. Hazardous manual cleaning of sewers and septic tanks
3. Survey of manual scavengers and their rehabilitation, in a time-bound manner

The main features of the Act are:

1. Definitions of manual scavengers and insanitary latrines widened to cover not only dry latrines but other insanitary latrines as well.
2. Offences under the Act are cognisable and non-bailable and attract stringent penalties.
3. Vigilance/Monitoring Committee at subdivision, district, state and Central Government levels.
4. National Commission for Safai Karamcharis (NCSK) would, inter alia, monitor implementation of the Act and inquire into complaints regarding contravention of the provisions of the Act.

5. Provision of construction of adequate number of sanitary community latrines in urban areas, within three years from the date of commencement of this Act to eliminate the practice of open defecation.
6. Prohibits the construction or maintenance of insanitary toilets.
7. Prohibits the engagement or employment of anyone as a manual scavenger.
8. Violations could result in a year's imprisonment or a fine of ₹50,000 or both.
9. Prohibits a person from being engaged or employed for hazardous cleaning of a sewer or a septic tank.
10. Calls for a survey of manual scavengers in urban and rural areas within a time bound framework.

The SRMS has been revised in November 2013 with the following major modifications, in line with the MS Act, 2013:

a. Definition of manual scavengers as per MS Act, 2013.
b. Provision of one-time cash assistance of ₹40,000.
c. Enhancement of the maximum project cost from the existing ₹5 lakh to ₹10 lakh, and ₹15 lakh in case of sanitation related projects.
d. Enhancement of capital subsidy from the existing maximum ₹20,000 to maximum of ₹3.25 lakh, based on the project cost.
e. Revision of the rate of monthly stipend during training from the existing ₹1,000 to ₹3,000 and the training period from one to two years.

The Ministry of Social Justice and Empowerment has associated reputed NGOs like Safai Karamchari Andolan, Rashtriya Garima Abhiyan and Sulabh International for identification of manual scavengers and their rehabilitation. The Ministry has assigned the responsibility of rehabilitation of the identified manual scavengers to the National Safai Karamcharis Finance and Development Corporation. Under SRMS, so far, out of the identified about 12,700 manual scavengers, one time cash assistance of ₹40,000 has been credited into the bank accounts of about 6,600 manual scavengers. However, despite having an attractive SRMS scheme, the task of comprehensive rehabilitation of the identified manual scavengers and their dependents is not picking up (NIC 2015).

The Ministry of Drinking Water & Sanitation under its SBM (Gramin) provides for an assistance of ₹12,000 (₹9,000 as Central grant and ₹3,000 as state/UT contribution). Although the SBM (G) also targets identification of insanitary latrines and their conversion, the pace of implementation of the scheme does not match the targets of eradication of manual scavenging. Under SBM (G), so far 1.89 lakh insanitary latrines have been identified, of which 1.56 lakh are dry toilets and 1.13 lakh have been converted into sanitary latrines. About 0.55 lakh dry toilets are yet to be converted into sanitary toilets. The Ministry of Urban Development, under the SBM (Urban), provides a grant of ₹4000 for conversion of insanitary latrines. The provision of the remaining fund for conversion will be made by the states/UTs (Ibid).

Under the Indira Awas Yojana of the Ministry of Rural Development, there is provision for providing assistance for construction of new houses and upgradation of kutcha or erumbling houses. Assistance of up to ₹75,000/- was provided to the eligible households. A provision has been made under the Indira Awas Yojana for special coverage of identified manual scavengers for providing them housing facilities in rural areas irrespective of their BPL status. The new scheme of "Housing for All" under the Ministry of Housing and Urban Poverty Alleviation aims at providing housing facility to all citizens of India.

Under the scheme of "Pre-Metric Scholarship to the Children of Those Engaged in Occupations Involving Cleaning and Prone to Health hazards", being implemented by the Ministry of Social Justice and Empowerment, the children of manual scavengers are also provided scholarship of ₹110 to ₹700 per month.

Problems in Elimination of Manual Scavenging

The states/UTs are slow in identification of insanitary latrines and manual scavengers as there is no time-bound plan for identification of insanitary latrines and manual scavengers. Further, in a case filed in the Supreme Court of India, many states/UTs gave affidavits stating there were no insanitary latrines in their jurisdiction. Due to fear of contempt of court, they hesitate to report the existence of insanitary latrines in their states/UTs.

At present, the work of conversion of insanitary latrines into sanitary latrines is being attended to as a part of the broad programme of construction of toilets. There is a need to have a time-bound approach as per the mandate of the MS Act, 2013, for conversion of insanitary latrines. There remain several challenges in implementing the legislation to ensure that manual scavengers can work and live with dignity. Hence, rehabilitation of manual scavengers is slow and in many cases not adequate due to various problems being faced, which include:

a. Time-frame within which land is to be allotted as part of the rehabilitation package for former manual scavengers as provided for in the 2013 Act.
b. Correct and timely identification of insanitary latrines and manual scavengers.
c. Implementation of provision regarding prohibiting "hazardous cleaning" of sewers and septic tanks.
d. While the Act is encouraging in that it focuses on the responsibility of officials to ensure its implementation, it does not outline administrative measures beyond conduct rules that can be imposed if officials do not implement the Act.
e. Manual scavengers are mostly illiterate and have no exposure to any work, other than sanitation related work. Many of them are old; they lack confidence for running self-employment projects. Many of them are not willing even to avail of any skill development training.
f. Banks are hesitant to provide loans to manual scavengers. Many state channelising agencies, due to low rate of recovery of loan from safai karamcharis, are not willing to extend loans to manual scavengers.

The National Safai Karamcharis Finance and Development Corporation, an apex corporation for the socio-economic development of safai karamcharis and manual scavengers and their dependents, is the nodal agency of the Government of India for rehabilitation of the identified manual scavengers and their dependents. The Corporation has adopted a camp approach for mobilisation of the target group and readying them to avail of the benefits of government schemes for their rehabilitation in alternative occupations. In these camps, apart from the manual scavengers and their dependents, various concerned departments of the state, training providers, and representatives of banks and NGOs are invited. All the stakeholders are made aware of the benefits to be provided to the target group and motivated to provide all possible cooperation and assistance for rehabilitation of manual scavengers and their dependents. With the camp approach, it is hoped that the goal of meaningful and sustainable rehabilitation of the identified manual scavengers will be achieved (NIC 2015).

Therefore, the Government of India has adopted a two-pronged strategy of eliminating insanitary latrines through demolition and conversion into sanitary latrines, and developing a comprehensive rehabilitation package for manual scavengers.

However, while manual scavenging, for many, may have ended as a form of employment, the stigma and discrimination associated with it lingers on, making it difficult for former or liberated manual scavengers to secure alternative livelihoods and raising the fear that people could once again return to manual scavenging in the absence of other opportunities to support their families. Correctly identifying manual scavengers remains a key challenge. A comprehensive rehabilitation package has been put together that includes livelihoods and skill development, access to education for children of former manual scavengers and alternative livelihoods.

A comprehensive rehabilitation package could (UN India, 2015):

a. Ensure discrimination-free, secure and alternative livelihoods by providing skill development and livelihood training to women, linking them to government employment schemes and entitlements as well as ensuring their land rights. Vocational training linked to employment for young people, and support to liberated manual scavengers in building alternative livelihoods could go a long way in ensuring steady, stable livelihoods for the future.
b. Create a favourable environment through community awareness and sensitisation of local administration.
c. Build the capacity of the community to promote rehabilitation efforts and self-reliance and also build leadership in the community with particular focus on Dalit women.

Other than specific strategies to eradicate manual scavenging and to rehabilitate them, the government has also focused on improving sanitation conditions throughout India, especially in rural areas. Sanitation means much more than building toilets. The most important requirement for safe sanitation is getting rid of human excreta, dirty water and household refuse. Also crucial is the way people think and behave, and whether they have hygienic and healthy habits. Sanitation improvement is a bigger process, aimed at the individual, the home and the community, which must include health and hygiene education as well as sustainable improved toilet facilities, water supply and methods of removal of dirty water and household refuse. Providing, improving and maintaining satisfactory sanitation affects all members of society. This policy must apply in all situations: in rich and poor communities, in rural and urban areas, and whether sanitation is for individual households or provided as a system for an entire community. The major aim of the national policy on community sanitation is to improve the health and quality of life of the whole population. Improved sanitation facilities will reduce the incidence of disease, but only if there is improved hygiene practice and behaviour as well.

Sulabh's Commitment and Achievement

The Sulabh International Social Service Organisation is dedicated to the Gandhian ideology of emancipation of scavengers. Sulabh has been working for the removal of untouchability and social discrimination against human scavengers. It is noted for achieving success in the field of cost-effective sanitation, liberation of scavengers, social transformation of society, prevention of environmental pollution and development of non-conventional sources of energy.

Dr Bindeshwar Pathak's strategy for liberation of scavengers was through the Sulabh movement, consisting of a mixed package of technology and rehabilitation, with alternative employment and social reform. The Sulabh approach to restore human dignity for scavengers has five distinct stages: liberation, rehabilitation, vocational training, proper education of the next generation and social elevation. The special features of these stages are discussed elsewhere in the book. Earlier, there was social stigma and psychological taboo attached to the handling of human excreta. It could also be due to the fact that only people of the lowest economic and social strata were supposed to be associated with this job. Due to the efforts of Sulabh, and financial viability, people from higher social status now compete to take up sanitation projects without psychological reservations.

Altogether there are 60,000 volunteers working with Sulabh which include technocrats, managers, scientists, engineers, social scientists, doctors, architects, planners and other non-revenue staff. Sulabh takes 30 years' maintenance guarantee for the toilet complexes constructed by it. With the efforts of Sulabh, it is proven that the task of total sanitation coverage in any country can be fulfilled only through close co-operation between local government and the community or local NGOs involved with such work. Neither the government nor NGOs/CBOs can fulfil the task alone, because the problem requires both technical as well as social aspects to be tackled. Therefore, it needs a holistic effort to overcome the problem. The strategy developed by Sulabh can easily be replicated in other developing countries to improve sanitation status and quality of life.

Skills-based training has enabled women manual scavengers to take up alternative sources of livelihood, like working as a beautician, and has helped them gain respect in society (Mathews, 2015). Women registered at the Sulabh training centre, Nai Disha, are taught various vocational skills like food processing, tailoring and beauty care apart from being imparted functional literacy.

Sulabh is moving in the direction of attending to the dangers of insanitation. One toilet can transform the entire life of a woman by making her safer and healthier; and women have the power to transform their families. Besides, it also undertakes social upliftment programmes especially for female scavengers. Despite the long cultural legacy of the caste system, around 200 women from Alwar and Tonk districts of Rajasthan took a bath at the famous Ramghat on the bank of the Kshipra River (Shipra) to promote egalitarian social inclusion. Sulabh also initiated a pragmatic step towards inclusion of female scavengers at Nai Disha, its vocational training centre in Alwar, Rajasthan. The decision regarding selection of courses is taken by the women scavengers themselves. Women have so far been trained in food processing, beauty care, embroidery and cutting and tailoring. The social transformation brought about can be gauged by the incredible fact that the same society that was averse even to touching a scavenger, today readily purchases products (even eatables) prepared by the hands of these very scavengers. The women are paid a monthly stipend so that they do not revert to their old profession of scavenging.

In 1988, Pathak took a group of Harijans to the Nathdwara temple in Udaipur to defy inhuman orthodoxy and promote social integration. He even organised a common puja and community meals for high caste Brahmins and scavengers to partake together. In 1992, an English-medium school was opened in Delhi for the children of scavengers, thus extending Sulabh's philosophy of overall socio-economic development of scavengers.

In this way, the strings of a dream of universal sanitation are being pulled by a spotlight-adverse organisation from behind the scenes. The overall objective is to promote the survival, protection and development of scavengers, especially women and children, and to promote behavioural changes essential to realising the full benefits of these services (Sulabh 2018).

The key objectives of Sulabh International are (Rastogi 2011):

1. To restore human rights and dignity.
   a. liberation of scavengers from unhealthy and subhuman occupation of manual handling of excreta by converting bucket privies into Sulabh shauchalayas (pour-flush latrine with twin pits for on-site disposal of human waste);
   b. rehabilitation of the relieved scavengers and their wards in other jobs after training;
   c. help in social upgradation of scavengers and their promotion as equals in society;
   d. setting up information and employment exchange centres to help scavengers get employment either in the government or NGOs;
   e. opening English-medium schools to provide education to the sons and daughters of scavengers along with others; and
   f. helping scavengers build their houses away from slums so that they can be taken out from the unhealthy environment.
2. Prevention of environmental pollution and improvement of health, hygiene and ecology.
   a. educate people not to defecate in the open, lanes, bylanes, parks, streets, by the side of roads,railway tracks, etc.;
   b. motivate people to get bucket privies converted into Sulabh shauchalayas and to have toilet facility in houses where none exists;
   c. provide community toilet complexes with bathing, laundry and urinal facilities on a "pay-and-use basis" in slums and for pavement dwellers, rickshaw-pullers, the floating population and also for those communities in whose houses latrines cannot be constructed due to space constraint;
   d. persuade people to plant at least five trees per family and also to plant trees around public toilets for environmental protection.

3. Harness non-conventional energy sources from human waste and other wastes and save fuel and forests.
4. Procure manure from Sulabh shauchalayas and Sulabh toilet complexes and use it to increase farm productivity.
5. Promote job-oriented education and primary healthcare.
6. Form groups of people from all walks of life throughout the country and abroad to build public opinion against social evils and for the cause of economically poor and neglected sections of society.
7. Create new job opportunities by training change agents for integrated rural development.
8. Promote consultancy, research and development in technical and social fields.
9. Diffusion of innovations, education, motivation and awareness through mass communication.

Liberating Scavengers

- The Sulabh technology has liberated and rehabilitated 60,000 scavengers so far from the demeaning practice of physically cleaning and carrying human excreta.
- In the state of Bihar, Sulabh has installed 30,000 units and converted 10,000 more from old dry-pit latrines.
- Sulabh has provided two-pit, pour-flush, water seal toilet systems to more than 6 million households (about 12,00,000 individual toilets) and 5,500 community centres in 1,100 towns in 26 states and three UTs of India.
- Over 10 million people in India use Sulabh toilets daily.
- This self-sustaining system has helped in ending the uncivilised practice of open defecation and making the urban life clean, particularly in squatter colonies and places of congregation.
- Sulabh is already operating and maintaining about 100 shauchalaya complexes at important railway stations.
- Sulabh is producing and using biogas from human excreta from its 100 plants.
- A combined Sulabh action plan on human waste disposal and social reforms has provided jobs directly to 35,000 people, and has created 10,000,000 man days of work; making 240 towns scavenging-free. Over 4,000 scavengers have been provided vocational training.
- It has set up an English-medium public school in New Delhi and also

a network of centres all over the country to train boys and girls from poor families, especially scavengers, so that they can compete in the open job market. (Barker 2006; Dutt 2008; Nelson 2006; Sulabh 2018)

Education of the Children of Scavengers

Education holds the key to any major change and development. Literacy and education in India are significantly low, particularly among Dalits and Balmikis. In recent years, the educational infrastructure has expanded considerably and schools have been set up on commercial lines. These schools offer physical and instructional facilities comparable to those in developed countries. But very few children coming from low-income households, particularly Balmikis, have access to these centres of quality education. Moreover, since most of these children are first-generation learners, parents are hardly inclined towards the education of their children, especially girls. With this objective of imparting quality education, Sulabh Public School was set up in Delhi in 1992. The school aims to prepare children from the weaker sections of society for a better life.

The school brings quality education within the reach of boys and girls from Balmiki families. Apart from English and Hindi, Sanskrit is also included in the curricula, not only to provide modern, but also the traditional learning, so that the children do not forget the roots of Indian culture. Previously, Balmikis were not permitted to learn Sanskrit. The school also offers a wide range of support facilities. In addition, it regularly organises co-curricular activities with a view to promoting social integration. This serves as a model to be replicated throughout India for providing quality education to poor students.

The Sulabh Public School has marked features that distinguish it from others. The ratio of the students is 60 per cent Balmikis and 40 per cent from the general category. Balmiki students are provided free tuition, uniforms, books and stationery. The school is recognised by the Directorate of Education, Government of Delhi. It provides education up to class X. In 2018, the school had about 400 students.

Chapter 6

OPEN DEFECATION AND SULABH SHAUCHALAYA

Open defecation is the practice of defecating outdoor (in open space) rather than in a toilet. People may choose fields, bushes, forests, ditches, canals or other open spaces for defecation. They do so because either they do not have a toilet at home or as a traditional cultural practice. The practice is common where sanitation infrastructure and services are not available. Even if toilets are available the practice still continues due to habit.

About 892 million people, or 12 per cent of the global population, practised open defecation in 2016; 76 per cent (678 million) of the 892 million people practising open defecation in the world live in just seven countries. India is the country with the highest number of people practising open defecation, around 525 million people (WHO and UNICEF 2017).

Ending open defecation is an indicator being used to measure progress towards SDG 6. Extreme poverty and lack of sanitation are statistically linked. Therefore, eliminating open defecation is thought to be an important part of the effort to eliminate poverty. Open defecation perpetuates the vicious cycle of disease and poverty and is widely regarded as an affront to personal dignity.

Defecating in the open is a very ancient practice. In ancient times, there were more open spaces and less population pressure on land. It was believed that defecating in the open causes little harm when done in areas with low population, forests or camping type situations. With development and urbanisation, open defecation started becoming a challenge and thereby an important public health issue, and an issue of human dignity. With the increase in population in smaller areas, such as cities and towns, more attention was given to hygiene and health. As a result, there was an increase in global attention towards reducing the practice of open defecation.

The term open defecation became widely used in the WASH sector from about 2008 onwards. This was due to the publications by the Joint Monitoring Programme for Water Supply and Sanitation (JMP) and the UN International Year of Sanitation. The JMP is a joint programme of WHO and UNICEF to monitor the water and sanitation targets of SDG 6.

For monitoring purposes, two categories were created: 1) improved sanitation and (2) unimproved sanitation. Open defecation falls in the category of unimproved sanitation. This means that people who practise open defecation do not have access to improved sanitation. In 2013, World Toilet Day was celebrated as an official UN day for the first time. The term open defecation was used in high-level speeches that helped to draw global attention to this issue. "Open defecation-free" (ODF) is a term first used in Community-Led Total Sanitation (CLTS) programmes. The original meaning stated that all community members are using sanitation facilities (such as toilets) instead of going into the open for defecation. This definition was improved and more criteria were added in some countries that have adopted the CLTS approach in their programmes to stop the practice of open defecation.

The Ministry of Drinking Water and Sanitation has defined ODF as the termination of faecal-oral transmission by, first, no visible faeces found in the environment or village and, second, every household as well as public/ community institution uses a safe technology option for disposal of faeces. The safe technology option means toilets contain faeces so that there is no contamination of surface soil, groundwater or surface water; flies or animals do not come in contact with the open faeces; no one handles excreta; and there is no smell and no visible faeces in the environment.

The reasons for open defecation are varied. It can be a voluntary, semi-voluntary or involuntary choice. Most of the time, lack of access to a toilet is the reason. However, in some places, even people with toilets in their houses prefer to defecate in the open.

A few broad factors related to the practice of open defecation are:

a. Lack of infrastructure; often, lack of toilets in their houses, or in the areas where they live.

b. Lack of toilets in other places away from people's houses, such as in schools or on farms, leads to defecation in the open.
c. Use of toilets for other purposes; in some communities, toilets are found to be used for other purposes, such as storing household items, keeping animals, farm products or even as kitchens. In such cases, people often go outdoors to defecate.

There are several factors related to not having access to a comfortable and safe toilet (O'Connell 2014; Routray et al, 2015):

1. Poor quality of toilet: Sometimes people have access to a toilet, but the toilet might be broken, or of poor quality. Outdoor toilets (pit latrines, in particular) are typically devoid of any type of cleaning and reek of odour. Sometimes, toilets are not well-lit, especially in areas that lack electricity. Others lack doors or may not have water. Toilets with maggots or cockroaches are also disliked by people and hence, they go out to defecate.
2. Risky and unsafe toilets: There may be a risk to personal safety. They may be dangerous to access at night due to absence of lights, presence of criminals around them, and the presence of animals such as snakes and dogs. Women and children, the aged and the disabled who do not have toilets inside their houses are often found to be scared to access shared or public toilets, especially at night.
3. Presence of toilet but not privacy: Some toilets do not have a real door, but have a cloth hung as a door. In some communities, toilets are located in places where women are shy to access them due to the presence of men.
4. Lack of water near toilet: Absence of supply of water inside or next to toilets causes people to get water from a distance before using the toilet. This is an additional task and needs extra time.
5. Too many people using a toilet: This is especially true in case of shared or public toilets. If too many people want to use a toilet at the same time, then some people may go outside to defecate instead of waiting.
6. Fear of the pit getting filled: In some places, people are scared that their toilet pit will get filled very fast if all family members use it every day. So they continue to go out to delay the toilet pit filling up. This is especially true in the case of a pit latrine.

Similarly, there are other general factors that are not related to toilet infrastructure but support open defecation.

1. Lack of awareness: People in some communities do not know about the benefits of using toilets.
2. Difficulty in change of behaviour: Some communities have toilets, yet people prefer to defecate in the open. These toilets are provided by the government or other organisations but people do not like to use them, or do not value them. They continue to defecate in the open.
3. Preference for being in nature: This happens mostly in less populated or rural areas, where people walk outside early in the morning and go to defecate in the fields or bushes. They prefer to be in nature and fresh air; instead of defecating in a closed space such as a toilet. There may be cultural or habitual preference for defecating in the open air, beside a river or stream, or even a bush.
4. Combining open defecation with other activities: Some people walk early in the morning to look after their farms. They make use of this time for defecate in the open fields.
5. Social norms: Open defecation is a part of people's lives and daily habits in some regions. It is an ancient practice and is hard for many people to stop. It is a part of a routine or social norm.
6. Faecal incontinence–lack of control over defecation, leading to involuntary loss of bowel contents, including flatus (gas), liquid stool elements and mucus, or solid faeces: This medical condition can result in abrupt "emergencies" and not enough time to access a toilet.

In developed countries, open defecation is considered a part of voluntary, recreational outdoor activities in remote areas. It is difficult to estimate how many people practise open defecation in these communities. But it is also of very little public health, environmental and human dignity concern. The situation is very different in developing and less developed countries and communities, where open defecation is of high public health and development concern. The practice of open defecation is strongly related to poverty and exclusion, particularly in case of rural areas and informal urban settlements.

The negative public health impacts of open defecation are the same as those described when there is no access to sanitation at all. Open defecation, and lack of sanitation and hygiene in general, is an important factor that causes various diseases, the most common being diarrhoea and intestinal worm infections, and also typhoid, cholera, hepatitis, polio, trachoma and others.

Certain diseases are grouped under the name of waterborne diseases, which are diseases transmitted via faecal pathogens in water. Open defecation can lead to water pollution when rain flushes faeces that are dispersed in the environment into surface water or unprotected wells. Open defecation was found by WHO to be a leading cause of diarrheal death. An average of 2,000 children under the age of five, die every day from diarrhoea. Young children are particularly vulnerable to swallowing faeces of other people that are lying around after open defecation, because young children crawl on the ground, walk barefoot and put things in their mouths without washing their hands. Faeces of farmed animals are equally a cause of concern when children are playing in the yard (Cavill 2015).

Those countries where open defecation is most widely practised have the highest number of deaths of children under the age of five, as well as high levels of malnourishment (leading to stunted growth in children), high levels of poverty and large disparities between rich and poor. Research in India has shown that detrimental health impacts (particularly for early life health) are even more significant with open defecation when the population density is high. The same amount of open defecation is twice as bad in a place with a high population density.

Gender Implications of Open Defecation

There are strong gender impacts of open defecation. Lack of safe and private toilets makes women and girls vulnerable to violence and is an impediment to girls' education. Women are at risk of sexual molestation and rape as they search for places to defecate, that are secluded and private, often during hours of darkness. Having to defecate in the open takes its toll on human safety and dignity. The loss of privacy is particularly pointed for women and girls in developing countries. They face the shame of having to defecate in public so they often wait until nightfall to relieve themselves. They risk being attacked after dark, though it means painful holding of the bladder and bowels all day. Women in developing countries increasingly express fear of assault or rape when having to leave the house after dark. Reports of attacks or harassment near or in toilet facilities, as well as near or in areas where women defecate openly, are common.

There are several strategies used to eradicate open defecation, one of which is behaviour change. Some of the key drivers used to fight against open defecation in addition to behaviour change are: political will, sanitation solutions that offer a better value than open defecation, stronger public sector local service delivery systems and creation of the right incentive structures.

Efforts to reduce open defecation are more or less the same as those to achieve the MDG target on access to sanitation. Key aspects here are raising awareness, behaviour change campaigns, increasing political will as well as demand for sanitation. CLTS campaigns have placed a particular focus on ending open defecation by triggering the communities themselves into action. Various Indian government-led initiatives are ongoing to reduce open defecation. There are some simple sanitation technology options available to reduce open defecation prevalence if the open defecation behaviour is due to not having toilets in the household and shared toilets being too far or too dangerous to reach, especially at night.

People might already use plastic bags (also called flying toilets) at night to contain their faeces. However, a more advanced solution of the plastic toilet bag has been provided by the Swedish company Peepoople. The company manufactures "Peepoo bag", a "personal, single-use, self-sanitising, fully biodegradable toilet that prevents faeces from contaminating the immediate area as well as the surrounding ecosystem". This bag is now being used in schools and urban slums in developing countries.

Bucket toilets are a simple portable toilet option. They can be upgraded in various ways, one of them being urine diversion which can make them similar to urine-diverting dry toilets. Urine diversion can significantly reduce odour from dry toilets.

Gravity of Open Defecation

As per the Swachhta Status report of the National Sample Survey Office (NSSO), in 2015, more than half of the rural population (52.1 per cent) of the country still defecated in the open. Eliminating open defecation in India by 2 October 2019, the 150th birth anniversary of Mahatma Gandhi, is one of the key aims of the Swachh Bharat Abhiyan. When compared with other countries, India fares poorly. According to data compiled by Research

Institute for Compassionate Economics (RICE), sub-Saharan Africa, which had 65 per cent of the GDP per capita of India, had only about half of the rural population defecating in the open compared to India. In Bangladesh, only 5 per cent of rural people defecate in the open, significantly lower than India.

The Swachhta Status report finds that 45.3 per cent of households in rural areas reported having access to a sanitary toilet whereas, in urban areas, 88.8 per cent households reported having sanitary toilets. A sanitary toilet is one which ensures safe confinement and disposal of faeces and does not require the need for human handling. Access to latrines has improved over the years both in rural and urban India. In 1993, 85.8 per cent of rural households didn't have access to a latrine. By 2012, the number was reduced to 59.4 per cent.

On the other hand, access to a toilet does not ensure usage. As per an NSSO survey, in 2012, 1.7 per cent of the households in rural areas and 0.2 per cent of the households in urban areas had access to latrine but were not using them. But the Sanitation Quality, Use, Access, and Trends (SQUAT) survey conducted by RICE found that 40 per cent of households that have a working latrine have at least one person who regularly defecates in the open. Further, less than half of the people who own a government latrine use it regularly; 47 per cent of those that defecate in the open say they do so because it is pleasant, comfortable or convenient (Bansal 2016).

The *Comptroller and Auditor General* (CAG) report said that of the constructed toilets, around 30 per cent were found to be dysfunctional. A NITI Aayog report of a subgroup of chief ministers on the Swachh Bharat Abhiyan states that the visible improvement in toilet coverage across states is deeply undermined by the poor quality of operation and maintenance of these facilities. As per the All India baseline survey conducted by the Ministry of Drinking Water and Sanitation in 2012–13, 1.39 crore of the total 7.41 crore household toilets in India were dysfunctional.

Behaviour change is a key priority of the Swachh Bharat Abhiyan as sanitation is a behavioural issue. It involves a change of mindset amongst people to stop open defecation and to adopt safe sanitation practices. But numbers tell a different story. Fewer funds are now being spent on IEC activities. According to Accountability Initiative, construction of Individual Household Latrines (IHHL) accounted for 97 per cent of the total expenditure between April 2015 and February 2016. IEC accounted for only 1 per cent of total expenditure. Expenditure on IEC reduced from ₹175 crore in 2013–14 to ₹109 crore in 2015–16 (Ibid).

The Ministry of Drinking Water and Sanitation says that adequate availability of water for toilets is also a concern. In rural India, the Swachhta Status report found 42.5 per cent of households had access to water for use in the toilet compared to 88 per cent in urban India. As of August 2016, only 17 of the 650 districts had been declared ODF by the government. Of the six lakh plus villages in India, 54,732 were declared ODF as of 31 March 2016. These figures are sourced from responses to questions in the Parliament.

In many rural areas the practice of open defecation is ritualised and bound in tradition. The behaviour and attitudes of the ethnic groups resist the use of latrines. Open defecation is related to factors specific to the culture of the ethno-linguistic group that practises it. Beyond their individual differences, the members of a group or society have particular ways of thinking and behaving, in the form of culture, and will react to situations in similar ways. Hence, the collective abandonment of open defecation will only be achieved through the modification of the social convention which regulates the practices of the group.

Open Defecation and Socio-Cultural Barriers

The whole concept of latrines has assumed a unique socio-cultural meaning in India. It is not the scarcity of water or simply a lack of access to toilets that pushes people to use alternatives such as agricultural fields as toilets. Some claim that the concept itself is alien to many, as ownership of toilets in north India has not had a bearing on the reduction of open defecation. While some choose to use the fields because toilets close to the vicinity of the house are considered to be polluting, others do not use toilets because the eventual cleaning of the latrines is perceived to be ritually degrading.

People wrongly believe that the pits of the latrines will get filled in a couple of months. This keeps people from using a latrine on a regular basis. Also, since emptying one's own latrine pit is socially unacceptable, as it is something they believe only an outcaste can do, households tend to use a latrine only for emergencies when someone is too weak (women, the elderly, children) or sick to go out in the open.

The ethno-linguistic groups involved in a study (Dittmer 2009) reported a number of socio-cultural factors or beliefs related to both their reasons for retaining the practice of open defecation and their resistance to changing their sanitation practices.

1. Shame or embarrassment of being seen approaching a toilet.
2. Excreta must be removed from the house due to bad smell.
3. Latrines are meant for wealthy people and you should not try to imitate them.
4. If someone feeds you, you should defecate in their field.
5. You may be possessed by demons if you use a latrine.
6. Use of latrines leads to the loss of magical powers.
7. Defecating in latrines shortens life span.
8. Continuation of ancestor's way of life.
9. Comfortable with the practice of open defecation.

Open defecation is also related to difficult socio-economic and geophysical conditions; including financial, technical and health-related issues.

Poverty: The cost of building a latrine is high in relation to household income in many rural communities, requiring unaffordable technical and financial resources. People who cannot afford chemical fertilisers encourage defecation in their fields, as it is a ready and cheap source of fertiliser. Building latrines in these communities is perceived as depriving growers of a useful resource. People often cannot think of sleeping in (thatched-roof) huts and hence to build latrines with cement and reinforcing steel just to defecate is beyond their resources; they give less importance to the latrines and do not want to invest in latrines.

Smell, heat and maintenance: Many traditional latrines are not well maintained, and a persistent complaint about traditional designs is that they generally do not allow for the escape of unpleasant smell and "heat" from the latrine. Many people prefer to defecate in an open space in the bush where the faeces will dry quickly in hot weather, rather than in a confined and unpleasant-smelling building. In some localities, poor hygiene standards in public latrines, especially during the rainy season when pits fill with water, discourages people from using them.

Safety: Latrines built using local materials are more affordable for poor people, but the absence of a cement slab to cover the hole means the structure is difficult to keep clean, and the use of the latrine can be hazardous, especially for small children who may easily fall into the pit. Many latrines are abandoned because the wood used in the place of the slab has broken or become rotten. Accidents are sometimes caused by poor construction.

Environmental constraints: The geophysical conditions in some locations make latrine construction more difficult, either because the ground is too hard or because it is too sandy and unstable. Construction in such areas requires technical and financial resources that people often cannot afford.

Swachh Bharat Mission

Swachh Bharat Abhiyan also called Swachh Bharat Mission or Clean India Mission, is a campaign that aims to clean up the streets, roads and infrastructure of India's cities, smaller towns and rural areas. The objectives of Swachh Bharat include eliminating open defecation through the construction of household-owned and community-owned toilets and establishing an accountable mechanism for monitoring toilet use. The mission aims to achieve ODF India by 2 October 2019.

The mission contains two sub-missions: Swachh Bharat Abhiyan (Gramin or rural), which operates under the Ministry of Drinking Water and Sanitation; and Swachh Bharat Abhiyan (Urban), which operates under the Ministry of Housing and Urban Affairs. Open defecation and sewage contamination of drinking and bathing water has been an endemic sanitary problem in India. As part of the campaign, volunteers, known as Swachhagrahis, or ambassadors of cleanliness, have promoted indoor plumbing and the Community Approaches to Sanitation (CAS) at the village level. Other NGOs also have extended their support towards this mission, especially Sulabh.

Sulabh has initiated concrete steps to stop open defecation and improve sanitary conditions in India. The innovations by Sulabh include: the scavenging-free, two-pit pour-flush toilet (Sulabh Shauchalaya); safe and hygienic on-site human waste disposal technology; a new concept of maintenance and construction of pay-and-use public toilets, popularly known as Sulabh Complexes with bath, laundry and urinal facilities being used by about 10 million people every day with generation of biogas and biofertiliser from excreta-based plants, low-maintenance wastewater treatment plants of medium capacity for institutions and industries. Other work includes setting up an English-medium public school in New Delhi and also a network of centres all over the country to train boys and girls from poor families, especially scavengers, for the job market.

The Central Rural Sanitation Programme was first launched by the Government of India in the First Five Year Plan, by Union Minister of Rural Development S.K. Dey. In 1953, the Community Development Block offices were opened, and the programme for building toilets in rural areas was executed through these offices. The *auger* (a tool consisting of a twisted rod or metal attached to a handle, used for making large holes in wood or in the ground) to dig the pit was sent to the villages, for which some money was given to the villagers. This programme was not successful. Therefore, till 1985, the Government of India did not take any interest in rural sanitation programmes. In 1986, another initiative was started under the Central Rural Sanitation Programme (CRSP), but it was confined to the BPL population. An amount of Rupees 500 was given for building the toilet which was inadequate, and the most disappointing part was that the government decided to construct only one-pit latrines, instead of the two-pit pour-flush toilets which Dr Pathak had invented in 1968–69, hoping that the beneficiaries would develop the habit of using twin-pit toilets, and would have the other pit built on their own. After a lapse of 22 years, the Ministry of Rural Development y decided to adopt two-pit latrines, and also tried to help the beneficiaries, who were now above poverty line. Even today, a substantial number of people in the villages have not been given any subsidy because they are from the higher income group. The amount of ₹12,000 given by the Government of India and the state governments is not adequate to build a good-quality toilet. Sulabh has built toilets as a model to demonstrate the standard needed for good-quality toilets.

Sulabh has built toilets in different parts of India under CSR partnership with Boeing Company, State Bank of India, ONGC, Maruti, HDFC and Bharti Foundation. The fundamental objective needed to make the programme successful is that there should be one donor, whether it is the government or a corporate agency or anybody who can do resource mobilisation. In this context, the role of an NGO becomes very crucial in the scheme. The volunteers of Sulabh fulfil this crucial role by visiting each household, to motivate and educate the members about the importance of toilets, and the subsequent benefits related to it, and those who build toilets under their close supervision get follow-up visits. The Sulabh model maintains quality control with disciplined supervision and follow-up, which paves the way for encouraging construction of good-quality toilets. With this qualitative process, the dream of having toilets in each house can be fulfilled and open defecation can be eliminated.

Dr Pathak has a meticulous plan; the scheme will be known as Open Defecation Free India or ODFI. India has 675 districts, 6849 blocks, 2.51 lakh panchayats and 6.46 lakh villages. The cost of a toilet is about ₹30,000 without stone while with stone, the cost goes up, ranging from ₹35,000 to ₹60,000. It depends on the type of toilet. One can donate a minimum of ₹30,000 which is the cost of one toilet; if there are 200 toilets needed in a village, the cost will come to ₹60 lakh. For one panchayat comprising of three villages, the cost will come to 1 crore 80 lakh. Similarly, the cost for covering a block or tehsil will be ₹60 crore and for a district, ₹600 crore. The Bharti Foundation had taken responsibility for one district, Ludhiana. If one decides to take responsibility for one toilet, or for a toilet in all homes of a village, a panchayat, a block or a district, the work will be carried out in the name of the donor or in the name of the company or organisation. Before taking the decision, there may be interaction with the people of the village for whom the work will be done. Dr Pathak has earnestly requested all to join hands to make India clean and open defecation-free, and thus, a fitting tribute to Mahatma Gandhi on his 150th birth anniversary (Sulabh 2016).

Uniqueness of Sulabh Shauchalaya

The Sulabh movement led by Dr Bindeshwar Pathak performs the most required social functions for the well-being of the most isolated and downtrodden population of the country.

Sulabh was envisioned as an agent of social and cultural change. Inspired by the Gandhian philosophy of truthfulness, non-violence and altruism, Sulabh believes and practices the Gandhian principle of trusteeship. Sulabh seeks to develop an egalitarian society, based on equal opportunity for every human being irrespective of caste, race and natural endowments. Sulabh adopts a holistic development approach and promotes the concept of a happy home.

Swachh Bharat is recent; the MDGs are post-2000. But Dr Pathak's vision for this mission started over five decades ago. His resolve to uplift the scavenger community paved the way for the biggest sanitation movement in India and the world. Every Indian knows of the Sulabh Shauchalaya, but not many know the story of the man behind it.

In 1973, Dr Pathak was given ₹500 to build two Sulabh shauchalayas for demonstration in the compound of Arrah Municipality in Bihar. Since then, Sulabh has converted about 1.3 million bucket toilets into Sulabh shauchalayas throughout the country; and more than a million scavengers have been liberated with more than 640 towns made scavenging-free. When Dr Pathak started his mission in 1973, he was the only one, not just in India but the world. In Bihar, when he went to talk about toilets, the man he was speaking to said, "Let's talk after tea. How can we talk about toilets while having tea?" During its journey of success, Sulabh replaced bucket toilets in Bihar. The people who earlier wanted a septic tank model, began demanding the Sulabh shauchalaya system. The pilot project that started in 1973 launched one of the biggest movements in sanitation across the world. The UNDP has a detailed report on the working and success of the programme.

Dr Pathak believes that in India, untouchables require social acceptance. He aligned his work with the guidelines given by Dr Ambedkar, to understand whether untouchability has been eradicated or not. "When everybody will go to a temple to worship, when everybody will take a bath in the same pond, everyone will draw water from the same well, and everybody will dine together." Dr Pathak fulfilled all these conditions in two towns, one of which is Alwar in Rajasthan.

Dr Pathak stresses the fact that education is key to development for all spheres in society. Any society that has grown is only because of education. Sulabh started giving the workers English and Hindi lessons, started giving them books; they are now able to apply for jobs that helps them earn ₹10,000 to 15,000 a month. The community has branched into other professions. Dr Pathak says, "I have not changed the caste; it's the same caste, status has changed. Now they're not called untouchables. They go with Brahmins and upper castes to dine and to sit together. This great change has happened in the country."

Despite a multicrore social enterprise, Dr Pathak is a humble man. He credits the change in the lives of untouchables in India to technological innovations in sanitation. His journey is one that will inspire many to look at social enterprise in a different light. Dr Pathak's story is also proof that technology, innovation and impact go hand in hand.

The rationale and key advantages of Sulabh flush composting toilets are:

- Hygienically and technically appropriate, and socio-culturally acceptable.
- Affordable and easy to construct with locally available materials.
- Design and specifications can be modified to suit the householder's needs and affordability.
- Eliminates mosquito, insect and fly breeding.
- Can be constructed in different physical, geological and hydro-geological conditions.
- Free from health hazards and does not pollute surface or groundwater, if proper precautions and safeguards are taken during construction.
- Can be located within the premises as it is free from foul smell and fly/mosquito nuisance, etc.
- Can be constructed on upper floors of houses.
- Pits are generally designed for three-year desludging intervals, but if desired, it can be designed for longer periods or reduced to two years.
- Maintenance is easy, simple and costs very little.
- Needs only 1.5 to 2 litres of water for flushing, while a conventional flush toilet needs 12 to 14 litres of water.
- Needs less space than a septic tank toilet system.
- Does not need scavengers for cleaning the pits or disposal of sludge. This can be done by the householder.
- Makes available rich fertiliser and soil conditioner.
- Can be easily connected to sewers when introduced in the area.
- A low-volume flushing cistern can be attached to avoid pour flushing.
- Sulabh flush compost toilets do not need vent pipes as gases are dispersed into the soil.

Chapter 7

SANITATION AND SOCIAL TRANSFORMATION

In India and around the world, the situation of having no toilet is a very important human development issue which the global community will have to address. It has drawn the attention of national and international organisations engaged in the promotion of sanitation-related programmes and activities. The toilet is a central subject of health and hygiene in India and other developing countries, which has become a tool for changing the structure of Indian society. This revolution has touched social, cultural, health, hygiene and sanitation related issues, leaving its powerful impact on the pace and progress of a wide variety of current initiatives; aimed at breaking the barriers of caste and changing its traditional structure and system in Indian society.

If governments do not see sanitation and hygiene for the people as of high priority, the situation will continue to prevail as it has since Independence. The greatest cause of loss of life in India, down the ages, is preventable infections caused due to poor sanitation and ignorant hygiene practices. The nation's considerable budget is spent on treating infected people while preventive measures would have saved lives and funds. The policies need to include providing needed lavatories and amenities to the public at large while introducing hygiene as a subject at primary school level and creating early awareness in children. Subsidies and technical advice are to be offered to the rural population and a nationwide campaign would get people to cooperate and change their behaviour.

Defecation in rural areas is done in the woods or near fields, where the excreta is always covered by soil and quickly converted to land nutrient in the presence of sunlight. So it is a nature-friendly method of recycling since ancient times. The same cannot be said about open defecation in slums and cities, where it is definitely unhygienic. It is a sorry state of affairs to have many people still defecating near the railway tracks.

Diseases, including cholera, which still affect some 3 million people each year, can be largely prevented when effective sanitation and water treatment prevent faecal matter from contaminating waterways, groundwater and drinking water supplies. Infected water supplies can be treated to make the water safe for consumption and use (Praeger). There have been five main cholera outbreaks and pandemics since 1825. In 1849, English physician John Snow published a paper "On the Mode of Communication of Cholera," in which he suggested that cholera might be water borne. During the 1854 epidemic, he collected and analysed data, establishing that people who drank water from contaminated sources such as the Broad Street pump died of cholera at much higher rates than those who got water from elsewhere (as stated in Nagla 2015).

India has 1.2 billion people and is far from achieving cleanliness. Less than one in three households in villages have toilets. Urban areas have more toilets but nevertheless suffer from poor sanitation and disposal mechanisms. The lack of public toilets for the urban poor and in rural areas leads to alarming rates of water borne diseases and affects women and children most. India also carries the shame of having manual scavengers, to clean human excreta from open lavatories, even today. In India, toilets are not just confined to sanitation issues, they involve abominable social oppression.

The 2011 Census reveals that half of India's population still defecates in the open. Only 46.9 per cent of the 246.6 million households have lavatories while 49.8 per cent defecate in the open. The remaining 3.2 per cent use public toilets (Nagla 2015). Open defecation lies at the root of many development challenges. More than half of the 1.2 billion people in India live without toilets. They squat at roadsides, in agricultural fields or at railway tracks and defecate in the open. Cultural and traditional reasons and a lack of education are the prime reasons for this unhygienic practice.

Access to improved sanitation can increase cognition among children. Further, Indian households defecating in the open and the absence of a toilet or latrine is one of the important contributors to malnutrition. According to UNICEF, hand washing with soap, particularly after contact with excreta, can reduce diarrheal diseases by over 40 per cent and respiratory infections by 30 per cent. Diarrhoea and respiratory infections are the number one cause of child deaths in India. With 638 million people defecating in the open and 44 per cent mothers disposing of their children's faeces in the open, there is a very high risk of microbial contamination (bacteria, viruses, amoeba) of water which causes diarrhoea in children. Children weakened by frequent diarrhoea episodes are more vulnerable to malnutrition and opportunistic infections such as pneumonia. About 48 per cent of children suffer from some degree of malnutrition in India. Studies suggest that open defecation is an important threat to human capital in developing countries. The survey figures mention that 54.7 of per cent households in the country are without toilets.

We need to view services such as the availability of functional toilets as part of the right to live a life of dignity and equality. Pathak observes that India lacks a culture of sanitation. The royalty and rulers might have had slaves to empty their waste, but much of India has had a late start in toilet training. Even the rural rich in the 1950s did not have toilet facilities in their mansions. Women went out in the open for defecation as did the men. However, today, India has made progress from a no-toilet scenario to providing nearly half of its population with latrines. Pathak says implementation of rural sanitation must be made a priority and speeded up. Sulabh is seeking ways to accelerate the installation of toilet facilities. The programmes include training youth in both rural and urban areas on health and sanitation pressing the government for fund allocation, and encouraging alternative livelihoods for caste groups that manually scavenge toilets.

The government is mechanically releasing the money and targeting toilet construction without paying any attention to community involvement. As a result, most of the toilets, especially in rural areas, are lying non-functional. People use these toilets for storing fodder or cow dung cakes (Nagla 2015). A UNICEF report mentioned that the national average of sanitation, hygiene and water safety in India is a mere 34 per cent. For the urban population it is 58 per cent whereas for people in the rural areas it is just 23 per cent. The situation is endorsed by the JMP report, which establishes that at least 40 per cent of the people from the poorest background have barely benefited from sanitation facilities meant for them in the last decade.

The government gives a subsidy for the construction of toilets but it does not reach the real beneficiary, be it a Dalit, tribal or extremely poor population or women, children and differently-abled people. WHO finds adequate sanitation a tool to ensure significant beneficial impact on health, both in households and across communities.

Toilets and Social Change

Human excreta is a source of infection. It is one of the main cause of environmental pollution. Every society has a responsibility for its safe removal and disposal so that it does not constitute a threat to public health. The health hazards due to improper excreta disposal are soil pollution, water pollution, contamination of food and propagation of flies. The resulting diseases are typhoid and paratyphoid fever, dysentry, diarrhoea, viral hepatitis and similar intestinal infections and parasitic infestations. These diseases are not only a burden on the community in terms of sickness, mortality and low expectation of life, but a basic deterrent to social and economic progress. Therefore, proper disposal of human excreta is a fundamental environmental health service without which there cannot be any improvement in the state of community health.

Nearly 70 per cent of India's population lives in rural areas and the majority of them go to the fields for defecation and thereby pollute the environment with human excrement. The situation is in no way better in urban areas. Surveys have shown that 58 per cent of the population goes out in the open for defecation; of them18 per cent are in urban India while in the rural areas it is 69 per cent (WHO-UNICEF, 2010). This habit of indiscriminate fouling of surroundings with human excrement is generations' old, and rooted firmly in the cultural behaviour of Indian villages. In urban areas, the latrine is considered a necessary part of a house. In rural areas, by and large, people have not accepted latrines with enthusiasm, and even when installed, only a few used them regularly. The problem in rural sanitation is to overcome the resistance of the villagers to use sanitary latrines. Research studies have indicated that there is only one way to solve the problem, i.e., through health education. Social scientists have also listed the reasons why villagers do not accept latrines.

It shows that people have a poor image of latrines in their minds. Secondly, using a latrine goes against their daily habit of going to the fields. The use of latrines involves a drastic change in the day-to-day behaviour of a large number of people. The solution to the problem is to teach people first the reason why latrines are important. The teaching should be undertaken by all known methods of health education: direct discussion, group discussion, demonstration on how to use latrines, use of visual aids and, above all, service facilities. The ultimate goal of health education will be to motivate the rural people towards acceptance and use of sanitary latrines. This will bring about real social change through sanitation.

The Sulabh International Social Service Organisation is exclusively engaged in promoting low-cost sanitation technology, eradication of manual scavenging and liberation and rehabilitation of scavengers. The toilet revolution that Sulabh ushered in the country has been a tool of social transformation that Pathak envisaged. It worked with the cooperation of a friendly voluntary workforce of over 50,000 people working full-time for a mission. Thus, Sulabh became a catalytic agent for sanitation and non-caste oriented transformatory social change. The Sulabh International social Service Organisation has engineered an innovative, affordable and environment-friendly toilet that has helped over one million marginalised people in India.

The Sulabh toilet is not only a unique technology for sanitation and preventing environmental pollution, but also for social reform. Required to remove human waste by hand, the Balmikis suffered occupational hazards of poor hygiene and health, in addition to being heartlessly marginalised by society for their unclean work. To change this, Dr Pathak created a technology to convert bucket latrines into two-pit, pour-flush toilets. These new toilets are being utilised across India.

Sulabh also provided alternative jobs to the Balmikis, who had lost their jobs due to the large-scale conversion of privy latrines into Sulabh toilets. Sulabh prioritised skill development, improving literacy and vocational training for Balmikis, including the children. It has set up many centres and institutions across the country to provide vocational training in many market-friendly trades. With the foresight that traditions take time to evolve and require initiative from all members of society, Sulabh implemented the concept of "social adoption". This is to formally and publicly adopt a Balmiki family. The pair of families closely interacts and visits each other's homes. At times, the adopting family helps the adopted family to overcome social adjustment problems. Adopters are typically persons of high social standing, and hence their approach and interaction become an example for others to reinforce the integration of the Balmikis into mainstream society.

Today, 1.2 million Sulabh household toilets have been constructed and 54 million government toilets are based on the Sulabh design. There are over 8,000 Sulabh community toilet blocks in the country and 10.5 million people use toilets based on the Sulabh design daily. As a result, Balmikis are not condemned to their traditional role. The major social reform endeavours of Sulabh International is that an upper caste elite closely interact with a family of a scavenger community include running the Sulabh Public School, where children of both high caste and low caste study under one roof and share meals. Here, through social mainstreaming programmes, efforts are made to prepare scavengers to get involved with mainstream society and they have made a dent in the rigidities of the caste system.

Sulabh International has recently undertaken a micro-level programme for the empowerment of women from the scavenger community. Through this the social status of these women is upgraded by providing them vocational education in economically rewarding occupations. Consequently, the eatables prepared by these women of the scavenger community are now being purchased by the so-called high caste groups.

A wide variety of programmes and activities of the Sulabh organisation are exclusively focused on social activities inspired and informed by the secularist mandate of the Constitution of India which seeks to abolish all forms of caste and creed based discrimination. The organisation has successfully pursued its agenda to include India's excluded castes in the social mainstream of society. One outstanding example of this has been to visit a Hindu temple which disallowed the entry of the so-called untouchable persons.

With reference to toilets, several kinds of social changes can be attributed to the invention of toilets, promotion of toilets and toilet-centred sanitation practices. These highlighted the social transformation process undertaken by Sulabh for liberating, rehabilitating and mainstreaming women scavengers into society and providing them sustainable livelihoods, thus fulfilling the dream of Mahatma Gandhi.

A class of people was condemned as scavengers and treated as untouchables for generations. Hardly anyone ever paused and wondered what could be done to help them until Gandhiji raised a cry against their suffering. India banned untouchability and the construction of dry latrines to obviate the need for scavenging. But the evil which had continued for centuries could not be ended overnight. Bindeshwar Pathak launched the

Sulabh movement, the main purpose of which is the liberation of scavengers from their shameful social condition. With his efforts, millions of scavengers have been freed from the task of carrying night soil as head-load. All over the country, over one lakh people, mostly women, are still engaged in this demeaning profession.

Pathak lived in a colony of scavengers in Bettiah, an outlying district of Bihar. The experience of living in a scavengers' colony made Pathak think and the solutions lay in replacement of the bucket toilet system. This led him to devise and implement the two-pit, pour-flush, compost toilet system technology for individual households and operating and maintaining public toilets linked with biogas plants attached to the Sulabh Effluent Treatment (SET) device, leading to liberation of scavengers from their demeaning profession. With this effort, Bindeshwar Pathak is proud to say that it has been possible to liberate them and thereby bring about social transformation.

After being liberated, it was taken care to ensure that the scavengers were able to find employment elsewhere and if unable to do so, were provided training by Sulabh in market-oriented trades, whereby they could secure gainful employment or be self-employed. Social transformation has been to the extent that the locals now consume eatables made by them, a fact which until a couple of years ago was unthinkable. They acquired self-confidence. Their grit and toil has helped them gain self-esteem and enhanced their social status.

Dr Pathak has taken the help of the media and journalists to promote the social cause. Journalists have interacted with the erstwhile women scavengers; talked to them, heard their real life experiences and written stories of their sorrows, the humiliation they suffered due to social ostracisation they faced living as scavengers. The book, *New Princesses of Alwar: Shame to Pride*, is an effort of members of the media and others who associated themselves to this endeavour.

'No toilets, No Marriage' It's easier for modern Indian women in the metros to walk into a shopping mall and find a toilet. But it is not so for their underprivileged counterparts who are poor or live in villages with no toilet facilities. Women and girls often defecate in public, harming their health and also inviting molestation and unwanted attention from men in both rural and urban areas.

In this connection, some instances have occurred where brides have left the homes of the grooms after finding the household did not have a proper toilet. It has forced some men to pose in photos beside a toilet in their home before seeking a bride in their villages. India's Supreme Court ruled in 2011 that every government school must provide toilets, especially for girls. Inability to do so would mean closing down the school. India has been encouraging rural communities to build toilets. But building sanitation systems in developing countries is not easy. Flush toilets are not always an option. Many poor communities live in water-stressed areas. Others lack links to sewage pipes or treatment plants.

Dr Pathak has talked extensively about how the toilet as a simple invention with tremendous civilising impact has played a vital role in enhancing the quality of life and in resolving some of the intricate social problems, like the practice of untouchability and the rigidities of India's caste system. In view of this, the sociological implications of the toilet revolution around the world, especially in India, have been most profound. The history of the evolution of toilets from 2000 BCE to date suggests many notable changes that have been brought about by this supposedly harmless but realistically important invention. History shows how an ordinary invention like that of the toilet has stirred the human mind, evoked passion, inspired imagination and kindled the hope and vision of many a social crusader around the world. In this context, the invention of the toilet is one of the winning ideas. This winning idea of toilet invention, evolution, propagation and action has demonstrated the power and potential that the toilet has had in the course of human history. The toilet is one single small-time invention that has made us civilised. This makes us feel that the toilet is one of the important achievements of mankind. The toilet revolution around the world has made its mark on modern civilisation, and its advances have been amazing, inspiring and, at times, horrifying.

The inadequate progress in sanitation makes India an outlier even among developing countries. Poor sanitation impairs the health of Indians, leading to high rates of malnutrition and productivity losses. India's sanitation deficit leads to losses worth roughly 6 per cent of India's GDP, by raising the disease burden of the country. Children are affected more than adults. The rampant spread of diseases inhibits children's ability to absorb nutrients, stunting their growth.

A large part of India's malnutrition burden is owing to the unhygienic environment in which children grow up. Poor sanitation and high population density act as a difficult situation for Indian children, half of whom grow up stunted. Public health in India has been neglected by the policymakers in post-Independence India, who focus on disease-specific intervention rather than on an overarching public health network focused on prevention. India is one of the few Asian economies that did not invest in an integrated public health system involving food safety, water management, waste disposal, vector control, sanitation systems, health education and other health regulations (Gupta 2005).

In India, social exclusion has been predominantly used in understanding caste-based discrimination. Caste-based occupational groups in India, like that of scavengers, including manual scavengers, constitute one such socially, economically, psychologically and politically marginalised section of the society. Excluded groups are often faced with double and triple discrimination. A Dalit or adivasi woman faces discrimination on account of her gender as well as caste, leading to increased vulnerability and exclusion from the process of development. For example, the male literacy rate in India is 82.14 per cent compared to the much lower female literacy rate of 65.46 per cent. This disparity is in itself alarming. However, it is the low rate of literacy among the SC and ST females at 41.9 per cent, and 47.8 per cent, respectively, which reflects the double disadvantage faced by the Dalit and adivasi women. Similarly, specific Dalit communities involved in manual scavenging are comparatively worse off than other Dalit communities.

Historical Development of Toilets

A toilet is a sanitation fixture used primarily for the disposal of human urine and faeces. They are often found in a small room referred to as a toilet, bathroom or lavatory. Through history, we can trace a variety of toilet systems adapted to different cultures, need and availability of technology, land and water. Flush toilets, which are common in many parts of the world, may be connected to a nearby septic tank or more commonly in urban areas via a large sewer pipe to a sewerage system. The water and waste from many different sources is piped in large pipes to a more distant sewage; treatment plant. Chemical toilets are used in mobile and many temporary situations where there is no access to sewerage, dry toilets, including pit toilets and composting toilets require no or little water with excreta being removed manually or composted.

Ancient civilisations used toilets attached to simple flowing water sewage systems including those of the Indus Valley Civilisation, like Harappa and Mohenjo-Daro (Yadav 2004) which are located in present-day India and Pakistan (Jutti and Wallenius 2005) and also the Romans and Egyptians who invented a version of the flowing water toilet. Although a precursor to the modern flush toilet system was designed in 1596 by John Harington, such systems did not come into widespread use until the late 19th century (Praeger). Thomas Crapper was one of the early makers of toilets in England.

The third millennium BCE was the Age of Cleanliness. Toilets and sewers were invented in several parts of the world, and Mohenjo-Daro had some of the most advanced system, with lavatories built into the outer walls of houses. These were primitive Western-style toilets made from bricks with wooden seats on top. They had vertical chutes, through which waste fell into street drains or cesspits. The toilets at Mohenjo-Daro were only used by the affluent classes. Most people would have squatted over old pots set into the ground or used open pits. The people of the Harappan civilisation in Pakistan and northwestern India had primitive water-cleaning toilets that used flowing water in each house that were linked with drains covered with burnt clay bricks. The flowing water removed the human wastes (Angelakis 2014).

Early toilets that used flowing water to remove the waste are also found in Orkney, Scotland, from about 3100 BCE until 2500 BCE. Around the 18th century BCE, toilets started to appear in Egypt in the time of the Pharaohs and in ancient Persia. In The Roman civilisation, toilets using flowing water were sometimes part of public bath houses.

But sitting toilets only came into general use in the mid-19th century in the Western world. The Roman toilets were probably elevated to raise them above open sewers which were periodically flushed with flowing water, rather than elevated for sitting. The Romans were not the first civilisation to adopt a sewer system. The Indus Valley Civilisation had a rudimentary network of sewers built under grid pattern streets and it was the most advanced seen so far. Squat toilets (also known as an Arabic, French, Chinese, Japanese, Korean, Iranian, Indian, Turkish or natural position toilet) are toilets used by squatting rather than sitting, and are still used by the majority of the world's population. There are several types of squat toilets, but they all consist essentially of a hole in the ground or floor with various provisions for human waste.

Chamber pots were in common use in Europe from ancient times, even being taken to the Middle East by Christian pilgrims during the Middle Ages. By the early modern era, chamber pots were frequently made of china or copper and could include elaborate decoration. They were emptied into the gutter of the street nearest to the home. During the Victorian era, British housemaids emptied household chamber pots into a slop sink that was inside a housemaids' cupboard on the upper floor of the house. The housemaids' cupboard also contained a separate sink, made of wood with a lead lining to prevent chipping china chamber pots, for washing the bedroom ware. Once indoor running water was built into British houses, servants were sometimes given their own lavatory downstairs, separate from the family lavatory (Lorenz 2014).

By the 16th century, cesspits and cesspools were increasingly dug into the ground near houses in Europe as a means of collecting waste, as urban populations grew and street gutters became blocked with the larger volume of human waste. Rain was no longer sufficient to wash away waste from the gutters. A pipe connected the latrine to the cesspool, and sometimes a small amount of water washed waste through the pipe into the cesspool. Cesspools would be cleaned out by tradesmen, who pumped out liquid waste, then shovelled out the solid waste and collected it in horse-drawn carts during the night. This solid waste would be used as fertiliser. The perception that human waste had value as fertiliser, and in ammonia production, delayed the construction of a modern sewer system in Paris as a replacement for the city's cesspool system. In the early 19th century, public officials and public hygiene experts studied and debated the matter at length, for several decades. The construction of an underground network of pipes to carry away solid and liquid waste was only begun in the 1880s, gradually replacing the cesspool system, although cesspools were still in use in some parts of Paris in the 20th century. The growth of indoor plumbing, toilets and bathtubs with running water came at the same time.

American lavatories followed the pattern of constructing cesspools in urban areas, using the practice already established in Europe, although the use of the outhouse near the family home was also common where more land was available, and keeping the waste well away from the well water. The indoor toilet invented in England in the 1880s, was soon introduced in the US, in the homes of the wealthy and in hotels. Flush toilets were introduced in the 1890s. Public awareness of germ theories about disease, as well as inexpensive manufacturing methods, helped the flushing toilet to spread to the middle class and even working class households (Stamp 2014). Various forms of flush toilets have become widely used in modern times; the amount of water used by modern toilets is a significant portion of personal water usage.

A pit toilet is a dry toilet system which collects human excrement and urine in a large container or trench and ranges from a simple slit trench dug in the ground to more elaborate systems with seating and ventilation systems. They are more often used in emergency, rural and wilderness areas as well as in much of the developing world. The waste pit or trench, in some cases, is large enough so that the reduction in the mass of the contained waste products by the ongoing process of decomposition allows the pit to be used more or less permanently. In other cases, when the pit becomes full, it may be emptied or the hole covered with dirt. Pit toilets have to be located away from drinking water sources (wells, streams, etc.) to minimise the possibility of disease spread. Army units typically use a form of pit toilet when they are in the field and away from functional sewerage systems.

Dry toilets, which use very limited or no water for flushing, include:

a. The pit toilet (a simple hole in the ground).
b. The composting toilet (which mixes excrement with carbon-rich materials for faster decomposition).
c. The incinerating toilet (which burns the excrement).
d. The tree bog (a simple system for converting excrement to direct fertiliser for trees).

The pig toilet, an outhouse linked to a pig enclosure by a chute, is still in use to a limited extent but the subsequent use of the pigs for food carries a significant risk for human health. The unsanitary "flying toilet" is used in slums in Africa where plastic shopping bags are first used as a container for excrement and then thrown as far away as possible. This practice has led to the banning of the manufacture and import of such bags in Uganda, Kenya and Tanzania. A toilet that pays its users has been opened in Musiri, Tamil Nadu, India. It is the first of its kind. The faeces it receives are composted, and the urine is used as fertiliser for bananas and other food crops.

Before the introduction of modern flush toilets, it was common for people to use a chamber pot at night and then to dispose of the night soil in the morning; this practice continued in prisons in the UK until recently and is still in use in the Republic of Ireland. Chemical toilets which do not require a connection to a water supply are used in a variety of situations. Examples include passenger train toilets and airplane toilets and also complicated space toilets for use in zero-gravity spacecraft.

A public toilet, frequently called a restroom, is accessible to the general public. It may be within a building that, while privately owned, allows public access. Access to a public toilet may require a fee (pay toilet), or may be limited to the business's customers. Depending on culture, there may be varying degrees of separation between men and women and different levels of privacy. In more luxurious variations there may be an attendant, towels and showers. A fairly common feature in more modern toilets is an area to change baby diapers.

The portable toilet is used on construction sites and at large outdoor gatherings where there are no other facilities. They are typically self-contained units that are made to be easily moved to different locations as needed. Most portable toilets are unisex single units with privacy ensured by a simple lock on the door. The units are usually lightweight and easily transported by a flatbed truck and loaded and unloaded with a small forklift. Many portable toilets are small moulded plastic or fibreglass portable rooms with a lockable door and a receptacle to catch waste in a chemically treated container. If used for an extended period of time, they have to be cleaned out and new chemicals put in the waste receptacle.

The high-tech toilets include features such as automatic flushing mechanisms that flush a toilet or urinal when finished, water jets or bottom washers like a bidet, blow dryers, artificial flush sounds to mask noises, and urine and stool analysis for medical monitoring. Matsushita's Smart Toilet checks blood pressure, temperature and blood sugar. Some feature automatic lid operation, heated seats, deodorising fans or automated paper toilet seat cover replacers. Interactive urinals have been developed in several countries, allowing users to play video games as with the Toylet, produced by Sega, that uses pressure sensors to detect the flow of urine and translates it into onscreen action.

A floating toilet is essentially an outhouse on a platform built above or floating on the water. Instead of wastes going into the ground they are collected in a tank or barrel. To reduce the amount of waste that needs to be hauled to shore, many use urine diversion. It was developed for residents without quick access to land or connection to a sewer system. It is also used in areas subjected to prolonged flooding.

A chamber pot is a receptacle in which one would excrete waste in a ceramic or metal pot. Among Romans and Greeks, chamber pots were brought to meals and drinking sessions. This method was used for hundreds of years; shapes, sizes and decorative variations changed throughout the centuries. This method is no longer used in developed countries, with the exception of hospital bedpans.

Garderobes were toilets used in the Middle Ages, most commonly found in upper-class dwellings. Essentially, they were flat pieces of wood or stone spanning from one wall to the other, with one or more holes to sit on. These would go into pipes that would lead outside the castle or manor. Garderobes would be placed in areas away from bedrooms to avoid the smell and also near kitchens or fireplaces to keep the enclosure warm.

Urinals were originally designed for males; although it is possible for urinals to be used by females. They are intended for the disposal of liquid waste, not solid waste. Urinals are meant to be used for the convenience of male users in a standing position. These fixtures are most commonly found in public places.

The squat toilet consists of a hole in the ground. To use this toilet, one is in a squatting position rather than sitting, by placing one foot on each side of the toilet and squatting over it. Modern versions are in separate stalls when they are in public lavatories, and include toilet tissue rolls for the user's convenience.

Technology and Sanitation

Human society has faced the problem of sanitation right from the beginning. However, sanitation practices have changed according to the will and the need of the community. Still, the societies, especially the developing societies, face the problem of disposal of human waste and the waste material generated in society. Technology has played an important role in sanitation. Without the aid of technology it would be difficult for humans to solve the problem of disposal of human and animal waste.

It is estimated, that 2.5 billion people worldwide lack access to safe sanitation, causing serious health problems, and in some cases, death. Food and water tainted with faecal matter result in child deaths. Most of these deaths could be prevented with the introduction of improved sanitation, along with safe drinking water and increased hygiene. It was only in the 16th century that a technological breakthrough came about that helped human beings to have clean toilets in houses.

Technologies do matter, but it takes a lot more in the field of sanitation. In many countries, sanitation technologies are piloted. Some work well and go to scale, while others break down or do not deliver the services they were intended to provide. There are very few standards for assessment and introduction of technology at local levels. The 18th century was a century of toilets. Despite the invention of the water closet by John Harington in 1596, which cost only six shillings and eight pence, it was not adopted on a large scale for almost 182 years.

The delays in actual use of inventions are common in human history. Toffler calls them the Cultural Gap. During this period, people used the earth closet. In these toilet,s instead of water, earth was used. So, the problem of cleaning remained. The world also saw the development of pan closets which, like a cigarette ash tray, threw the material at the bottom. This, too, required manual cleaning. At the same time, chamber pots, close stools and open defecation remained. In comparison to this, Harrington's toilet under the name, Angrez, was being used in France, though not introduced on a large scale in England. In 1738, Brondel introduced the valve type flush toilet. Alexander Cummings further improved the technology and provided a better device in 1775. In 1775, Scottish inventor Alexander Cummings invented a water closet which presented the S-shaped trap still used to this day, and was awarded the patent for it.

The world was yet to witness further technological developments. In 1870, S.S. Helior invented the flush type toilet, called Optims, an improvement over Blummer's design. From 1880 onwards, however, the emphasis has been more on aesthetics to make cisterns and bowls decorative. The bowls were so colourful that some suggested using them as soup bowls. It was in 1880 that toilet curtains made their appearance. The trend was called the age of Belle Époque in France and Edwardian (opulence) in England. During 1890, we had the first cantilever type toilet. Since then the world has not witnessed any significant technical change except some change in the shape of toilets and reduction in quantity of water per use. It was around 1900 that the institution of the bathroom came into vogue in Europe (Pais 2015).

In India, the institution of the gusalkhana (bathroom) was established by the Mughal emperors in 1556. Oppressed by the heat and dust, they constructed luxurious bathing and massage facilities. But this was only for the rich. The ordinary citizens lived in insanitary conditions. In contrast, the 20th century has given pride of place to toilets in the home and they are more luxurious, more spacious than at any time in the past. While the provision of a toilet in the house solved the household problem of cleanliness, the challenge remained as to how to dispose of human waste at city level. This was also solved when the sewerage system was introduced. Human waste was transported manually with the help of carts, an unhygienic situation. Around the same time, the sewerage system was introduced in Calcutta (present day Kolkata) the capital of colonial India. However, its extension in the country was and remains slow as it is capital-intensive and beyond the resource capacity of the economy even today.

Realising that the sewerage facilities will remain out of the reach of society at large, in 1970, Sulabh International introduced a pioneering technology; twin-pit pour-flush latrine and human excreta-based biogas plants. It has constructed, in the last 25 years, over 6,50,000 toilet-cum-bath complexes and 62 human excreta-based biogas plants and is maintaining them. This gives an appropriate solution to dispose of and recycle human waste into fertiliser, electricity and gas which can be used in kitchens.

Modern Technology in Sanitation

Sanitation technology is used all over the world according to society's capacity and the technology itself. In fact, a lot depends on the geography regarding the appropriate sanitation technology. The technology used in the hilly regions may be less expensive but may not be usable in flat land topography. The application of sanitation technologies depends on the economic capacity of the public or the capacity of the government. Some of the modern technologies used in the field of sanitation are (Pais 2015):

Hands-Free Toilets

Long accepted as a great convenience for people with mobility or dexterity problems, to enable independent toilet use, automatic shower toilets are also more hygienic. Almost 80 per cent of infectious diseases are passed on by human contact, as only half of people wash their hands after using the toilet. Hands-free toilet without the need for toilet paper is a healthier option. Germs are passed on by hand/body contact, so removing that contact improves hygiene. Washing with water rather than wiping is also more effective.

Sewage Technology

Throughout the world different kinds of technologies are used to manage sewage water. The technologies include advanced oxidation process, aerated lagoon, aerobic granular reactor, aerobic granular sludge technology, aerobic treatment system, anaerobic clarigester, anaerobic digestion, anaerobic filter, API oil water separator, anaerobic lagoon, batch filter technology, belt filter, bioconversion of biomass to mixed alcohol fuels, bio filters, bioreactor and septic tank. Septic systems are a type of On-Site Sewage Facility (OSSF). In Europe, septic systems are generally limited to rural areas. Since a septic system requires a drain field that uses a lot of land area, they are not suitable for densely built cities. A septic tank is a key component of the septic system, a small-scale sewage treatment system common in areas with no connection to main sewage pipes provided by local governments or private corporations. Other components, typically mandated and/or restricted by local governments, optionally include pumps, alarms, sand filters and clarified liquid effluent disposal means such as a septic drain field, ponds, natural stone fibre filter plants or peat moss beds. Periodic preventive maintenance is required to remove the irreducible solids that settle and gradually fill the tank, reducing its efficiency.

Sullage or Grey Water Technology

This is a household based technology mainly for rural areas to treat grey water that comes from the kitchen sink and bath for reuse. A kit designed to treat household wastewater for reuse could be one of the ways to tackle water scarcity in rural areas. The kit consists of two large PVC barrels, each able to contain up to 200 liters of water, pipes and sand. Before reaching the barrels, the wastewater goes through a separate filter where things like small bits of food are removed. The barrels are filled with sand; there is an anaerobic digestion of the organic matter when the water goes through the sand filter and becomes cleaner.

Drainage Technology

Drainage technology allows the flow of wastewater through open or underground pipes to the sea or tanks of filtration. In a hilly region, it is easy to carry the drain water to the sea. In a flat region, electronic pumps or machine pumps are used for the flow of wastewater.

Street Cleaning Technology

A street sweeper or street cleaner may refer to either a person's occupation, or a machine that cleans streets. A street sweeper cleans the streets, usually in an urban area. Street sweepers have been employed in cities since sanitation and waste removal became a priority. A person who sweeps streets would use a broom and a shovel to clean the litter, animal waste and filth that accumulates on streets. Later, water hoses were used to wash the streets. Modern street sweepers are equipped with water tanks and sprayers to loosen particles and reduce dust. The brooms gather debris into a main collection area from which it is vacuumed and pumped into a collection bin or hopper. A regenerative air street sweeper uses forced air to create a swirling effect inside a contained sweeping head and then uses the negative pressure on the suction side to place the road debris inside a hopper. Debris is removed from the air by centrifugal separation and reused, keeping particulate matter inside the hopper.

There is a need for innovators and creative thinkers to solve the sanitation challenge. And technology is one part of the puzzle. In addition to improving technology, we need to reflect on what we already know, understand what sanitation options people want and strengthen the enabling environment for sanitation services that last. This requires investing in formative research and behaviour change, strengthening governance and accountability, working on better supply chains as well as in technology that is not only innovative, but also appropriate.

The second challenge is that there are a lot of reasons why existing technologies fail, that are related to the technology, but not (only) technical. The technology is unaffordable for the poorest, construction materials are not available, and local workmanship is of low quality.

Third, to ensure that technologies are used, we need to understand what consumers want. It is households which make the decision to invest in a toilet. The process of technology introduction, demand creation and hygiene behaviour change is a crucial factor in determining if the technology will be taken up.

In 2011, the Bill & Melinda Gates Foundation launched the Reinvent the Toilet Challenge–a programme created to design toilets that capture and process human waste without piped water, sewer or electrical connections, and transform waste into useful resources, such as energy and water, at an affordable price. This toilet challenge is the second effort targeted at a specific country and is a testament to the research and development capabilities in India. One uses microwave energy to transform human waste into electricity. Another captures urine and uses it for flushing. And still, another turns excrement into charcoal. The Reinvent the Toilet Challenge is designed to spur innovation and bring creative thinking to solve the problem of dealing with human waste.

Sanitation is the only way for a better life in the modern world. As society is developing, the threat to human life is increasing in different forms. The threat of human waste is one of the important things which humans cannot ignore. So, the management of human waste in a particular manner may help humans to live better in society. Lack of sanitation should not become a reason for an unhealthy situation in society. Considerably, we can say that it is better to prevent something before it turns into a problem. So, modern society has to understand the importance of sanitation and that prevention is better than cure.

Some of the important measures for the prevention of poor sanitation are (Pais 2015):

Construction of Toilets in the Required Area

The toilet has been one of the important requirements of human beings in society. It is very important to have a toilet for personal use. The requirement of toilets in public places is more. So, wherever the requirement for a public toilet is there, the public authority should take proper measures to construct toilets to prevent unhealthy environment.

Construction of Sewage or Drainage System

Construction and maintenance of a drainage system for the purpose of carrying away wastewater is one of the important things to be taken care of. Mismanagement of wastewater can lead to several diseases. So, construction of wastewater drainage in a systematic and scientific way is important.

Providing Drinking Water Facilities

It has been observed that people face the problem of drinking water and due to impure drinking water, they fall sick. Providing safe, clean drinking water can avoid these problems. The requirement for safe drinking water is the first need of society. Panchayats, town and city municipalities and city corporations should consider it a priority.

Proper Disposal of Human and Animal Waste

Human and animal waste are threats and have to be tackled. The latest technology to dispose of human and animal waste should be used. It should not be dumped in the river or the canals, as this makes people get diseases. Management of human and animal waste can help to establish a better environment. It should be implemented in both rural and urban areas.

Creating Awareness about Sanitation

Lack of awareness about sanitation is also one of the important reasons for poor sanitation in society. When people are aware about sanitation and its importance, they will try to avoid unhealthy conditions in their surroundings for better health. Generation of awareness among people is also considered one of the important aspects of society. Both adults and children should be educated. Children could be educated in the schools.

It is not the problem of sanitation which is causing health problems or any other social problems, it is the ignorance of people and their negligence. Thus, it is understood that one should take responsibility to prevent unhealthy surroundings by not contributing to pollution and developing a better sanitation system in society.

Sulabh's Initiatives

Sulabh plays a major role in transforming society by initiating alternative sanitation systems. Mentioned below are some of its major strategies.

Community Toilet Technology

These are for those households which cannot afford an individual TPPF, and have no space to have one. Such a facility is also needed for commuters, pavement dwellers and the floating population mainly in urban settlements.

Sulabh studied the behaviour and attitude of people who did not use available public toilets in towns and cities and came up with the idea of providing community toilet complexes with bathing, laundry and urinal facilities on a pay-and-use basis.

The main features of a community toilet complex are:

- There is no burden on the public exchequer.
- A nominal charge is collected from each user.
- Children, differently-abled and the poor are exempted from payment.
- No charge is taken for use of urinals.
- The earnings are used for operation and maintenance of the complex.
- Attendants man each complex round the clock.
- Lighting at night and 24-hour water supply are maintained.
- Soap for washing hands is provided free for the users.
- Aesthetically pleasing architecture together with tree plantation around the complex.

Sulabh's largest community toilet complex is at Shirdi. It contains 148 toilets and 108 bathrooms; with space for dressing, babysitting and breastfeeding and 5,000 lockers to store the belongings of the pilgrims. The electricity made available through biogas generation from human excreta lights the complex. Up to 50,000 visitors use these facilities every day.

Excreta-based Biogas and Biofertiliser Technology

Dr Pathak is probably the first person in the world who has promoted, on a massive scale, the idea of obtaining biogas from human excreta collected in large public toilets. The successful and satisfactory functioning of this plant encouraged him to replicate the project all over the country. Biogas so produced is used for lighting, cooking, etc., and the effluent is a rich fertiliser. The biogas plant is attached to the Sulabh effluent plant where the effluent is made colourless, odourless and pathogen-free, fit for discharge into any water body, promoting a better and healthier environment.

Wastewater Treatment through Duckweed

Duckweed has natural properties which can treat even the toxic waste discharged from cities except for oil. The oil should be separated before the water is discharged into duckweed ponds. Only 20 per cent of urban India has sewerage systems for treatment and disposal of wastewater. Wastewater pollutes natural streams like rivers and the environment. It currently afflicts almost all the towns and cities of India, posing a big challenge to ensuring a safe and healthy living environment for the ever increasing number of city dwellers. One of the major problems with wastewater treatment methods is that none of the available technologies has a direct economic return. The available technologies are unaffordable due to high capital and maintenance costs.

The water is purified and treated to the extent that the quality of water is good even for pisciculture. One can rear fish in such water and based on analyses of the brains and livers of the fish, it have been found that they have no harmful bacteria and, are thus perfectly edible. This technology is suitable for towns with a population up to 50,000. Sulabh has taken up research-cum-demonstration projects on duckweed-based low-cost wastewater treatment in collaboration with concerned government agencies. The ambitious projects are underway in some rural as well as urban areas with direct economic return from pisciculture and use of duckweed as nutritious feed for poultry and animals.

Sulabh International Centre for Action Sociology (SICAS)

The purpose of this agency is to meet the problems and challenges directly, and also to equip people to face the future challenges. One activity of the centre is Sulabh Public School, established in Delhi in 1992 with an objective of imparting quality education to children of the scavenger community. The second is the vocational training centre, with an objective of making individuals skilled and independent. The first Sulabh centre was started in Patna in 1985. Subsequently, other vocational training centres were started in Mumbai and Delhi.

Sulabh International Institute of Technical Research and Training (SIITRAT)

SIITRAT runs refresher and training courses for interested persons for skill building in construction, operation, and maintenance of various low-cost water supply and sanitation schemes, and human excreta-fed biogas plants. SIITRAT has also developed a new technology – Sulabh Thermophilic Aerobic Composter (STAC) for making compost from any biodegradable waste, without any manual handling. This technology is able to convert organic waste into manure and soil conditioner, to prevent spread of weed and disease.

Sulabh International Institute of Health and Hygiene (SIIHH)

SIIHH is an outcome of Sulabh's emphasis on development of an integrated healthcare approach, with an added emphasis on yoga, use of medicinal plants, hygiene and a health-conscious attitude, and safe and clean food and drinking water. The focus of this integrated health planning is on women, children and youth in rural areas and urban slums.

Sulabh International Museum of Toilets

The museum has artefacts and replicas from different civilisations. The purpose of this museum is to educate students and the general public about the historical development of toilets and to provide information to researchers.

All these innovative activities from Sulabh have proved successful and functioning efficiently towards the transformation of the society in relation to sanitation. The Sulabh technology is user-friendly and replicable.

- All the technologies under the project are simple and indigenous.
- Their operation and maintenance are easier than for other technologies.
- The on-site waste disposal technology can be replicated in various geological conditions.
- The public toilet complexes are most suitable for slums, railway stations, bus stands, court compounds and such other places. There are various designs of public toilets to suit space constraints and different incomes. Cultural heritage is also taken into view while designing a toilet complex.
- Local skilled persons can be trained to implement the whole system, which enhances its replicability chance in any locality.
- Biogas technology is also very simple and replicable at any place. The design is suitable even in low temperatures as it can bear temperature variation due to its underground structure.
- None of the technologies developed by Sulabh is patented; they are accessible to anyone interested in sanitation.

Therefore, the chance of replication is high. More than one million. TPPFs have been constructed by the organisation itself.

Sulabh also provides efficient service delivery:

- The Sulabh sanitation technologies are easily marketable due to their comfort, cleanliness, dignity, privacy and aesthetics.
- The Sulabh toilet technology has been globally accepted as the most suitable, affordable and absolutely safe for developing countries by international agencies like the UNDP, World Bank, UNICEF and WHO.
- Sulabh's cost-effective and appropriate sanitation system was recognised as a global "Urban Best Practice" by the United Nations Centre for Human Settlements at the Habitat-II conference held at Istanbul (Turkey) in June 1996.
- Sulabh has been granted Special Consultative Status by ECOSOC in recognition of its outstanding service to mankind.
- St. Francis Prize for the Environment 'Canticle of all Creatures' was conferred on Dr Pathak in 1992 in recognition of his services to the cause of the environment and social upliftment of the oppressed people.
- National and international media like the BBC, Doordarshan, Zee TV and All India Radio have widely acknowledged the achievements of Sulabh.
- *The New York Times, The Washington Post, Nation* (Bangkok), *The Times of India, The Hindustan Times, The Statesman, The Indian Express, India Today, Dinman, Water World, The Telegraph* and *Source* (UNDP monthly magazine) have published articles lauding the achievements of Sulabh in the fields of low-cost sanitation, liberation of scavengers, harnessing of energy from human excreta and environment improvement.

Sustainability and Future Plans of Sulabh

Believing in Gandhian philosophy and willing to work till the last breath of life for holistic social development of the deprived, Dr Pathak is still very enthusiastic about the plans he has for expanding the work of Sulabh. He terms Sulabh a movement, not an organisation, which has to keep on working till the last human is served. However, he is worried about the lack of interest and fresh talent in this field (Sinha 2015).

Sanitation as an Economic Activity

Sanitation as a business uses sanitary systems for the purpose of business. Providing a toilet facility by collecting money can be called as sanitation business. The process of bettering society in the name of sanitation is established and in the name of collecting money, business is accomplished. Nowadays, it is observed in society that public toilets are also managed by private organisations for better maintenance. It is true that paid toilets are cleaned compared to free toilets.

Following are some of the ways through which sanitation can be turned into business.

Paid Toilets

In order to maintain better sanitation levels, the government and NGOs are establishing paid toilets in public places and slum areas. These public toilets charge a nominal amount for use.

Biogas Plants

Biogas plants generate gas for domestic use from human and animal waste which generates income for the family. Earning money from waste also helps in establishing sanitation in society. Toilets which are constructed for human defecation can be used for income generation also. There are many companies which have made building biogas plants a business for homes in rural areas.

Sanitary Art and Design

No one has given any thought to the toilet as a piece of art, but in terms of business, it is. Sanitary design is an important aspect in the sanitary business. The art of sanitary systems is nowadays gaining more attention in upper middle class society. People are paying lakhs of rupees for paintings and sanitary fittings. Some families wish to install toilet fittings which are imported. These attitudes have helped to establish sanitation as a business. Sanitary items are generating more income for people. Sanitation was a necessity, now it has turned into much more.

Every business needs an investment. Sanitation is a low-margin business in society. You invest less amount and get assured profit throughout life. There is no fear of decreasing demand; there will always be demand as it is a necessity for people. So, sanitation has turned into a better business in metropolitan cities like Delhi, Kolkata, Mumbai and Bangalore. Sanitation can be considered one of the faster growing businesses requiring less skill and less investment with assured profits. Moreover, NGOs are taking more interest in the sanitation business than the government, though they are non-profit organisations.

Sanitation as Dignity

Dignity is social status which will uphold a person in society on the basis of his economic assets and socio-political power. The dignity of a person can also be measured on the basis of his job which is more socialistic in nature. We can observe two kinds of dignity when we refer to sanitation dignity. One is sanitation commodities which will increase human value in society; and the other is the dignity of human labour in the field of sanitation. Dignity with commodity is more economic in nature; dignity with labour is more socialistic in nature.

We need to understand sanitation as dignity in both ways: dignity in terms of commodities as well as dignity of labour in sanitation work. Dignity of labour in sanitation deals with the social status of the sanitation labourers, as they have low status in society. The dignity of sanitation labour is in the caste hierarchy. Martin Luther King has said, "All labour that uplifts humanity has dignity and importance and should be undertaken with painstaking excellence" (as quoted in Pais 2015). According to Max de Pree (2004), American businessman and writer, we need to give each other the space to grow, to be ourselves, to exercise our diversity. We need to give each other space so that we may both give and receive such beautiful things as ideas, openness, dignity, joy, healing and inclusion. Sanitation as dignity can gain a wider meaning when it is considered in terms of economical aspect; the attitude of the people contributes to dignity through sanitation. Considerably, people are not only using sanitation for the purpose of health, they maintain well-designed sanitary systems like bathtubs, imported showers, basins and some electronic sensor watertaps; people think that the expenditure on sanitary systems can upgrade status in society, thus the dignity is improved. Sanitation has a strong connection not only with personal hygiene but also with human dignity and well-being, public health, nutrition and even education.

Sanitation contributes to gender equality, access to education and dignity. It also enhances dignity, privacy and safety, especially for women and girls. It improves convenience and social status. Sanitation in schools enables children, especially girls reaching puberty, to remain in the educational system. Restricted toilet opportunities increase the chance of chronic constipation and make women vulnerable to violence if they are forced to defecate at night and in secluded areas. In some areas, it is considered having a toilet at home is more important than any gold assets, basically a woman needs a toilet more than anything else. Providing improved sanitation facilities is equal to liberating women and girls and also providing substantial benefits for the whole community. Toilet facilities provide privacy and prevent women from experiencing abuse while defecating openly. As domestic caretakers of the sick in many societies, women benefit the most from a healthy community. Thus, women can defecate with dignity at home with a toilet facility. Their own health is safeguarded while they gain time to further their education and contribute to their family's well-being.

Clean toilets contribute to poverty eradication by protecting one's health and the ability to work. Good sanitation in school is essential for keeping children in school, particularly girls during their menstruation. Sanitation is considered a part of dignity with changing modern society. The concept of dignity not only relates to the exterior of the house like owning a car; it is also related to the interior of the house. It is a common practice when the groom's side visits the girl's house during a proposal to also see the toilet. It is also the case when the girl's side visits the groom's house. In such instances, both families take care to see that both the house and toilet are clean. Nowadays, Indian families consider sanitation as dignity and they are spending more money on the toilet and bathroom than the hall where people come and go. Sanitary systems are getting costlier as it is considered dignified and the development of sanitary systems is taking place not only with the notion of necessity but dignity. On an average, the Indian middle class family spends nearly ₹1.5 lakh on their sanitation at home. In some of the homes in large cities, people have gold-plated toilet fittings.

Sanitation saves lives and the faster we act the more lives we can save. A child's life could be saved every 20 seconds if safe drinking water and basic sanitation are available. This improvement could reduce 80 per cent of all sicknesses and diseases; it could save more lives per year than are lost due to war. A dramatic improvement in health would permit more dignified lifestyles – providing each man, woman or child with more time to work, learn or care for the family. Urinating and defecating are basic human needs just like eating, drinking, sleeping or breathing. Every human being should be able to fulfil that need with dignity. Sanitation provides privacy and protects everyone in the community. It is time we recognise the potential of sanitation for human development and act concertedly to make a difference.

Sulabh strategically emphasises promoting quality healthcare by providing hygienic conditions and proper sanitation, in rural as well as urban areas. The efforts are focused on creating awareness about toilets and providing economical and reasonable toilets, which are cheaper to build and easy to maintain.

The key programming approaches of Sulabh also include energy generation through renewable and non-conventional source of energy, skill set development and training for livelihoods.

Sulabh Sanitation Mission Foundation focuses on:

1. Capacity building, awareness and training
2. Construction, maintenance and housekeeping
3. Energy generation through renewable non-conventional sources of energy
4. Skill development and training for livelihoods
5. Programme implementation and monitoring
6. Publications for awareness generation
7. Posters for awareness generation

Capacity building and training activities aim to train people on hygiene practices and sanitation awareness and to motivate them to avoid open defecation.

This is achieved by organising:

1. Agricultural camps
2. Block-level sensitisation meetings with religious leaders, teachers, NGOs' representatives and parents, to ensure maximum attendance of children in schools

3. Training of adolescence girls
4. Block-level sensitisation meetings on sanitation/hygiene
5. Making of motivational murals
6. Workshop at block-level in villages
7. Technical options for integrated low cost sanitation in urban areas
8. Training module for district-level master trainers under the Total Sanitation Campaign in rural areas
9. Training for motivators to enhance demand generation
10. Guidelines for provisioning of washing arrangements (hand washing) including maintenance in schools

One of the primary focus areas of Sulabh Sanitation Mission Foundation towards proper sanitation has been the eradication of the practice of open defecation through construction of toilets. Sulabh has an expertise in the construction of two-pit toilet blocks in schools, individual households as well as community toilets. It also maintains the toilets by employing local staff who will clean them daily as well as designating volunteers to check proper usage and cleanliness of these toilets. Sulabh Sanitation Mission Foundation takes housekeeping contracts for corporations, public and private sector enterprises. The trained staff is experienced and skilled to take care of various day-to-day activities of housekeeping.

There are a few projects executed by Sulabh Sanitation Mission Foundation as sanitation initiatives. These include: construction and maintenance of school toilets, renovation of public toilets, construction and maintenance of toilet complexes and total sanitation in town and village panchayat areas.

Human excreta-based biogas technology remained unnoticed for long due to the fact that the available technology was not socially acceptable, as it required manual handling of human excreta, which contains a full spectrum of pathogens. The design developed by Sulabh does not require manual handling of human excreta and there is complete recycling and resource recovery from the wastes. The digester is built underground into which excreta from public toilets and other biodegradable waste flows under gravity. The biogas, thus produced, is stored in an inbuilt liquid displacement chamber. Methane is the only combustible constituent, which is utilised in different forms of energy.

The Sulabh Sanitation Movement was started with the objective to liberate and elevate the status of scavengers. Towards this, it adopted a technology that would reach sanitation facilities even to the poorest, and to bring scavengers in to the mainstream of Indian society. Sulabh International branched into several inter-related activities meant not only to rehabilitate, socially and economically, those weaned away from scavenging, but also to restore their self-esteem and self-respect. Education holds the key to any major change and development. With this objective of imparting quality education, Sulabh Public School was set up in Delhi.

The Sulabh vocational training centre aims to provide development and training in diverse skills to boys and girls from weaker sections of society, especially from Balmiki households, so that they use their newly acquired talents to the fullest and achieve better economic and social adjustment. Its main objectives are: to mobilise boys and girls from the weaker sections to pick up market-oriented trades and thus enable them not only to earn a living, but also to help them towards developing confidence, self-esteem and reliance.

The courses are so designed that they help students acquire skills which help towards self-employment. There is a follow-up programme to monitor the progress of each student in later life. The first Sulabh vocational training centre was set up at Patna in 1985. It offered vocational training to young boys and girls in several trades. By all accounts, it was a great success. Shortly thereafter, another centre in collaboration with the government of Maharashtra was set up in Mumbai. It offered adolescents vocational training programmes in keeping with market demands. It has been quite successful and continues to attract the attention of both trainees and employers. Yet another centre was opened in Delhi in 1992. Presently, it offers one-year training in English stenography, cutting and tailoring, beauty care, computers, dress designing, embroidery, English and Hindi typing, electrical work and audio-visual work.

Chapter 8

LEADER OF SANITATION

Sanitation is a massive social problem in India, both in the urban and rural context. With increasing population, the problem is growing. Open defecation in rural areas and lack of facilities in the urban regions has created a situation that needs urgent attention. This is one of the largest problems that the country faces. The Central Government has launched several programmes focussing on different spheres and in different regions to improve the conditions of sanitation. Alongside, there are other agencies that are working and collaborating for the same cause. Sulabh is one of the prominent organisations that has committed to the cause of sanitation. The story of Sulabh International is well known all over India and abroad.

However, there are also other initiatives that have been taken up to make toilets more accessible:

3S (Sanitation Solutions Simplified)

One of the pioneers in the field, 3S provides portable restrooms, affordable solutions, luxury restroom containers and cleaning services. Most suited for construction sites and events, this company was started by Rajeev Kher in Pune in 1999. Currently, the organisation manages 155 million litres of liquid waste, serving more than 1,55,000 people daily (Mehta 2017).

Basic Shit

As the name suggests, Basic Shit aims to create a clean and safe environment for public sanitation. Started in 2014 in Dwarka, New Delhi, by Ashwani

Aggarwal, Basic Shit builds hygienic, low-cost, portable urinals that can be set up by unskilled labourers in public areas where people urinate in the open frequently. The urinals are connected to the sewers through manholes to ensure correct disposal of the waste and are made from 20-litre water jars (biodegradable recycled plastic) with tin sheds to cover a unit (Ibid).

Svadha

Started by Garima Sahai and K.C. Mishra in 2014, Svadha integrates the entire sanitation value chain. It establishes an army of entrepreneurs to provide access to quality, affordable and sustainable sanitation solutions. Svadha does this by owning the full stack from enabling partners, getting supply and tech, and training implementing partners. Supported under Toilet Board Coalition's first accelerator programme, Svadha operates from Odisha (Ibid).

Ekam Eco Solutions

Based in New Delhi, Ekam Eco Solutions was started in 2013 by Vijayraghavan Chariar and Uttam Banerjee. It works in the domains of sustainable sanitation, value-added bamboo products and sustainable livelihoods. The company has developed a waterless urinal called Zerodor, which is a completely non-consumable and non-chemical-based mechanical device. Conventional water flush urinals use approximately 2-4 litres of water for flushing, and Zerodor solves this problem by giving a simple attachment that can be installed in less than 10 minutes with existing urinals (Ibid).

Samagra

Started by Swapnil Chaturvedi, the "'Poop Guy'" of Pune, Samagra is in the business of making good quality and accessible toilets for the urban poor. Supported by the Bill and Melinda Gates Foundation, Swachh Bharat Abhiyan and more partners, Samagra works primarily with design and behaviour change to reach a more sustainable future. The company builds toilets that have basic services like lighting and ventilation, and goes a step further by providing regular maintenance services, sanitary dustbins and kids' accessories. They also encourage behaviour change with workshops and door-to-door surveys (Ibid).

Banka BioLoo

Started by Namita Banka in Telangana in 2012, the company is engaged in promoting and developing innovative environment-friendly products and services for human waste management systems. The company deals with manufacturing, supplying and installation of biotanks for digestion of human waste as a complete solution, rentals and AMC of mobile biotoilets, consultancy for development of large biotanks, wastewater treatment and recycling solutions (Ibid).

Safai Karmachari Andolan

Safai Karmachari Andolan (SKA) is a national movement committed to the total eradication of manual scavenging and the rehabilitation of all scavengers in dignified occupations. SKA was initiated in 1995 by children of those engaged in manual scavenging for liberation from their horrible occupation and indignity. Since then, it has grown progressively to become a national movement spread over 25 states of India, with the national secretariat in New Delhi. Under the guidance of the National Advisory Group, SKA's programmes are executed by the National Core Team working closely together with state conveners, organisers and animators across the country (SSVK 2013).

While primarily focusing on the rights of manual scavengers, SKA is also committed to working with all those engaged in "unclean" occupations such as sewage workers, pit workers and sweepers who fall within the ambit of "safai karmacharis". SKA was instrumental in eradicating manual scavenging; it works in close cooperation and collaboration with other Dalit and human rights organisations committed to the rights of Dalits and other marginalised communities in general and safai karmacharis in particular.

In 2003, SKA, headed by Bezwada Wilson, approached the Supreme Court by way of a writ petition seeking implementation of the 1993 law that prohibited manual scavenging. The petition, grounded in the Constitution, unambiguously stated that manual scavenging is both a source and a result of the horribly cruel social exclusion rooted in notions of pollution, and therefore the continued practice of this "disability" has no place in the vision of an independent India.

Since the Parliament outlawed manual scavenging in 1993, the very existence of a dry latrine became illegal. Wilson's SKA, which began in Andhra Pradesh and Karnataka, took a crowd of former manual scavengers, mostly women, to demolish dry latrines wherever they could find them. Further, SKA members went on a yatra in Andhra Pradesh, lobbying with Dalit MLAs, and got the government to demolish most of the dry latrines in the state.

Wilson has spent the past many years getting the law implemented, and getting the Central and state governments to rehabilitate manual scavengers. The organisation undertook massive all-India surveys to identify manual scavengers, and then do everything they could to make them leave the work. Since manual scavenging paid them so little, Wilson's organisation motivated them to leave it and find alternative work; anything that would pay more. There were those who hid their caste, migrated and found work as house helps. Others started small roadside shops or took to basket weaving. Thus, Wilson has worked to make lives better for those who worked to clean sewage lines and septic tanks, often leading to deaths. For his work Wilson has been awarded the Magsaysay Award.

For Navsarjan, the solution to manual scavenging and untouchability is loud activism and alternative employment. There are programmes that provide manual scavengers with loans to set up small businesses. SKA, a Dalit organisation, prefers direct action over empty promises, and often demolishes dry latrines by hand. Dr Pathak, however, preferred not to destroy toilets, but to build them.

One could never ever imagine that caste-based de-humanising activities of such nature could exist in India even to this day. It was a matter of immense shame for a nation that such a practice has gone unchecked for several decades. These initiatives are examples of people who have shown tremendous grit to work for a problem that seems so large at the outset. The developing world needs more and more of these initiatives, and a movement towards better sanitation globally.

Mahatma Gandhi

Mahatma Gandhi championed the issue of sanitation by voicing his strongest opposition to the employment of manual scavengers from select SCs in 1917. Yet, almost a century later, the practice of manual scavenging is still going on. The "toilets for all" and the proposed Clean India goals of the SBM by 2 October 2019 would be an apt homage to the Mahatma.

The 2011 Census reports 7.9 lakh toilets in India are serviced by humans, 5.9 lakh of which are in rural areas and the rest, about 2 lakh toilets, are in urban regions. It also reveals an astounding 13.1 lakh toilets disposing night soil directly into drains, out of which about 3.7 lakh exist in rural areas and 9.4 lakh in urban sections. These are the toilets that have been directly contributing to the demand for manual scavenging and have been recognised as insanitary. Toilets which are connected to sewers, septic tanks and pits also sustain the practice of manual scavenging in the absence of proper waste management (Bhol 2015).

Due to these reasons, this degrading practice still exists in India, including insanitary toilets, inadequate waste management and the discriminatory and iniquitous caste system. The Prohibition of Employment as Manual Scavengers and their Rehabilitation (PEMSR) Act, 2013, stems from The Employment of Manual Scavengers and Construction of Dry Latrines (Prohibition) Act, 1993. Both these have been catalysts for the sanitation sector in India. These Acts derive from the zealous efforts of Mahatma Gandhi to end the malicious practice of manual scavenging.

Pathak founded Sulabh International in 1970. It is now India's largest charitable organisation, with over 50,000 on its staff. Millions of Indians have installed the Sulabh Shauchalaya latrine. Every day, 10 million Indians use a Sulabh toilet, because they are in railway stations, airports and on the main streets of India's cities. Pathak's toilet blocks are so common, Indians now say, "I'm going to the Sulabh," and the word *toilet* can be left silent.

Pathak's ideals were those of Gandhiji's. The father of the modern Indian nation was one of the few political leaders in history to publicly talk about toilets. There is a scene in Richard Attenborough's biopic film where Gandhiji argues with his wife because she refuses to clean their latrine. She says it is the work of untouchables; he tells her there is no such thing.

At the 1901 Congress party convention, Gandhiji told delegates it was a disgrace that manual scavengers were being used to clean the latrines. He asked delegates to clean their own latrines and when they did not, he publicly cleaned his own. The eradication of manual scavenging was a recurrent theme throughout Gandhiji's life. He called the practice "the shame of the nation". He wrote, "evacuation is as necessary as eating; and the best thing would be for everyone to dispose of his own waste".

Gandhiji realised that effective steps should be taken to abolish untouchability if only to save Hindu society from disintegration. He made a countrywide tour and used the tool of mass awareness to eradicate the practice of untouchability. Millions of people heard his speeches and thousands of them, inspired by his thoughts, stopped the practice of treating Harijans as untouchables and started fraternising with them. From the beginning he sought the cooperation of the municipalities and other local bodies in ameliorating the working and living conditions of sweepers and scavengers. The response had been slow but drawing the attention of these bodies to the lot of sweepers and scavengers was a beginning. While emphasis is to be laid on improved methods of working for the sweepers, it was clear in their intention and their aims that the ultimate goal was to make it unnecessary for man to carry or clean human excreta and therefore, there was emphasis on better types of latrines.

Time and again Mahatma Gandhi observed that unless one had a toilet in his house, he must put earth on excreta after defecation (tatti par mitti) to prevent diseases and foul smell. While Gandhiji was in Phoenix Ashram,he used a trench latrine and human excreta was used as manure. Even during the freedom movement, he recommended the use of trench latrines. He virtually designed a new concept of the latrine, which was later named "Wardha type latrine". The concept was adopted in different parts of the country to ensure proper sanitation and liberate scavengers (Jha 2004). Dr Pathak launched Bhangi Mukti (scavengers' liberation) after three decades; translating Gandhian thought and vision into practice, and liberated lakhs of scavengers.

Mahatma Gandhi on Manual Scavenging

The work of cleanliness is sacred; and that work can be done only by a Brahmin or by a Bhangi. The Brahmin does it in his wisdom, and the Bhangi in ignorance. If either of the two disappears from Hinduism, Hinduism itself will disappear. And since service was dear to Gandhiji's heart, the Bhangi was dear to him. In fact, he expressed his desire to belong to the status of a Bhangi; and wished to sit at meals with a Bhangi. (Navayana 2014).

Gandhiji said it was simply superfluous for him to say anything about untouchability. He expressed his aspiration to be born a Bhangi in the next birth. A Bhangi is not a born sinner. There are countless Bhangis who deserve veneration and many among Brahmins are to the contrary. He wished to serve the Bhangis in numerous ways by being born into that caste. But they should not detest and hate the Brahmin (*Navajivan, 11 January1925).*

Speaking on Varnashrama and untouchability, Gandhiji said, if untouchability is attached to birth, it is hideous and must be rooted out; if it attaches to occupation it may be a sanitary rule of great importance. It is of universal application. A collier, while he is engaged in his work, refuses to shake the hand extended to him, saying that he is too dirty. But after his work is finished, he takes his bath, changes his clothes, and very properly mixes with the highest in the land. Therefore, we must remove the taint of birth, i.e., the idea of superiority and inferiority attached to birth, and purify Varnashrama. The children of scavengers may remain scavengers without being or feeling degraded, and they will be no more considered untouchables than Brahmins. The fault does not lie in recognising the law of heredity and transmission of qualities from generation to generation, it lies with the faulty conception of inequality.

Varnashrama was not conceived in any narrow spirit. It gave the labourer, the Shudra, the same status as the Brahmin. It provided for the accentuation of merit and elimination of demerit, and it transferred human ambition from the general worldly sphere to the permanent and the spiritual. The aim of the Brahmin and the Shudra was common Moksha or self-realisation, and not realisation of fame, riches and power. Later on, this conception of Varnashrama became degraded and came to be identified with mere empty ceremonial assumption of superiority by some, and imposition of degradation upon others. This is a demonstration of the weakness of human nature. He suggests that the reformer should seek to end the curse of untouchability and to restore Varnashrama to its proper place. Gandhiji had immutable faith in the capacity of Hinduism to purge itself of all impurities from time to time. (*Young India*, 13 August 1925).

The humiliation heaped upon Bhangis are too many and too horrible that enough amends cannot be made even if we scraped off our own skins and presented them with shoes made from them. It is no calamity to be a sweeper. One can become a Bhangi in two ways. Somebody may call one a Bhangi by way of abuse, as if a sweeper is a burden to society, though he does the very useful work of cleaning latrines and sweeping streets. Or one may call that man a Bhangi whose service to others reaches its acme. The Bhangi's service is like that of our mothers, but we never call them untouchables. The mother is revered as a goddess worth remembering during our morning prayers. The Bhangi therefore is a true servant of society. The mother serves the child with love and she gets love in return. But the sweeper gets a salary for his service in return. Just as we cannot live without mothers, we cannot live without sweepers.

Gandhiji called himself a scavenger by choice, and literally cleaned hundreds of cheris. He called scavenging one of the most honourable occupations. It is not an unclean occupation by any means. One has to handle dirt. Every mother has to do it. But nobody says a mother's occupation is unclean. And yet the scavenger's occupation is considered unclean. Therefore, those who call themselves caste Hindus commit a sin when they consider themselves higher than Harijans. (*Harijan*, 19 January 1934).

The ideal Bhangi would be a Brahmin par excellence, possibly even out do him. It is possible to envisage the existence of a Bhangi without a Brahmin. But without the former, the latter could not be. It is the Bhangi who enables society to live. A Bhangi does for society what a mother does for her baby. A mother washes her baby of the dirt and ensures his health. Even so, the Bhangi protects and safeguards the health of the entire community by taking care of sanitation. The Brahmin's duty is to look after the sanitation of the soul; the Bhangi's that of the body of society. But there is a difference in practice; the Brahmin generally does not live up to his duty, the Bhangi does. Society is sustained by several services. The Bhangi constitutes the foundation of all services.

And yet Indian society has branded the Bhangi as a social pariah, set him down at the bottom of the scale, held him fit only to receive kicks and abuse, a creature who must subsist on the leavings of high caste people and dwell on the dung-heap. He is without a friend. His very name has become a term of reproach. This is shocking and the origin of this inhuman conduct is not known, but by looking down upon the Bhangi, Hindus deserve the contempt of the whole world. Our villages have today become seats of dirt and insanitation and the villagers come to an early and untimely death. If only we had given due recognition to the status of the Bhangi as equal to that of a Brahmin as he deserves, our villages today no less than their inhabitants, would have looked a picture of cleanliness and order. We would have to a large extent been free from the ravages of a host of diseases which directly spring from our uncleanliness and lack of sanitary habits.

An ideal Bhangi should have a thorough knowledge of the principles of sanitation. He should know how the right kind of latrine is constructed and the correct way of cleaning it. He should know how to overcome and destroy the odour of excreta and the various disinfectants to render them innocuous. He should likewise know the process of converting night soil and urine into manure. But that is not all. An ideal Bhangi would know the quality of night soil and urine. He would keep a close watch on these and give a timely warning to the individual concerned. Thus he would give timely notice of the results of his examination of the excreta. That presupposes scientific knowledge of the requirements of his profession. He would likewise be an authority on the subject of disposal of night soil in small villages as well as big cities and his advice and guidance in the matter would be sought for and freely given to society. He would have the usual learning necessary for reaching the standard laid down for his profession. Such an ideal Bhangi, while deriving his livelihood from his occupation, would approach it only as a sacred duty. In other words, he would not dream of amassing wealth out of it. He would consider himself responsible for the proper removal and disposal of all the dirt and night soil within the area which he serves and regard the maintenance of healthy and sanitary condition within the same as the summum bonum of his existence. (Harijan, 28 November 1936)

There are certain matters in which strikes would be wrong. Sweepers' grievances come in this category. Just as man cannot live without air, so too he cannot exist for long if his home and surroundings are not clean. One or other epidemic is bound to break out, especially when modern drainage is put out of action. A Bhangi may not give up his work even for a day. And there are many other ways open to him for securing justice. *(Harijan,* 21 April 1946) When everything else fails should the Bhangi continue his service on starvation wages, living in dirt and squalor? In such cases the proper remedy is not a strike, but a notice to the public in general and the employing corporation in particular that the Bhangis must give up the sweeping service which consigns those reserved for that service to a life of starvation and all it means. There is a wide distinction between a strike and an entire discontinuation of service. A strike is a temporary measure in expectation of relief. Discontinuance is giving up of a particular job because there is no expectation of relief. Proper discontinuance presupposes fair notice on the one hand, and prospect of better wages and freedom from squalor and dirt on the other. This will wake up society from its disgraceful slumber, resulting in a proper scavenging of the overgrowth that has smothered public conscience. At a stroke, the Bhangis will raise scavenging to a fine art and give it the status it should have had long ago. (*Harijan*, 23 June 1946).

Where there is ample supply of water, modern sanitation can be introduced without any hardship for the poor. Gandhiji was opposed to machinery which displaces labour. Whether the flush system will remove the curse of untouchability is open to grave doubt. It will not disappear through such means as has been suggested. Not until we all become Bhangis and realise the dignity of the labour of scavenging and latrine-cleaning will untouchability really be exorcised." (*Harijan*, 15 September 1946).

Gandhiji strongly and repeatedly condemned the Indian practice of hiring people from the lowest rungs of the Hindu caste system, who were once called untouchables, to manually clean out primitive dry latrines or collect waste from fields where villagers relieved themselves, urging his countrymen to clean up after themselves. Although outlawed, manual scavenging continues to persist in India as do other infrastructure failings hindering efforts to improve sanitation in the country. Almost half the population still defecates in the open, and the practice is more prevalent in the countryside where government figures indicate that almost 70 per cent of households don't have access to proper toilets.

Some of Gandhiji's thoughts on sanitation and cleanliness appear in "Music of the Spinning Wheel" by Sudheerna Kulkarni (2012):

Sanitation is more important than political independence

While leading a non-violent movement for India's independence from the British in 1947, Gandhiji spoke about the need to improve hygiene and cleanliness in the country. "Sanitation is more important than political independence," he said. In an address on waste management and cleanliness, Mr Pranab Mukherjee, when he was President of India, reiterated Gandhiji's decades-old exhortation.

Religion and sanitation

In 1915, Gandhiji went to the Kumbh Mela, a triennial festival that rotates between four Indian cities. That year, it was held in the Hindu holy city of Haridwar in India's north on the bank of the river Ganges. After seeing millions of devotees take a dip in the sacred river in an attempt to wash away their sins at Haridwar, Gandhiji wrote in *Young India*, an English weekly he edited from 1919, "I had gone there full of hope and reverence. But while I realised the grandeur of the holy Ganga and the holier Himalayas, I saw little to inspire me in what man was doing in this holy place. To my great grief, I discovered insanitation, both moral and physical…There is defilement of the mighty stream even in the name of religion." Thoughtless ignorant men and women use for natural functions the sacred banks of the river where they are supposed to sit in quiet contemplation and find God. They violate religion, science and the laws of sanitation (Malhotra 2015).

A lavatory must be as clean as a drawing room

In May 1925, in an edition of Navjivan, a weekly newspaper that Gandhiji edited from 1919, he wrote about the importance of keeping lavatories clean. "I learnt 35 years ago that a lavatory must be as clean as a drawing room. I learnt this in the West." The cause of many of our diseases is the condition of our lavatories and our bad habit of disposing of excreta anywhere and everywhere (Ibid).

Perfect sanitation makes an 'ideal village'

In 1937, to a question on how he would perceive an "ideal village", Gandhiji responded (as it appeared in *Harijan*), "An ideal village will be so constructed as to lend itself to perfect sanitation…The very first problem the village worker will solve is its sanitation."

Sanitation for ministers and menials alike

In a speech in New Delhi in September 1946, Gandhiji stressed the need for equal levels of hygiene in bungalows that ministers lived in as well as the servants' quarters tucked away in these massive houses. What was so distressing is that the living quarters of the menials and sweepers employed in the viceroy's house were extremely dirty.

Gandhiji's Guidelines for Cleanliness

- "So long as you do not take the broom and the bucket in your hands, you cannot make your towns and cities clean."
- When he inspected a model school, he told the teachers: "You will make your institution ideal, if besides giving the students literary education, you have made cooks and sweepers of them."
- To the students his advice was, "If you become your own scavengers, you will make your surroundings clean. It needs no less courage to become an expert scavenger than to win a Victoria Cross."
- The villagers near his ashram refused to cover excreta with earth. They said: "Surely this is *bhangi's* work. It is sinful to look at faeces, more so to throw earth on it." Gandhiji personally supervised the scavenging work in villages. To set an example, he used to go to the villages with a bucket and a broom. Friends and guests went with him. They brought bucketfuls of dirt and stool and buried it in pits.
- All scavenging work in his ashram was done by the inmates. Gandhiji guided them. People of different races, religions and colours lived there.
- No dirt could be found anywhere on the ashram ground. All rubbish was buried in pits. Peelings of vegetables and left-over food were dumped in a separate manure pit. Nightsoil, too, was buried and later used as manure. Wastewater was used for gardening. The farm was free from flies and stink though there was no *puccca* drainage system.
- Gandhiji and his co-workers undertook sweepers' work by turn. He introduced bucket-latrines and bicameral trench latrines. Gandhiji showed this innovation to all visitors with pride; rich and poor, leaders and workers, Indians and foreigners, all had to use these latrines. This experiment slowly removed aversion for scavenging from the minds of orthodox co-workers and women inmates of the ashram.
- The sight of a *bhangi* carrying a nightsoil basket on his/her head made him sick. He explained how, with the use of proper instruments, cleaning could be done neatly.
- He wrote, "Village tanks are promiscuously used for bathing, washing clothes and drinking and cooking purposes. Many village tanks are also used by cattles. Buffaloes are often seen wallowing in them. The wonder is that, in spite of this sinful misuse of village tanks, villages have not

been destroyed by epidemics. Medical evidence shows that lack of pure water supply in villages is responsible for many of the diseases suffered by the villagers." (*Harijan,* 8 February 1935), (Rathi 2015).

B.R. Ambedkar, on manual scavenging, said Gandhism is a paradox. It stands for freedom from foreign domination, which means the destruction of the existing political structure of the country. At the same time it seeks to maintain intact a social structure which permits the domination of one class by another on a hereditary basis which means a perpetual domination of one class by another. The first special feature of Gandhism is that its philosophy helps those who have to keep what they have and to prevent those who have not from getting what they have a right to get. The second special feature of Gandhism is to delude people into accepting their misfortunes by presenting them as the best of good fortunes.

The Hindu sacred law penalised the Shudras for acquiring wealth. It is a law of enforced poverty unknown in any other part of the world. Gandhism does not lift the ban. It blesses the Shudra for his moral courage to give up his property. To quote Gandhiji on owning property: "The Shudra who only serves as a matter of religious duty, and who will never own any property, who indeed has not even the ambition to own anything, is deserving of thousand obeisance. The very Gods will shower down flowers on him."

On perpetuating scavenging, Gandhiji said, "The sacred law of the Hindus lays down that a scavenger's progeny shall live by scavenging." In Hinduism, scavenging was not a matter of choice; it was a matter of forced labour. Gandhism seeks to perpetuate this system by praising scavenging as the noblest service to society.

What is the use of telling the scavenger that even a Brahmin is prepared to do scavenging when it is clear that according to Hindu Shastras and Hindu notions, even if a Brahmin did scavenging he would never be subject to the disabilities of one who is a born scavenger? For in India a man is not a scavenger because of his work. He is a scavenger because of his birth, irrespective of the question whether he does scavenging or not. If Gandhism preached that scavenging is a noble profession with the object of inducing those who refuse to engage in it, one could understand it. But why appeal to the scavenger's pride and vanity in order to induce him and him only to keep on scavenging by telling him that scavenging is a noble profession and that he need not be ashamed of it? To preach that poverty is good for the Shudra and for none else, to preach that scavenging is good for the untouchables and for none else and to make them accept these onerous impositions as voluntary purposes of life, by appeal to their failings is an outrage and a cruel joke on the helpless classes which Gandhiji can perpetuate with equanimity and impunity.

In this connection one is reminded of the words of Voltaire who in repudiation of an "ism"' very much like Gandhism said: "Oh! Mockery to say to people that the suffering of some brings joy to others and works well to the whole. What solace is it to a dying man to know that from his decaying body a thousand worms will come into life?" This is the technique to make wrongs done appear to the very victim as though they were his privileges (Navayana 2014).

If the untouchables skin and carry the dead animals of the Hindus, it is because they have no choice. They are forced to do it. They would be penalised if they refused to do it. The penalty is legal. In some provinces the refusal to do this dirty work is a breach of contract. In other provinces it is a criminal offence involving fines. In provinces like Bombay the untouchables are village servants. In their capacity as village servants they have to serve the government as well as the Hindu public. In return for this service they are given lands which they cultivate and on the produce of which they maintain themselves. One of the duties of the untouchables is to skin and carry the dead animals of the Hindus in the villages. If the untouchables refuse to perform these duties for the Hindu public, the land which they live on is liable to be confiscated. They have to choose between doing the dirty work or face starvation.

In provinces like the United Provinces, refusal to do scavenging by sweepers is made an offence. The United Provinces Municipalities Act II of 1916 contains the following provisions: Section 201 (1) "Should a sweeper who has a customary right to do the house-scavenging of a house or building fail to perform such scavenging in a proper way, the occupier of the house or building or the board may complain to a Magistrate." (2) "The Magistrate receiving such complaint shall hold an inquiry and should it appear to him that the customary sweeper has failed to perform the house-scavenging of the house or building in a proper way or at reasonable intervals, he may impose upon such a sweeper a fine which may extend to ₹10, and upon a second or any later conviction in regard to the same house or building, may also direct the right of the customary sweeper to do the house-scavenging of the house or building to be forfeited and thereupon such right shall be forfeited."

An exactly similar provision is to be found in Section 165 of the Punjab Municipalities Act of 1911. The Punjab Act is an advance over the U.P. Act, in as much as it provides for punishment of a sweeper who is not a customary sweeper but a contract sweeper. The Punjab Act adds: "(3) Should any sweeper, who is under a contract to do house-scavenging of a house or a building, discontinue to do such house-scavenging without fourteen days' notice to his employer or without reasonable cause, he shall on conviction be punishable with a fine which may extend to ₹10." Every order of forfeiture under Section 165 shall be subject to an appeal to the next superior court, but shall not be otherwise open to appeal."

People may be shocked to read that there exists legal provision which sanctions forced labour; this is slavery. Under slavery a breach of contract of service is an offence which is punishable with fine or imprisonment. Under free labour a breach of contract of service is only a civil wrong for which the labourer is liable only for damages. Judged in the light of this criterion, scavenging is a legal obligation imposed upon the untouchables which they cannot escape.

According to Mr Rice, the origin of untouchability is to be found in the unclean and filthy occupations of the untouchables. The filthy and unclean occupations which the untouchables perform are common to all human societies. In every human society there are people who perform these occupations. Such people are not treated as untouchables in other parts of the world (Ambedkar 1948).

Dr Bindeshwar Pathak

"The man who transformed teenage rebellion into a toilet revolution."

For a great politician to talk freely about such things in public was impressive, but Gandhiji's position had its critics. Quite a few Dalits object to Gandhiji's comparing scavengers with mothers looking after others' children, when the children are upper-caste Indians content to keep these "mothers" in a state of servitude. The great Dalit thinker, Dr B.R. Ambedkar, who thought that "inequality was the soul of Hinduism," wanted caste to be abolished, not tinkered with. In 1969, the idealistic young Pathak began to volunteer with the Gandhian Centenary Committee in his home state of Bihar. The committee's job was to organise three years of programmes and celebrations in honour of their hero's birth. Their hero cared about scavengers, so the volunteers were supposed to do the same. It scandalised his orthodox Brahmin family.

Dr Pathak, when he was still a child, wanted to know why some people were untouchable. He wanted to see what would happen if he touched one, so he did. His grandmother made him eat cow dung and sand, made him drink cow urine and then then take a ritual bath. How can cow dung be clean? Purification rituals that seem to defy logic are common in many cultures: the ancient Mesopotamians carried dung around their necks to ward off evil; Hindus decided that cow dung is holy. Such classifications of what is dirty and what is pure are obviously not about reality, but they serve a purpose. Investing dirt with power makes it more manageable. Deciding that some people are irreversibly impure makes them more manageable too. They can be kept in their place. Even so, writes Virginia Smith in *Clean,* her history of hygiene, "Distancing yourself from poisons, dust and dirt is one thing, but distancing yourself from invisibly 'unclean' people and objects is quite an achievement of the imagination." It was a leap of imagination that Pathak refused to make.

Gandhiji's tactics of encouraging brotherly love across caste boundaries and urging Indians to clean their own latrines had failed miserably. The status quo was too convenient. Pathak had a better solution in providing an alternative technology. Not by knocking down the dry latrines, but by providing a better latrine model that didn't require humans to clean it and at the same time was cheap and easy to construct.

It had to be on-site, because India has neither water nor sewers enough to install expensive water using treatment systems. Indian urban wastewater treatment consisted of dumping it in rivers. Pathak called his new latrine the Sulabh Shauchalaya (Easy Latrine). It was twin-pit and pour-flush. It could be flushed with only a cupful of water, about a litre, compared to almost a bucket full of water needed to operate flush toilets. There was no need to connect it to sewers or septic tanks, because the excreta could compost in one pit, and when that was full, after two to four years, the latrine owner could switch to the other, leaving the full pit to compost. This is a Gandhian concept. The Mahatma had used the phrase tatti par mitti (soil over shit) and would dig a pit for his own excreta then cover it with soil when it was full. The Easy Latrine leached its liquids into the ground but supposedly without polluting groundwater. And it was cheap, with the most inexpensive model.

The Sulabh model consisted of more than the latrine. It was also a method. Pathak saw how the aid and grant-making world worked. Budgets and donor cycles are fixed. They can be withdrawn after a few years with little notice. Pathak decided that Sulabh would not accept grants. It would make sanitation a business that paid for itself. He thought people would pay, so he developed a range of models for all budgets and tastes. His social service organisation would be non-profit, but it would be a business. This thinking was new.

Gourisankar Ghosh, who was working as an engineer in India in the 1970s before he went on to head the UN's Water Supply and Sanitation Collaborative Council, concedes Pathak and Sulabh have been revolutionary. He states, "In the 1970s in India, no one was talking about sanitation. Worldwide, not even the World Bank was addressing it. People were suspicious of Pathak because he's a self-made man. So he did it on his own, without UNDP or state support. He's a visionary and a path maker" (Rose 2008).

A British sanitation expert who knows Pathak expresses astonishment at "the amazing cult of personality around him". In a foreword to Sulabh history, Pathak writes, "I do not claim the eminence of Faraday, who invented the dynamo, Lazslo Biro, the inventor of the ball-pen, ... Einstein, or the unknown Assyrian who invented the wheel, or the caveman who 'invented' fire but one thing is common between me and those great names: none of them was an engineer" (Ibid).

Pathak's efforts have won him awards. In 1992, he became the first man to take the topic of latrines to the Vatican, where Pope John Paul II awarded him a St. Francis of Assisi medal. In 1995, he was the Limca Records (the Indian Guinness) Man of the Year. Indian journalist S.P. Singh wrote that Pathak remains "indifferent to fame and fortune", seeking only to rescue scavengers from the tyranny of the social system in which one man's excreta is another man's head load.

This Easy Latrine didn't bring in enough revenue to cover Sulabh's running expenses. Pathak decided to build public toilets too. In the 1970s, public facilities in India were a rare sight. The few in existence were squalid and offered little advantage to defecating on the pavement outside, so people often chose the street instead. Pathak had an idea that was simple, new and apparently doomed. If people had a clean toilet with water and light, they'd probably be willing to pay for it.

In 1973, the first Sulabh public toilet opened in Patna, the state capital of Bihar. It had water, electricity, and round-the-clock attendants. Sulabh charged ₹1 for toilet use, while urinals for men were free (women could also urinate for free, but they had to specify their needs to the caretaker). A wash cost ₹2. On the first day, Pathak said, 500 people used it.

Gourisankar Ghosh, working in 1980 in an office in Kolkata reports what he saw in Kolkata. "One morning I saw a lot of activity and someone told me someone was building a toilet. ...I never thought it would work but once it was built I saw women and men coming to use it. I was amazed. It cost one-fortieth of a dollar and they were using it happily" (Rose 2008).

Sulabh's concept of pay-and-use was not new; a similar government programme had been tried and failed several years earlier. The business model was; instead of funding toilets with government grants, Sulabh approached authorities and municipalities and suggested something different. If the authority paid for the cost of constructing the toilet and provided the land, Sulabh would run it for a set number of years and keep the profits. The business model was an attractive one to municipal authorities who could not be bothered with sanitation. Pathak said that in the beginning no one was willing to tender to construct toilets. The upper castes wouldn't consider it. They wouldn't even come for the meetings.

Pathak's other great achievement was to make toilets a topic to talk about. In India until a few years ago, nobody could imagine that any politician, bureaucrat or businessman of some standing would like to associate his name with anything even remotely connected to something as ordinary as a toilet. Now, most prominent politicians, including ministers and chief ministers, high-ranking bureaucrats and well-known businessmen readily agree and rarely decline to inaugurate the opening of public toilets in the country. When Sulabh set up an "adopt-a-scavenger" system, top politicians invited scavengers into their homes to share food and sponsored their education.

Dr Pathak, a Brahmin, has translated Gandhian thought and vision into practice. Dr Pathak is known around the world for his wide ranging work in the sanitation field to improve public health, advance social progress, and improve human rights in India and other countries. His accomplishments span the fields of sanitation technology, social enterprise and healthcare education for millions of people in his native country, serving as a model for NGO agencies and public health initiatives around the world. Over a span of five decades Bindeshwar Pathak has advanced his vision for a safe, just and dignified India through the introduction of dramatically improved sanitation. His project, Sulabh International, is improving India's sanitation, weakening the caste system and helping those in the untouchable caste move into safer, more dignified jobs. Pathak's systems are supported by municipal and user fees.

Pathak founded Sulabh International, which works to promote human rights, environmental sanitation, non-conventional sources of energy, waste management and social reforms through education. His work is considered one of the pioneers in social reform especially in the field of sanitation and hygiene. He received various national and international awards for his work with this organisation.

A prolific writer and speaker, Pathak has authored several books, the most well-known of which is *The Road to Freedom*, and he is a frequent participant in conferences on sanitation, health, and social progress around the world. His other major works are: Constitutional Safeguards for Weaker Sections and the Minorities in India, Rural Violence in Bihar and Agricultural Engineering in Development: Human Resource Development training and Education Programme (Nagla 2015). He wanted to become a lecturer in criminology but had to abandon his plans and later joined an organisation that was celebrating Gandhiji's birth centenary. As work progressed, he was transferred to another department and assigned the work of looking after the interests of manual scavengers.

The journey ahead to the success of Sulabh Shauchalaya took many years to materialise into reality; there were many hurdles from the government and many other events that hindered progress, but slowly things changed and Sulabh became what it is today. However, the greatness does not lie in the large-scale construction of latrines in houses and public places across India, but in the simple but grand vision of the man–to restore the lost individuality and dignity of the scavengers; to make them realise that they too are human beings entitled to live a dignified life just like others.

Dr Pathak sends the children of the scavenger community to school, and assists financially in the marriages of their girls. Today, women who used to clean toilets in the houses of upper caste who did not even give them water in a glass, are now running small businesses and go to the same houses where they cleaned toilets and sit on the sofa and talk to those upper caste women. They enter temples where they could not earlier go. Pathak often takes women who were scavengers to 5-Star hotels in Delhi for dinner and spends lakhs of rupees just to make them realise that they too can go there.

Dr Pathak also wants to empower women and he made Usha Chaumar,, who was once a scavenger, the president of Sulabh,. Today she walks the ramp with some of India's top models, meets dignitaries, gives speeches and accepts awards on behalf of Sulabh. He also sends his employees to the UN assembly and other places around the world to attend conferences and provides them with 5-Star accommodation.

Even though Pathak wrote his doctoral dissertation on scavenging, he realised that academia could not solve social problems. This is the starting point of his "Action Sociology" in his commitment to human rights and human dignity that he built up Sulabh as a systematic response to deal with the problem of manual scavenging. An inventor by nature, Pathak ultimately focused on building an alternative to bucket toilets that was affordable and culturally acceptable. He combined theory with practice, and launched Sulabh International. He has transformed societal approaches to sanitation, built an enduring infrastructure for public sanitation and attracted new talent and skilled persons to the sanitation sector.

Pathak travelled throughout India, living with families of scavengers as part of his Ph.D. research. Drawing on that experience, he resolved to take action, not only out of sympathy for the scavengers but also in the belief that scavenging is a dehumanising practice that would ultimately have a destructive impact on modern Indian society.

Sulabh International advances transformative change in diverse communities. His solution brings together design, financing, public will, municipal resources and technologies that are basic and low-cost. The pour-flush compost toilet (Sulabh Shauchalaya) is outfitted with biogas converters to generate energy and reduce toxins and environmentally damaging practices such as dumping waste into rivers. By introducing a scalable, self-financing solution for sanitation, Pathak eliminates scavenging.

The infrastructure Pathak has built is successfully used all over the country. Many of his approaches have been adopted in other countries like Bhutan and Afghanistan.. Additionally, he is contemplating starting a University of Sanitation that will be a central resource centre for everyone who needs to know about sanitation—users, technologists, municipal leaders, renewable energy experts and rights workers—to learn, share ideas, expand and deepen the work, and develop new ideas.

In 1878, an Act was passed under the British rule to implement public toilet systems. Even though the system was tried in some places in India, the toilets were too expensive to maintain and fell into disrepair. In the face of that failure, the subject of public sanitation was put aside, and defecation in public places continued. Due to the dirty undertones of the sanitation sector, people in respectable fields such as engineering, business and science, traditionally did not wish to work in the sector. The job fell to scavengers. Scavengers manually clean bucket toilets using rudimentary tools such as shovels and other buckets. They are relegated to the caste of untouchables and suffer discrimination. They have very little access to education, social services or job mobility. With low literacy levels and few marketable skills, the scavengers' lives perpetuate a cycle of poverty.

Pathak's goal is to transform the sanitation sector and provide more opportunities for everyone. By making the sanitation sector more suitable for investment, he is increasing the rewards of working in the sector. Further, his programmes are rehabilitating the scavengers and integrating them into society in a more respectful manner.

Under Sulabh International Academy of Environmental Sanitation, Pathak has been able to spread sanitation knowledge to citizen organisations, nurses, doctors and officers from Central, state and local governments. He has held training workshops to enhance knowledge and skills in project planning and implementation of sanitation technologies through on-site construction, technical visits and maintenance. He has also educated interested parties on various sanitation systems being implemented in the developing world, including biogas, biofertiliser, water treatment, duckweed technologies, solid waste management and environmental protection. By institutionalising sanitation education, he brings people from all sectors together and loosens age-old taboos. Toilets are now becoming a source of economic gain, and he is able to engage top business professionals, engineers and academics in the sanitation sector. Even though his organisation is sanitation-oriented, it holds true to its fundamental mission to liberate scavengers and remove social discrimination and untouchability. Toilet technology has become a tool for social transformation. Along with sanitation programmes, Pathak is providing technology and vocational training to help empower and generate alternative employment opportunities for scavengers.

Since scavengers traditionally have been trapped in a cycle of poverty and societal disenfranchisement, he is breaking that cycle through training and restoring dignity to the population. Through a combination of technological innovation and educational programming, he is using Sulabh to create a social revolution. Adopting flush toilets would end scavenging, enabling scavengers to pursue alternative forms of employment.

Pathak the Humanist

Dr Bindeshwar Pathak is a great humanist and social reformer of contemporary India. He is compassionate to the weaker sections of society. He has the vision of a philosopher and the undying zeal of a missionary. He is the icon of a new culture which embraces the poor and extols the dignity of labour. His boundless love for the downtrodden finds expression in several and tangible ways. Those who know him intimately swear that Dr Pathak was born to help the helpless. He is the leader of a national crusade for restoration of human rights and dignity to millions of scavengers; and for providing safe and hygienic human waste disposal systems to millions of Indians who go outside for open defecation along roads and railway tracks. He has himself identified with the problems of the untouchables.

Dr Pathak's multi-pronged efforts in bringing scavengers into the mainstream of national life has taken the shape of a movement for social justice. Moreover, he is an internationally acclaimed expert on sanitation and has developed and implemented a low-cost and appropriate toilet technology recommended by UN bodies for about 2.6 billion people across the globe. He gets the credit for sensitising Indians towards sanitation and those engaged in the sanitation work. Apart from low-cost sanitation, his contributions are widely known in the areas of bioenergy and biofertiliser, SLWM and poverty alleviation. Pathak combines in himself the traits of a social scientist, an engineer, an administrator and an institution-builder. What is remarkable is that he has ingeniously utilised all this expertise to enrich and empower the oppressed classes.

Environmental cleanliness and sanitation was the dearest subject of Mahatma Gandhi who proclaimed, "Cleanliness is next only to godliness". Gandhiji had two ideas in mind while talking about sanitation: one,that no one should clean and carry human excreta of others just to earn one's livelihood. There must be some scientific method of human waste disposal. Finding no other affordable alternative during his lifetime, Gandhiji had suggested 'tatti par mitti' (cover human excreta with soil) or use of the trench latrine which he himself used while living in Phoenix Ashram in South Africa. Secondly, Gandhiji wanted those engaged in sanitation work not to be treated as untouchables. They should get equal respect in the society, he took pains to emphasise, and in his typical style went on to declare that "the Bhangi (scavenger) is as important as the Viceroy".

After Gandhiji, Dr Pathak is the man who has championed sanitation and upliftment of the untouchables as the mission of his life. For the last three decades he has been working relentlessly to keep the ecosystem clean and bring the marginalised sections of society in the mainstream. His contribution in abolishing the inhuman practice of scavenging is seminal and unparalleled in the sense that he not only studied the social evil but provided its categorical solution through a low-cost toilet technology and developed a self-sustaining sanitation system across the country. In the process of providing an alternative to scavenging and rehabilitation and social upgradation of scavengers, Dr Pathak created a pan-Indian network with 50,000 volunteers and founded his Sulabh Sanitation Movement. "Nobody should go outside for defecation and every house in India should have a toilet" is the passionate obsession of Dr Pathak. In 1991, for his distinguished social service, Dr Pathak was conferred the Padma Bhushan by the President of India, R.Venkataraman.

Dr Pathak's epic struggle has helped the world to understand that the technology of Sulabh Shauchalaya that he modified and developed and implemented on a large scale could be a safe and hygienic human waste disposal system. Expensive systems like sewerage and septic tanks are not cost-effective and affordable for the teeming millions in third world countries. When he came up with the Sulabh technology in 1970, it was first greeted with scepticism and mockery; but in 1996 it was declared a global "Urban Best Practice" at the Habitat-II conference held at Istanbul and the Economic and Social Council of United Nations has granted Special Consultative Status to Sulabh in recognition of its outstanding service. Sulabh was also the recipient of the Dubai International Award for "Best Practice to Improve the Living Environment" in 2004.

Dr Pathak travelled all over the country, visited and lived with scavengers in their villages, studied their habits and social mores, their history and geographical spread to eventually declare that scavengers were a special class united in their miseries and social degradation. He said, "Let us save them from squalid conditions and in doing so we will be saving the national conscience." Significantly, he knew that slogans alone will not help and, hence, developed a technology which has become a credible alternative to scavenging in India.

He observed after studying scriptures that scavenging has no religious sanction and, hence, those who practise untouchability commit a sin; it is unproductive and revolting to manually clean excreta and we are wasting the waste which can be profitably used to raise farm production and produce biogas. He subsequently demonstrated this successfully. The union of theory and practice distinguishes Sulabh from other movements of a similar nature. Dr Pathak sought to abolish scavenging not only out of sympathy for scavengers but also out of the belief that it is a primitive, expensive and unhygienic practice.

Technology has played a decisive role in the Sulabh Sanitation Movement. During Mahatma Gandhij's lifetime and even thereafter, several attempts were made to develop a low-cost toilet technology but no tangible result emerged. Dr Pathak intervened successfully, gave the solution, applied the technology and showed to the engineers, administrators, planners and masses the how it functioned. It was a breakthrough in the Government of India's programme for the eradication of scavenging as the Sulabh system is affordable, acceptable to the masses and could be set up with the available local facilities.

The year 1974 is a landmark in the history of sanitation when the system of operating and maintaining community toilets with bathing, laundry and urinal facilities (Sulabh Shauchalaya Complex) with attendants' service round the clock was initiated on 'pay-and-use' basis in Patna. Now, Sulabh is operating and maintaining more than 6,000 community complexes across the country. These complexes have electricity and 24-hour water supply. The complexes have separate enclosures for men and women. The users are charged a nominal sum for using the toilets and bath facilities. Some of the Sulabh complexes are also provided with bath with shower facility, cloak rooms, telephones and primary healthcare facilities. These complexes have been widely welcomed, both by the people and the authorities, due to their cleanliness and good management. The pay-and-use system ensures self-sustainability without any burden on the public, government or local bodies. The complexes have also improved the living environment considerably.

An acknowledged pioneer of Action Sociology, Dr Pathak has been advocating the introduction of this novel discipline into the academic curriculum. Recently, sociology of sanitation was introduced in the syllabus at the university level by some universities. Sulabh is now diversifying into a number of innovative and environment-friendly development projects to uplift the lot of the poor. Under the dynamic and inspiring leadership of Dr Pathak, a dedicated team of sociologists, scientists, engineers, journalists and public-spirited people has built a large national network and Sulabh is all set to write glorious pages in the chapter of sanitation in India.

Besides being a recipient of several awards, laurels, and distinctions, Dr Pathak is a member of numerous national and international agencies, committees on environmental sanitation, urban development and related areas. He is also closely associated with many social, cultural, and philanthropic organisations. He has rendered excellent service to make our society and environment more healthy and harmonious. He did what no other social reformer managed to achieve; he blended his humanitarian philosophy with an environment-friendly technology. It is for these remarkable achievements that he has become a household name in India and is held in high esteem by a grateful society. Mulk Raj Anand, the writer, has correctly observed, "What Abraham Lincoln did for Blacks in America, Dr Pathak has done for scavengers in India. Both are great redeemers."

Sulabh Movement in India

Sulabh has taken bold steps in introducing social well-being activities and innovative initiatives to eradicate manual scavenging and open defecation as well as to rehabilitate those who once depended on manual scavenging. The prominent initiatives are:

1. Community toilet technology
2. Excreta-based biogas and biofertiliser technology
3. Wastewater treatment through duckweed
4. Sulabh International Centre for Action Sociology (SICAS), Sulabh Public School and Vocational Training Centre

5. Sulabh International Institute of Technical Research and Training (SIITRAT)
6. Sulabh International Institute of Health and Hygiene (SIIHH)
7. Sulabh International Museum of Toilets

It was noted earlier that Dr Pathak was given two books to read. One published by WHO, *Excreta Disposal for Rural Areas and Small Communities* by two sanitation engineers, Edmund A. Wagner and J.N. Lanoix; and the other in Hindi by Rajendra Lal Das. The WHO publication was subject to very close study, and many passages of it left a lasting impression on the young Pathak's mind. Out of the heterogeneous mass of latrine designs produced all over the world, the sanitary pit privy emerges as the most practical and universally applicable type. The WHO publication laid out the following seven conditions to meet the criteria for a sanitary latrine:

1. The surface soil should not be contaminated.
2. There should be no contamination of the groundwater.
3. There should be no contamination of the surface water.
4. Excreta should not be accessible to flies or animals.
5. There should be no handling of fresh excreta. Or when this is indispensable, it should be restricted to the barest minimum.
6. There should be freedom from odours or unsightly conditions.
7. The method used should be simple and inexpensive in construction and operation.

However, the suggestions in these books were for the application of this technology only in rural areas. Applying his mind, Pathak thought the soil conditions of rural and urban areas are the same. So, the same technology can also be used in urban areas. Therefore, he concluded that this technology, after some improvement, could be a viable alternative to scavenging. Accordingly, he innovated, modified and developed alternatives to suit the urban conditions, at the same time making 4 to 5 new designs for different site conditions such as congested areas and restricted spaces.

Perusal of the WHO's books helped Dr Pathak develop a technology which has proved to be revolutionary. The two-pit pour-flush technology is remarkable for its many advantages; it is hygienically appropriate, cost-effective and easy to construct and maintain with locally available materials. The design and specifications can be modified to suit the needs and the paying capacity of the user. The toilet can be located inside the house or outside. It can be constructed in different physical, geological and hydrological conditions and does not pollute surface or groundwater. Its maintenance is simple and does not require the services of a scavenger or large volumes of water. There is a potential for upgradation as it can later be connected to sewers, once sewage is introduced in the area. A low-volume flushing cistern can be attached and the whole set-up needs very little space. Additionally, fertiliser is generated. Earlier the world had only two technologies, the sewer system and septic tanks. Both require excessive water for flushing, unlike the Sulabh technology.

Dr Pathak lived with scavengers for four months, ate their food and shared their lives with them. In this simple but very direct way he set out to free himself of caste prejudice, and elevate himself, technologically and socially, to be capable of finding alternatives, not only to methods of scavenging but, more importantly, to restore some semblance of human right and dignity to scavengers. He returned from the scavenger colony totally converted and firm in his resolve that he would thenceforth dedicate his life for the cause of scavengers.

Dr Pathak solved the problem of entry of Harijans into Nathdwara temple in Udaipur, Rajasthan, in 1988. The controversy over entering the temple had taken a serious turn and so many attempts, made by others had failed. The situation became so serious that the then President of India, R. Venkataraman, himself wanted to lead the Harijans into the temple. Even political leaders and the state government officials had to go to the temple with police protection. This attracted Dr Pathak's attention and, with 100 scavengers and orthodox Vedic Maithil Brahmins, he entered the Nathdwara temple, offered prayers and recited bhajans and kirtans. The scavengers and the whole group took their meal together. This programme was performed without police protection.

Dr Pathak launched a campaign to help the SCs offer prayers in temples and perform puja at their homes with Vedic Brahmins. Also, in 1989, he started common puja and dining programmes where members of the SCs do fasting, sit at the puja and prepare prasad. They also prepare food for lunch or dinner. After the puja is over, the prasad and food are distributed by the SCs to all, including Vedic Brahmins, who eat it with them.

To improve the social status of scavengers in India, Sulabh started a social upgradation campaign. One high-status family in society has to "socially adopt" a scavenger family who will be treated like family members.

The association with these high-status people will raise the status of the scavengers. This programme has taken off very well. So far more than 5,000 scavenger families have been "adopted" by high-status people, including judges, advocates, journalists, ministers and planners.

Sanitation as a Global Concern

Sanitation is a global challenge which is faced by all, the underdeveloped, developing and also the developed countries. The solutions to better sanitation is demanded by all sections of people without any discrimination throughout the world. Sanitation is a challenge which is related to human health. For this reason, all countries are highly concerned about sanitation issues without any political bias. They believe that better sanitation can contribute to better socio-economic life. Hence, this has brought the nations together to work for better sanitation. We can witness some international organisations that are committed to facing the sanitation challenges.

Sanitation as an issue can be a reason for socio-economic development of a nation and it can also be a hindrance towards socio-economic development. There are different organisations which are working for the sanitation challenge throughout the world. Among them, we can identify WHO and UNICEF as the major ones. There are thousands of NGOs which are working for the betterment of sanitation conditions in different nations throughout the world with aid provided by WHO.

WHO is the directing and coordinating authority for health within the UN. It is responsible for providing leadership on global health matters, shaping health research agenda, setting norms and standards, articulating evidence-based policy options, providing technical support to countries and monitoring and assessing health trends. In the 21st century, health is a shared responsibility, involving equitable access to essential care and collective defence against transnational threats.

Around 1.1 billion people globally do not have access to improved water supply sources whereas 2.4 billion people do not have access to any type of improved sanitation facility. About 2 million people die every year due to diarrhoeal diseases; most of them children less than five years of age. The most affected are the populations in developing countries, living in extreme conditions of poverty, normally peri-urban dwellers or rural inhabitants. Among the main problems which are responsible for this situation are: lack of priority given to the sector, lack of financial resources, lack of sustainability of water supply and sanitation services, poor hygiene behaviour and inadequate sanitation in public places including hospitals, health centres and schools. Providing access to sufficient quantities of safe water, the provision of facilities for sanitary disposal of excreta and introducing sound hygiene behaviour are of capital importance to reduce the burden of disease caused by these risk factors.

The UN General Assembly declared 2008 as the International Year of Sanitation (IYS). The resolution expressed concern on the slow and insufficient progress in providing access to basic sanitation services at the global level and recognised that progress can be attained through active commitment and action by all states, as well as UN agencies, regional and international organisations, civil society organisations and other relevant stakeholders.

Over the last 50 years, WHO has generated, evaluated and shared new knowledge on safe disposal of excreta, sewage and community waste, and has been at the forefront of exploring linkages between water, sanitation and health. It has collaborated with key partners on international development efforts to raise the profile of sanitation, such as the International Drinking Water and Sanitation Decade (IDWSSD) (1980–1990) and the Johannesburg World Summit for Sustainable Development (2002).

WHO has recognised the importance of sanitation since its inception; the first ever World Health Assembly defined sanitation as a priority, and to this day, WHO continues to recognise its importance. WHO will continue to ensure that objective, balanced information is available to support policymaking and decision-making, advocate investment in sanitation as a cost-effective health intervention, increase impact by enhancing existing and new partnerships, and assist key partners at all levels by sharing the tools and guidelines it develops. Lack of sanitation is an affront to human dignity.

In response to the call for action of the UN General Assembly, WHO will provide support to the objectives of the IYS 2008 to accelerate progress on sanitation and hygiene and ensure that related health concerns are addressed. Strategically, WHO is best placed to:

- Advocate for policy changes to improve coverage;
- improve stakeholders' access to sanitation and health information;
- enhance partnership and linkages with key stakeholders and programmes.

UNICEF was created by the UN General Assembly on 11 December 1946, to provide emergency food and healthcare to children in countries that had been devastated by World War II. In 1953, UNICEF became a permanent part of the United Nations System and its name was shortened from the original United Nations International Children's Emergency Fund to United Nations Children's Fund. However, it has continued to be known as UNICEF, the popular acronym based on its previous title. UNICEF relies on contributions from governments and private donors. Governments contribute two-thirds of the organisation's resources; private groups and some 6 million individuals contribute the rest through the National Committees. It is estimated that 91.8 per cent of their revenue is distributed to programme services (Pais 2015). UNICEF's programmes emphasise developing services at community level to promote the health and well-being of children.

Inadequate access to safe water and sanitation services, coupled with poor hygiene practices, kills and sickens thousands of children every day, and leads to impoverishment and diminished opportunities for thousands more. Poor sanitation, water and hygiene have many other serious repercussions. Children, particularly girls, are denied their right to education because their schools lack private and decent sanitation facilities. Women are forced to spend large parts of their day fetching water. Poor farmers and wage earners are less productive due to illness, health systems are overwhelmed and national economies suffer. Without water, sanitation and hygiene, sustainable development is impossible. UNICEF works in more than 100 countries around the world to improve water supplies and sanitation facilities in schools and communities, and to promote safe hygiene practices.

UNICEF has been working in India since 1949; it is the largest UN organisation in the country. It is fully committed to working with the Government of India to ensure that each child born in this vast and complex country gets the best start in life, thrives and develops to his or her full potential. UNICEF uses its community level knowledge to develop innovative interventions to ensure that women and children are able to access basic services such as clean water, health visitors and educational facilities, and that these services are of high quality. At the same time, UNICEF reaches out directly to families to help them to understand what they must do to ensure their children thrive.

UNICEF has given certain facts about sanitation among children (Pais 2015):

- Hand washing with soap, particularly after contact with excreta, can reduce diarrhoeal diseases by over 40 per cent and respiratory infections by 30 per cent. Diarrhoea and respiratory infections are the number one cause for child deaths in India.
- Hand washing with soap is among the most effective and inexpensive ways to prevent diarrhoeal diseases and pneumonia.
- With 594 million people defecating in the open and 44 per cent mothers disposing their children's faeces in the open, there is a very high risk of microbial contamination (bacteria, viruses, amoeba) of water which causes diarrhoea in children.
- Children weakened by frequent diarrhoea episodes are more vulnerable to malnutrition and opportunistic infections such as pneumonia. About 48 per cent of children in India are suffering from some degree of malnutrition. Diarrhoea and worm infection are two major health conditions that affect school age children, impacting their learning abilities.
- Adequate, well-maintained water supply and sanitation facilities in schools encourage children to attend school regularly and help them achieve their educational goals. Inadequate water supply and sanitation in schools are health hazards and affect school attendance, retention and educational performance.
- Adolescent girls are especially vulnerable to dropping out, as many are reluctant to continue their schooling because toilet facilities are not private, not safe or simply not available.
- Women and girls face shame and a loss of personal dignity and safety risk if there is no toilet at home. They have to wait for the night to relieve themselves to avoid being seen by others.
- Only 31 per cent of India's population use improved sanitation (2008).
- In rural India 21 percent use improved sanitation facilities (2008).
- 145 million people in rural India gained access to improved sanitation between 1990 and 2008.
- 211 million people gained access to improved sanitation in all of India between 1990 and 2008.

- India is home to 594 million people defecating in the open; over 50 per cent of the population.
- In Bangladesh and Brazil, only 7 per cent of the populations defecate in the open. In China, only 4 per cent of the population defecates in the open.

World Toilet Organization

World Toilet Organization (WTO), founded on 19 November 2001, is a global non-profit organisation committed to improving toilet and sanitation conditions worldwide. It was founded by Jack Sim with the stated aim of being a global network and service platform wherein all toilet and sanitation organisations can learn from one another and leverage media and global support to influence governments to promote sound sanitation and public health policies. WTO empowers individuals through education, training and building local marketplace opportunities to advocate for clean and safe sanitation facilities in their communities. It was established with the aim to break the taboo around toilets and the sanitation crisis. Since 2001, WTO has lobbied governments, public and private sector stakeholders and the international community to prioritise sanitation in the development agenda.

World Toilet Summit

The World Toilet Summit is a unique global event established by the WTO to bring together various sanitation stakeholders under one roof to connect and collaborate on innovative inventions, projects and products in the sanitation sector. This annual event is jointly organised by a host government and the WTO. The World Toilet Summit aims to empower delegates, exhibitors and sponsors to exchange knowledge, expertise and resources in scaling up impact and innovation in the sanitation marketplace.

In late 2011, WTO established its centre in India to increase access of rural households to safe and affordable sanitation. On the ground, WTO works closely with local implementing partners eKutir, a for-profit social enterprise, based out of Odisha, and Sattva, a media and social business consulting firm based out of Bangalore. The pilot project was set up in Odisha where eKutir had established its strong rural base. By deploying eKutir's micro entrepreneurs to further the centre's mission in providing safe and affordable sanitation to the rural population, this partnership allows the WTO and eKutir to create more livelihoods, and boost health and dignity among the farming households. eKutir has been able to establish 25 micro entrepreneurs working for the sanitation cause in three different states of India. With the establishment of the centre, farmers have access to low-cost and affordable toilets. As a result, households reduce their medical expenses as they do not fall sick as often and this increases their savings. With a proven track record of impact in the pilot villages of Odisha, WTO and eKutir are collaborating on broadening this impact to other states in India.

NGOs and Sanitation

NGOs are citizen-based associations that operate independently of government, usually to deliver resources or serve some social or political purpose. The World Bank classifies NGOs as either operational NGOs, which are primarily concerned with development projects, or advocacy NGOs, which are primarily concerned with promoting a cause. NGO is any non-profit, voluntary citizens' group which is organised on a local, national or international level. Task-oriented and driven by people with a common interest, NGOs perform a variety of service and humanitarian functions, bring citizen concerns to governments, advocate and monitor policies and encourage political participation through provision of information. Some are organised around specific issues, such as human rights, environment or health. They provide analysis and expertise, serve as early warning mechanisms and help monitor and implement international agreements.

The majority of NGOs have considerable strengths and play important and varied roles in the sanitation sector. NGOs have assisted in facilitating better access to sanitation services for the poor and typically offer on--ground impact in increasing access to services within relatively short time-frames through established community relationships. They often have the ability to reach remote places or illegal settlements where service provision is challenging and have been shown to be adept at setting sanitation within a holistic development frame, commonly taking an integrated and longer-term programmatic approach in meeting community needs. They are adaptable to circumstance and taking on different roles in response to the local community and policy contexts. At the same time, NGOs are able to draw on national and also international experience through their networks of practitioners, facilitating the exchange of new ideas from one area to the next. The various roles played by NGOs in the sanitation sector can be broadly grouped into six categories (Charles 2010):

1. Facilitation of service delivery including direct service provision (particularly in emergency and humanitarian relief contexts or in areas characterised by extreme poverty or geographical remoteness) or playing an intermediary or broker role between communities and service providers.
2. Community education, awareness raising, sanitation and hygiene promotion and marketing including stimulating demand, gender sensitive approaches, supply chain strengthening and implementing behaviour change programmes.
3. Building partnerships and promoting networking between different sector actors including representing community views to governments and service providers and translating and communicating national policies and regulations to the local level.
4. Capacity building for local governments, service providers, in-country civil society groups and end users (households and communities).
5. Research and innovation including demonstration and piloting of innovative and locally adapted approaches and technologies.
6. Engaging in policy dialogue including promoting proven approaches and technologies, communicating lessons learnt, communicating community needs, advocating gender equity and monitoring the effectiveness of programmes and government initiatives.

The broad strengths NGOs bring to these roles need to be considered with reference to limitations of their roles and activities. While there are many examples of success, it is also true that NGOs have at times played potentially detrimental roles (though through good intentions). NGOs are taking funds from various donor agencies. Though they operate within the legal framework of the country, in most cases they are accountable to the donor agencies.

Pathak as a Visionary

Dr Bindeshwar Pathak is a great humanist and social reformer of contemporary India. To the weaker sections of society especially, his is the compassionate face of a paternal redeemer. He has the vision of a philosopher and the undying zeal of a missionary. He is an icon of sanitation and social reform who has made a difference in the lives of millions of people. Dr Pathak will be remembered in history for his innovative strides in the field of sanitation as well as social reform. With his efforts, erstwhile untouchables have been allowed by society to intermingle with them and to live on par, dining with them and allowed them to offer prayers in the temples. He has created a new culture which embraces the poor and extols the dignity of labour.

Dr Pathak's contribution to the field of sanitation, eradication of manual scavenging and the rehabilitation initiatives for the manual scavengers is acknowledged worldwide. His action sociology of eradication of manual scavenging is not by knocking down the dry latrines but by providing alternatives, new technology which does not require manual scavenging. Having earned his master's in sociology, Dr Pathak wanted to become a professor of sociology, unfortunately, his wish was not fulfilled. However, he has achieved this in action; he has professed and lived sociology in action. Truly, he is the founder of sociology of sanitation in India; and the founder of action sociology with his unique technological initiatives to transform the society in the field of sanitation. Dr Pathak fought against not only the eradication of manual scavenging but also against the feminisation of manual scavenging and caste-base sanitation work.

Dr Pathak is a model for the present generation, in bringing about social change, in breaking the shackles of caste exploitation without violence; his strategies were directly issue-based, not against any caste, any religion or region. Yet another significant contribution of Dr Pathak is generating study and reading material in sociology of sanitation. About a decade back, there was no literature easily available to read on sanitation, the area being disliked or even considered as taboo. Now we find books on sociology of sanitation, with different titles, discussing a wide range of issues relating to sanitation.

There is a dangerous trend among the young scholars today, of reductionism. Reducing a person or his contribution to one particular thing; leaving aside the whole range of thinking and debate on a wider perspective. For example, Gandhiji is reduced to Swatchhatha and Dr B.R. Ambedkar to the Constitution, while debunking their noble thoughts on democracy and humanism. Similarly, we should not reduce Dr Pathak to sanitation. He is a visionary. He is the originator of a movement in India, in the right direction; a revolution to transform society. It is a (silent) war against caste and gender discrimination. He has come out with technological solutions to the problems of sanitation; with alternatives which are non-violent, affordable and replicable. That was his beginning, but now, he has focused on other concerns of humanity. Presently, Sulabh has extended its activities to the destitute, victims of violence and natural disasters and also the widows of Vrindavan. Dr Pathak has realised that education is a powerful instrument to reach the target of his mission. Hence, Sulabh is giving importance to education of the young and the old. Further, the vision is to introduce sociology of sanitation at the higher learning level, and in social research.

Chapter 9

ACTION SOCIOLOGY AND SANITATION

In many ways, sociology has long been the danger field of the social sciences, labelled as "having no respect". Students flock to psychology programmes, counselling programmes, economics or social work programmes and even anthropology programmes but not sociology, maybe because they think that graduates with those programmes can get a real job (Price 2009). There are always faculty positions for sociologists, but rarely do we see a classified advertisement, "sociologist wanted". Part of the reason is that we have historically been so concerned to get sociology recognised as a "real" social science. The division between "pure" sociology and "practical" sociology is as old as sociology itself. We keep forgetting and rediscovering this part of our history over and over again.

In the late 1970s, there evolved the Association for Applied and Clinical Sociology and the Sociological Practice and Public Sociology section within the American Sociological Association. Now, teaching and training programmes in applied and clinical sociology have started that attract an increasing number of students; even the traditional sociology programmes. Sociologists have been finding more and more ways to go from "thinking about sociology" to "doing sociology". There is something deeply satisfying about taking our theories and methods and applying them to the "real world".

Sociology has freely given the concepts and methods to virtually all other social science disciplines, unlike other social science disciplines. The focus groups and survey research are developed from sociology. The diversity of sociological careers ranges much further than we were aware of. People from sociology just don't talk about it because they are not widely recognised by the business world. And practitioners have not been supported by organised sociology. But now it is changing.

Doing sociology means not just analysing sociology or talking about social issues, we're actively engaged in practising what we preach. We are university professors, community college faculty, sociologists working in state and federal government, and even sociologists in private practice. What sociologists are doing ranges from the application of statistics and survey methodology to using qualitative, ethnographic and field methods to help communities solve real problems; from applied research to straight forward clinical practice. Today, we need to come away from the book and understand what sociologists do outside of teaching in universities. Sociologists are engaged in communities, so that they can do something with sociology.

In some of the roles sociologists play in doing sociology, sociological practitioners differ from others who might work in similar roles and on similar problems, through the background and application of sociological theory to whatever they are doing. A fascinating example is in a clinical sociologist working with people with substance abuse, a context far from the usual safe, academic setting,. At the juncture, applied sociology and public sociology are doing collaborative research to facilitate and improve community policing and crime prevention.

Education and the educational system is also an area of great interest to sociologists and sociology. Another major interest of sociologists is sociological practitioners' work with communities. It can be in projects designed to do community research with social change, through a sociologically informed assessment of the needs and assets; or a project in which the consultants create evaluation tools designed to foster development of housing and other environment, meeting the needs of our aging population. All those who do sociology have somehow joined or at least work within the system. Some sociologists apply what is commonly termed a "critical sociology" perspective to their practice. Applied sociologists also play a significant role while working in government settings; as sociologists, they can transform and enhance the methodologies; not only to get the information but to apply sociology in order to enhance the quality of that information.

Sociology is a discipline of study which focuses on human group life, communities and societies. Sociology can also be considered a way of viewing human behaviour that focuses on the patterns of relationships among individuals rather than solely the individuals themselves. This distinguishes sociology from the field of psychology. The sociological perspective offers a way to view facts, conditions and people, and a way to perceive and understand the world around us. In a very real sense, all sociology is applied. C. Wright Mills (1959) described the "sociological imagination" as a way of understanding the complex relationship between individual lives and the larger social world in which they live. For Mills, the personal troubles experienced by individuals are always connected to and impacted by larger public issues. Building on this notion, all of social life is a potential outlet for the study and application of sociological principles and ideas. Sociologists study a wide range of institutions, from families to political structures and the economic development of nations, and the unique nature of how these various institutions interrelate and impact each other. The applications of sociology are evident everywhere. Sociologists engage in all types of work as they study the conditions, people and issues of society. Public opinion, market analysis, community needs assessments, policy analysis and the study of social problems, are often the domain of sociologists. Understanding crime rates, population shifts and growth, and trends in the media are all more fully understood through the sociological perspective (Price 2009).

Sociology can be used to gain a more basic understanding of the fundamental aspects of social phenomena. However, sociology can also be applied with the goal of making practical, real world applications to individuals and organisations. Applied sociology tends to have a "client centred" focus where some group, agency or corporation is drawing upon the essential skills of the sociologist in a community based setting, where an actual or "real world" issue is in need of being resolved or considered. Further, clinical sociologists are often asked to be part of a team where the goal is to alter a problematic social relationship or to restructure some social institution. Here, the sociologist as a consultant is brought on board to assist a corporation in the midst of significant change or may be asked by therapists to research a new form of group therapy for their client. Other clinical sociologists themselves do therapy, community development or other work as change agents (Glassner and Freedman 1979).

Sociology is also in many ways a public enterprise. A public sociologist is a public intellectual who applies sociological ideas and findings to social issues about which sociology has something to say (Gans 1999: 265). We need to demonstrate how sociologists are taking sociology to publics beyond the university, engaging them in dialogue about public issues that have been studied by sociologists (Burawoy 2005). Applied, clinical and public sociologists participate in grassroots organising, community-based non-profits, government agencies, policy think tanks and research organisations. They do consulting work, research proposal writing, administer programmes, census research, market analysis, environmental impact studies, and work in the fields of criminal justice, education, healthcare and governance, among others.

Sociologists are interested in applying sociological knowledge to improving society's conditions and people's lives. In general, sociologists play three different roles in doing sociology:

1. They conduct research to systematically analyse social conditions and possible solutions to problems in the conditions.
2. They develop models, theories and perspectives to further help us understand how the social conditions might be changed for the better.
3. They facilitate improving the social conditions as policymakers and activists.

Probably, their most common role is conducting research; searching for possible causes of problems and evaluating possible solutions. A review of a number of sociological associations indicates that their main focus is research. Similarly, in the US, about 75 per cent of sociologists are in academic institutions (Price 2009). Less commonly, doing sociology might include direct intervention, including things like improving access to clean water or training people on how to advocate for their rights.

Sociological conditions of this kind can serve as indicators of what kinds of sociological activities or practices are possible. With a close look at this, people can develop a better understanding about what sociologists do, around the world. People can then see how and where sociology would be useful in understanding, explaining and helping to change the world. Sociology not only explores methods of data collection but also sees how to relate theory to practice. It also goes further and examines the philosophy underlying different approaches to sociological research.

Application of the mind is more important than mere knowledge alone. Knowledge can be borrowed but not the mind nor the art of its application. With the academic background of an "action sociologist", Pathak was deeply motivated and inspired by the ideals of Mahatma Gandhi for the removal of scavenging and untouchability from society and the promotion of environmental sanitation by eliminating open defecation. An in-depth study of the sanitation scenario in India, during the pre-Independence and post-Independence era, convinced him that neither the sewerage nor the septic tank systems, would be able to address the gigantic problem of lack of sanitation in urban and rural India. He came across a WHO publication *Excreta Disposal for Rural Areas and Small Communities* by Edmund A. Wagner and J.N. Lanoix (1960), which led him to design the twin-pit, pour-flush compost toilet. The present designs and specifications were developed through years of experimentation and pilot studies.

Contribution of Dr Pathak to Action Sociology

The contribution of Dr Pathak can be seen in the activities of the organisation he started. The International Academy of Environmental Sanitation and Public Health (IAESPH) is a not-for-profit NGO and have been working for the promotion of global environmental sanitation in the public's interest. This academy was formerly known as Sulabh International Academy of Environmental Sanitation and Public Health (SIAESPH). With the same functioning and objectives, it was renamed in 2004 to Sulabh International Institute of Technical Research and Training (SIITRAT), established in 1984 for promoting research, development and consultancy services in the sanitation sector.

The academy's main thrust is to contribute towards sustainable sanitation solutions through capacity building, skill upgradation, knowledge sharing, technology transfer and social transformation to enhance the quality of life of billions of underprivileged people in the developing world. With a view to strengthening these areas of operation, the academy undertakes design, construction, operation and maintenance of sanitation services, monitoring and evaluation of sanitation projects and continuing research and development in the sector.

The academy has a well-planned institutional framework demonstrating the technological solutions coupled with a well-equipped scientific laboratory for research and development. The academy possessed a rich knowledge pool and multi-disciplinary professionalism including sanitation experts, health professionals, social scientists, engineers, architects, administrators, ecologists and world-wide networking of scholars and eminent professionals with proven abilities from related areas. The academy is dedicated to promote PEACE in the developing world through:

Poverty alleviation
Environmental sanitation
Awareness and motivation
Children as agents of change and
Education for all

In environmental sanitation, "safe water and basic sanitation" is the foundation of life and health and personal hygiene is the key to happy living.

Sulabh is aimed at shouldering a much larger mandate of performing as an international centre of holistic learning and education on all issues relating to environmental sanitation and public health. The aim is to treat environmental sanitation and public health as a major field of education and disseminate knowledge and skills to all walks of life at national, regional and global levels, predominantly through capacity building and training, knowledge management and technology transfer, consultancy services, research and development, project management, action sociology and gender mainstreaming.

The specific objectives include:

- Capacity building and training for both national and international professionals
- Curriculum development, documentation, networking, etc.
- Applied and fundamental research and action sociology in environmental sanitation
- Formulation, monitoring and implementation of projects relating to environmental sanitation with focus on water, sanitation, health and hygiene
- Consultancy services on issues relating to social, environmental and technological development in the area of environmental sanitation and public health
- Contributing to achieving localised MDGs for sanitation among developing countries through knowledge sharing and technology transfer

In concurrence with the objectives set, the academy has formulated action-oriented activities:

- Preparation of professionals of national, regional, local and international repute on the issues of water, sanitation, health and hygiene
- Globalisation of appropriate, affordable, eco-friendly and culturally acceptable sanitation technologies to widen the sanitation coverage, particularly to SAARC and other developing countries
- Research and development in water, sanitation, health and hygiene sector
- Social reforms and mobilisation
- WASH campaign involving schools as "agents of change" for sanitation and hygiene
- Rehabilitation of women and children of weaker sections through education and vocational training
- Alternative sources of livelihood for liberating scavengers through skill upgradation and upscaling their capacities for sustainable development
- Awareness generation and creation of demand for safe access to water and sanitation through community participation and participatory democracy

Sulabh is envisioned as a centre of holistic learning and education in environmental sanitation. Its core competence is seen in:

- Capacity building and knowledge management
- Research and development
- Project formulation and implementation
- Consultancy services
- Water resources management
- Waste management
- Environmental protection;
- Health and hygiene
- Action sociology
- Rural sanitation
- Gender mainstreaming

The core competence is well diversified and mainly emphasised on on-site application of innovative sanitation solutions in the areas of:

- Toilet-related sanitation and its application for the utilisation of society at individual household as well as at community level with unique advantage of on-site disposal of human excreta
- Promotion of towns/cities and villages free from open defecation
- Water quality and surveillance
- Water conservation through rainwater harvesting and wastewater management by recycling and reuse through treatment
- Solid waste management including composting
- Developing scavenger-free towns by relieving the scavenging community of the menace of manual cleaning of toilets and bringing them on a par with the mainstream society
- Encouraging school sanitation and creating school sanitation clubs as children, the future citizens of society, are the agents of change for promoting the safe sanitation movement

Sulabh believes in decentralisation of its activities for effective performance. Its professional networking is spread all over the country in association with international organisations like UN-Habitat, UNICEF, UNDP and WHO. The organisation has also established its regional training centres at Patna and Kolkata. The Regional Centre in Patna, Bihar, has the facilities of a sanitation park, training centre and hostel accommodation, catering to the need for training of all the stakeholders of the region. The centre has gained a reputation as being one of the most effective and efficient training organisations in the area. It has undertaken and completed various research studies sponsored by WHO India, including "Disease burden due to inadequate water and sanitation facilities in India", "Perceptions and practices of sanitation and hygiene in five states of Eastern India, West Bengal, Bihar, Orissa, Jharkhand and Assam and the impact on community health" and "Development of guidelines for water safety plan for different water supply systems used in rural India". Apart from these studies, the centre provides collaborative support to the Institution of Public Health Engineers for organising national seminars and workshops on issues related to urban health, sanitation, disaster management, public health engineering materials and equipments. The centre has helped in developing an encyclopaedia on Sanitation. It also collaborates with International Scientific Forum on "home hygiene" for promotion of hygiene behaviour issues internationally and supports WASH India and *Water Supply and Sanitation Collaborative Council* (WSSCC) in their activities.

Efforts towards Toilet Related Sanitation

Sulabh promotes its twin-pit, pour-flush compost toilet for household use, public toilets on pay-and-use basis for community use and bioenergy systems by generation of biogas from biogas plants linked to public toilets as well as utilising animal wastes like cow dung. The biogas emanating from the biodigester linked to the public toilets is being utilised as cooking gas, for electricity generation, street lighting and body warming. It also propagates the effluent treatment technology by which the effluent from the human excreta-based biogas plant becomes colourless, odourless and pathogen-free water which can be used safely for aquaculture, agriculture purposes or for discharge into any water body. The Government of India and international agencies including UN-habitat, WHO and UNICEF have recognised these efforts. Sulabh promotes these proven technologies through capacity building and skill upgradation to all the related functionaries, not only from India but also from the countries of the developing world. It also provides technical assistance as well as project-based consultancy services for design, construction, operation and maintenance of these technologies with its endeavour to contribute for sustainable sanitation.

Awareness Creation and Promotion of Open Defecation-Free Habitats

Sulabh ensures upscaling the mindset of the community towards quality living in a pollution-free environment, while extending sanitation services. Villagers are predominantly poor and vulnerable. The diversion of these people from the age-old practice of open defecation, which has been the cause of health hazards and environmental pollution, is a unique demonstration of the concerted efforts of Sulabh.

The organisation considers it significant to facilitate creating sensitised citizenry with awareness, motivation and participation in sanitation, intensive and responsive involvement of all stakeholders with a more effective role of civic bodies and the private sector, a proactive mindset regarding towards sanitation, hygiene and environmental protection, a public-private-people partnership, creating awareness through school children and teachers as agents of change and improved health, hygiene and sanitation in society.

Gender Mainstreaming

Sulabh gives equal importance to gender mainstreaming. It supports all activities that bolster women's empowerment with dignity. The scavengers, who traditionally clean and carry away human waste have been enabled with dignity and social status. Among them, the women are the worst sufferers. An innovative approach called Nai Disha (new direction) has been initiated to change the course of life of manual scavengers, particularly women, by liberating them from scavenging and rehabilitating them to bring them into the mainstream of society through education and gainful employment. The scavenger rehabilitation programme is the academy's prime agenda. Supporting training programmes, vocational education for achieving self-employment are among the main considerations of the academy's capacity building and training effort.

Achieving Scavenging-Free Societies through Social Transformation

Another significant activity is the rehabilitation of scavenging communities in the mainstream of society through education, developing market-oriented vocational skills and thereby ensuring their dignity and freeing them of social discrimination.

Water Conservation and Wastewater Management

Sulabh considers rainwater harvesting essential for water conservation as well as recharging groundwater. It has prepared detailed project reports for rainwater harvesting for five 5-Star hotels of the Taj Group (Agra, Jaipur, Chennai and two hotels in Goa) as well as for Scindia School Gwalior; DIN Cooperative Group Housing Society, Dwarka, New Delhi; and the Ramakrishna Mission Sewashram, Lucknow, implemented in collaboration with the International Rainwater Harvesting Alliance (IRHA), Switzerland. The stakeholders of the concerned projects were imparted the necessary training for design and execution. The treated effluent from the biodigester also contributes to recycling and reuse of treated wastewater. In addition, Sulabh also propagates use of duckweed for wastewater treatment and promoting pisciculture for economic gain.

Sulabh has made a significant dent in the Clean Yamuna Manch Project under Yamuna Action Plan II (YAP) sponsored by the Government of India and JBIC, Japan, at different locations including Agra, Gurgaon, Faridabad, Yamuna Nagar and Noida with its main objectives enhancing public awareness and participation; developing greater understanding and popularity for all YAP sewerage and non-sewerage components; promoting higher visibility, positive image and support among policy-makers and the general public; promoting behavioural change towards adoption of environment-friendly practices among the public; creating a network of stakeholders which shall gradually take over activities of the Clean Yamuna Manch beyond the project period; and sensitising civic bodies about YAP.

Sulabh assisted the environmental improvement project at Kanpur and Mirzapur towns under the Ganga Action Plan in collaboration with the Netherlands-based consulting firm (Haskoning and Euroconsult) in preparing project reports on low-cost sanitation to prevent pollution of the Ganga. It was involved in the National River Conservation Plan of the Government of India and is assisting the state governments and local bodies in preventing pollution of other rivers in the country.

Solid Waste Management

Solid waste management constitutes a serious problem, particularly in mega cities. It is observed that garbage disposal, waste recycling and urban poverty are closely linked. In most of the cities, the system of waste collection is visible at municipal dumping sites. The waste pickers have an intrinsic role in the handling of the cities' garbage and play an important role in the existing solid waste management in most of the cities. There are five major steps involved in the management of garbage viz. collection, segregation, transportation, treatment and disposal. Sulabh emphasises solid waste management mechanisms including vermi-composting in all its projects and consultancy services, wherever appropriate, as an instrument of improving environmental practices, employment generation and energy promotion and adopts it in an integrated manner.

Sulabh has completed a Government of India project sponsored by UNDP on "National Strategy for Urban Poor on Solid Waste Disposal through Vermi-composting and Improvement of Environment by strengthening Community-based Organisations". The project was aimed at improvement of environmental practices for the management of solid waste; demonstrating to the community that recycling is a viable source for employment generation; gender sensitisation; setting up of an institution at the community level to sustain the system; reorganisation and reuse of open spaces to improve the micro climate and ensuring accessibility of the people (improvement of water bodies and plantation for soil improvement).

The activities undertaken were mainly awareness generation, cleanliness drive, school sanitation and cleanliness of school premises, demonstration of rain harvesting, vermi-composting, training and gender sensitisation, greening, and improvement of local organisations through workshops and meetings and discussions.

School Sanitation

Sulabh emphasised promotion of school sanitation as students serve as a medium for spreading the message of sanitation in each home and influence their parents to build toilets. Since teachers command the respect of the community, they prove very helpful in motivating people to construct toilets in their houses. In the promotion of school sanitation, Sulabh has been encouraging establishment of "School Sanitation Club" with a goal to mould the total personality of the individual student in relation to th ecommunity and thereby to the ecosystem as a whole. The focus is towards the child as the "key human resource" and the schools as "knowledge centres".

Research and Development

Sulabh's applied research on various issues relating to social, environmental and technical developments has resulted in carrying out several important studies on social issues of scavengers' rehabilitation, their skill development and brought out significant research on sustainable technologies like biogas plants, duckweed ponds, materials and designs of the pan and trap of toilets, wastewater disposal and treatment, solid waste management and biomedical waste management. The outcome of these research studies and designing capabilities are tested and validated on ground realities and propagated for community use through capacity building and training. Sulabh aims at bringing sanitation into the sharp focus of academic activities and research at national, regional and global levels by revitalising capacity building, training, professional studies and counselling.

Capacity Building and Training

Sulabh has well-established infrastructure to provide capacity building and training and on-site demonstration of sanitation technologies and related areas with respect to household toilets of different designs and varying costs, toilet complexes for community use linked to biogas plants and effluent treatment, composting technology, and wastewater treatment through duckweed technology. Sulabh performs regular on-site training/ demonstration of these technologies for people from all walks of life for transfer of knowledge and technologies.

The experience gained over the years has inspired Sulabh to create trained manpower and professionals to handle the sector in a more effective manner in the 21st century. It has taken up this initiative to prepare national and international professionals, planners, elected representative, functionaries of the Central/state/local governments, private sector, NGOs, CBOs, educational institutions including universities, colleges and schools and all those engaged in the implementation of the sanitation programmes by augmenting their capacities through workshops, and training programmes, enablingthem to widen the sanitation coverage. Sulabh offers demand-driven programmes based on Training Needs Assessment (TNA) for specific target groups in specific areas.

Sulabh has developed appropriate curricula and modules for capacity building and training on various themes including project planning, implementation and monitoring of on-site sanitation for household use and community use, bioenergy systems, wastewater treatment, solid waste management systems, rainwater harvesting, health, hygiene, school sanitation, environmental protection and community participation. It works closely with various stakeholders and uses knowledge sharing and technology transfer instruments in innovative ways to reach larger audiences in the sector. This process in a continuous manner upscales sanitation performance. The modules developed by Sulabh for capacity development fits in perfectly in a holistic way to widen the water and sanitation coverage not only in India but also abroad, with suitable modification.

The academy mostly organises Training of Trainers (TOT) programmes so that these trained professionals further impart training locally for promotion of sanitation services. Such illustrations include Sulabh's capacity building programme on "Sanitation Technologies" in 14 African countries in collaboration with UN-Habitat. After completion of the training, the technologies have been implemented in these countries. Sulabh also conducted skill development programmes in Bangladesh and Ethiopia.

Internship Programmes

Sulabh provides internship programmes to national and international university students in water, sanitation, and the health and hygiene sector, as an integral part of their curriculum with practical dimensions. The students are oriented on sanitation technologies, bioenergy and wastewater treatment systems developed by Sulabh as well as its other initiatives, including women's empowerment, through interactive sessions, on-site demonstration and technical visits to different cities/towns in India. A number of students not only from Indian universities, colleges and the wards of various embassies, but also from African and Asian countries including Zambia, Nigeria, Cameroon, Ghana, Uganda, South Africa, Cambodia, Nepal and Japan have benefitted from these programmes.

Contact Programmes for Developed Countries

Developed countries like France, the US, Japan, Australia and Singapore also benefitted from the efforts of Sulabh in sanitation. It provides two to three months' placement programmes in the water, sanitation, and health and hygiene sector.

Human Resource Development

Sulabh has taken up various initiatives for human resource development (HRD). Regular training courses are organised for hospital nurses, doctors and technical officers of the Forest Research Institute, Dehradun; officers and trainees of the Human Settlement Management Institute (HSMI) of

HUDCO; NGOs; and many other departments of Central, state and local governments.

Training for Grassroots Functionaries

The academy organises skill development programmes for grassroots functionaries on "Sanitation and Housekeeping" periodically to upgrade their skills in the area of a clean environment and its maintenance. The objective is to build a cadre of professionalism among the functionaries with appropriate skills and techniques in sanitation, health and hygiene and in housekeeping services for efficient functioning in their respective trades.

Sulabh considers masons and skilled workers as an important tool for creation of demand and promote construction activities through social marketing. It organises practical training and workshops for these functionaries on how to construct toilets, particularly at the household level. The workshops organised by the academy in Bangladesh, Ethiopia and Bihar include masons' skill up gradation as part of the agenda.

The capacity building efforts through training and internship programmes had a significant effect in knowledge sharing and technology transfer to a number of professionals from national and international agencies in Uganda, Ghana, Cameroon, Nigeria, Mexico and Zambia.

Collaboration with UN-Habitat

UN-Habitat Nairobi, recognised Sulabh for its capacity development on environmental sanitation of professionals from the developing countries. Fourteen African countries including Ethiopia, Mozambique, Uganda, Cameroon, Burkina Faso, Kenya, Tanzania, Cote d'Ivoire, Mali, Ghana, Rwanda, Senegal, Nigeria and Zambia have benefited through capacity building on "Sanitation Technologies" in collaboration with UN-Habitat, as a part of the implementation of the Habitat Agenda in achieving the MDGs set for sustainable development in water, sanitation, health and hygiene sector and also a part of the worldwide global initiative to promote clean living and good health.

This capacity building programme provided an opportunity to the participant countries to exchange ideas on sanitation and discuss sanitation technologies and try them out in their own countries with adaptations.

This programme has been a step towards strengthening and promoting South-South cooperation for sharing experiences and exchanging ideas on appropriate technologies. The ambassadors of Ethiopia and Kenya in India felt a need for technological exchange for the common good of the peoples of India and Africa and urged getting these new techniques to improve sanitation facilities in their respective regions.

South Asian Countries

Several South Asian countries including Nepal, Sri Lanka, Bhutan, Cambodia, Bangladesh and Afghanistan are also implementing/starting implement programmes to address the respective country's sanitation issues. The academy has initiated a health and hygiene awareness programme concomitant with toilet construction at the five sites of construction in Kabul under the Government of India's relief and rehabilitation package for the war-torn nation, which included one hospital and four marketplaces with adjoining slums. The municipal officials and engineers working in the sanitation sector were trained and their capacities were enhanced so as to understand the various issues of sanitation. The rehabilitation package also includes a baseline survey on WASH, an awareness campaign for promotion of better hygiene practices covering schools, colleges and other educational institutions, and advocacy of safe drinking water, appropriate sanitation and usage of community toilets constructed under the programme.

With Support from WHO

The academy has not only been working closely with UN-Habitat, it has also made significant contribution to bridging the sanitation gap with WHO and UNICEF through projects and studies. Some of the significant projects done with the support of WHO include the Delhi Healthy Urban Project (DHUP), a pilot initiative for implementing WHO's Healthy City Programme in Delhi; the "Preparedness of Rural Health Centres on Water, Environmental Sanitation and Infrastructure Management Services in the Disaster-Prone Areas of India" project; and fact sheets on Water and Environmental Sanitation in Urban India for WHO Water Day.

The DHUP pilot project has contributed in providing a new paradigm shift in the overall governance process for promoting sustainable city development. The pilot project has enabled establishing a change with WHO's public health initiative of healthy Cities Programme (HCP) wherein the focus of governance is centred on health, which becomes an integral component of city planning though innovative strategies for settlement management and development with equitable economy, environment and social values. Similarly, the WHO PHC Study Project contributed to promoting an effective, efficient and sustainable healthcare delivery system in the study areas, and also brought about a proven change in the functioning process of the rural health centres. These projects became models for replication in similar habitats.

In Association with UNICEF

Sulabh, through its Regional Centre in Patna and in association with UNICEF and the government of Bihar provided capacity building and training, particularly for the grassroots workers to support the scaling up of the Total Sanitation Campaign and the Swajaldhara programme, a government-launched reform in the water supply and sanitation sector to emphasise awareness generation for creating demand in rural areas. The Lal Ganj and Hazipur blocks of Vaishali district, Bihar, were chosen for demand generation of sanitation and safe handling of drinking water among the rural population. The block coordinators and panchayat coordinators were trained along with assured delivery of sanitary materials to the rural people with appropriate technology in order to provide safe sanitation in the least possible time. Masons were also trained for creation of demand and construction activities. This project was a good example of strong partnership amongst NGOs, government bodies and international agencies focusing on unified goals. On the initiative of UNICEF Uganda, efforts are on the way for the academy to promote appropriate sanitation with biogas facilities in Kampala and Karamoja.

For Republic of Mozambique

Sulabh developed social and technical guidelines on Health, Hygiene and Sanitation Education for the Republic of Mozambique, which was aimed at implementing their rural sanitation programme including health and hygiene and provides sanitary technological options to the beneficiaries to choose as per their needs, choice and financial capacity. The main purpose was to improve the health of the rural population by introducing good hygiene and sanitation practices within households and giving them access to protected water supply and adequate sanitation. The guidelines dealt in detail with the social and technical issues of rural sanitation and appropriately set objectives for enhancing the awareness levels, promoting behavioural change, creating a network of stakeholders and sensitising the civic bodies in achieving the goal. They were designed for use of the implementing agencies and also for assisting the local authorities in rural sanitation development with appropriate training programmes covering social, technical and administrative issues.

Royal Government of the Netherlands

At the request of HUDCO, the academy carried out an evaluation study of low-cost sanitation programmes in four towns, namely, Balghat, Dewas, Durg and Sarni of Madhya Pradesh. The Human Settlement Management Institute (HSMI) of HUDCO, in collaboration with the Institute of Housing and Urban Development Studies (IHS), Rotterdam, took up a Government of Netherlands-assisted collaborative project on "Capacity Building for the Urban Environment: A Comparative Research, Training and Experience Exchange". The experiences obtained through the research study on the operational strategies of best practices for urban environmental management were presented in Habitat II, the second UN conference held at Istanbul in June 1996.

Waste consultants from the Netherlands sought to prepare a document on methods of household human excreta collection from dry bucket privies in various towns in China, Ghana, India, Tanzania and the Netherlands. The study for India was entrusted to the academy. The case illustration from India was related to scavengers who collect and dispose of human waste in Ghaziabad town, their internal organisation, socio-economic relationships with the residents of the neighbourhood and their contribution to the town's sanitation system. The role of the local authority and privately employed scavengers and of private-sector organisations was distinguished in all the stages of human excreta collection and disposal. The study report was presented by Sulabh at the international workshop organised by Waste Consultants in Colombo, Sri Lanka.

Japan International Cooperation Agency (JICA)

The JICA awarded Sulabh the feasibility study and preparation of the Water Quality Management Plan for the Ganga in Varanasi city with an aim to reduce the pollution load on the river. The academy carried out a feasibility study under non-sewerage schemes for the city of Varanasi, focusing on a low-cost sanitation programme for slum communities to prevent open defecation and construction of new dhobi ghats and improvement of existing ones to reduce discharge of pollutants into the river. Other activities carried out were survey of slums and dhobi ghats, organising workshops on low-cost sanitation and dhobi ghats, public participation/public awareness(PP/PA) activities with stakeholders, focus group discussions (FGDs) with representatives of slum areas and preparation of the feasibility report, guidelines and a manual for low-cost sanitation and dhobi ghats.

World Bank

At the request of the World Bank, Sulabh carried out evaluation of the status of rural water supply in scarcity villages in seven states, viz, Andhra Pradesh, Bihar, Gujarat, Himachal Pradesh, Madhya Pradesh, Rajasthan and Uttar Pradesh.

Projects Completed and in Progress

Around 100 projects and studies relating to capacity building, water supply, and water conservation including rainwater harvesting, sewerage, sewage treatment, low-cost sanitation, biogas production from human and animal wastes, health and hygiene issues, and waste management, have been completed or are in progress by Sulabh which are sponsored/funded by the Central, state or local governments, public and private sector organisations, international institutions like UN-Habitat, WHO, UNICEF, UNDP, NGOs, universities and other related institutes. Indeed, capacity building and training is an integral part of most of the projects and studies undertaken by Sulabh.

Publications

Sulabh has brought out several publications. *Social Marketing of Sanitation* seeks to serve as the link between UN-Habitat and other agencies engaged in promoting socially and environmentally sustainable towns/cities and to provide shelter for the poor. The publication analyses the barriers in promoting sanitation and experiences in social marketing with case studies from Asia and Africa, and provides strategies and solutions. It is extremely useful for professionals engaged in improving the quality of life by promoting sanitation and is a guideline to policymakers, field workers and experts in the area of water and sanitation. A decade back, there was no literature and study material on sociology of sanitation. In the last couple of years, Sulabh has brought out several volumes. A few more are in progress on special themes of sanitation and the activities of the Sulabh Academy.

With the rise of organisations like Sulabh a new force has emerged in support of civil society. Along with administrative organisation we need the stream of communication to reach the civil society. Clear objectives and ideology has to be reached to common people. Good literature and research make this handy and instrumental to build a sound civil society. In this sense, publications, in the form of research papers, books and journals play an important role. The present society needs charismatic leaders like Bindeshwar Pathak to motivate people. His leadership with collective creativity can transform the society.

Social choice of Sulabh consists in measuring economic and social growth in terms of poverty reduction, education to all, environmental sanitation and especially eradication of all evil practices built around manual scavenging. This is the holistic approach and the publications intend to cut across the states and cultures. Such literature is with a vision, a vision of hope and destiny to multitude of people. Columbus was ambitious, his challenge of sailing off to his death turned out into a vision that has led the future generations into a tomorrow. This is the vision of Bindeshwar that the oppressed have a tomorrow that they get their rights and build a future.

It is said, kings, captains or modern politicians make headlines by winning wars or making peace. But there are people who miss the headlines but make history. Bindeshwar Pathak working to eradicate manual scavenging, open defecation, improve environmental sanitation and hygiene is close to solve a great social problem of sanitation; in the process, making a history which will be remembered much after everything is lost in the silence of time. The publications, and literature is them, bear witness to the road he trod with his vision; a vision Gandhiji had a century ago.

The Way Ahead

Sulabh has fulfilled its vision of becoming one of the world's leading knowledge hubs for facilitating appropriate, affordable, eco-friendly and culturally acceptable sanitation development, free from environmental pollution and bringing social transformation in achieving the sanitation target set for the MDG among the developing countries.

Examples of Institutional Growth

Sulabh International Social Service Organisation is taking steps to open a *Sulabh International University of Sanitation* that will help in bringing hygiene and sanitation related awareness among the youth and the general public at large. Students passing out of the university will work as missionaries of sanitation that will result in a clean and liveable environment.

The Sulabh International University of Sanitation will be committed to excellence in research and development in environmental science and engineering and will provide sustainable technological solutions to the environmental problems faced by governments, industries and the society as a whole, especially for the underprivileged in India.

A dream project of Dr Pathak, the University will also help the country to propagate the message of Mahatma Gandhi and Sulabh. The ripple of Swachhata initiated by Dr Pathak about four decades ago has become a big wave today. When it gets realised, it will be the first university of its kind in India. It will produce consultants and professionals to work in the field of development and public health, providing an in-depth understanding of how to deliver effective, modern, water supply, sanitation and other public health interventions in urban and rural areas in low-income and transitional economies. It will serve as an education and training resource centre for sanitation and environment management experts.

With the visionary ideas of Dr Pathak, the University will concentrate its efforts in the areas of research and development; provide public/private consultancy services as well as tertiary education. The University will be dedicated solely to training and increasing the capacity of our human resource to analyse, design and implement effectively the solutions that will help make not just India but the planet clean. It will have a strong focus on the development of practical and policy skills and will address the critical future challenges of climate change, population growth and urbanisation. Emphasis will be laid on technical interventions in water supply, sanitation and solid waste management.

The University will provide different courses for youth, consultants and professionals working in international development and public health sectors. These courses will train students in the essential skills and knowledge required to plan and implement, along with communities, water supply and sanitation projects and programmes worldwide, particularly in less developed countries. What will make it stand out will be its outreach to practitioners, using its knowledge base and applied research to develop the capacity of individuals and organisations throughout the world, promoting the integration of social, technical, economic, institutional and environmental activities as a prerequisite for development.

Chapter 10

SANITATION RESEARCH

Research is something basic and important to any discipline, not only to establish itself but also to grow and expand. In its march towards eradication of manual scavenging and open defecation, Sulabh has passed through several stages, inducting and testing different methods. In research, Dr Pathak has gone a step further, in application of Action Research and Participatory Research.

A lot of research has been taken up and also been completed in the area of sanitation. However, much of it focuses on water and environmental sanitation and related areas. Not much research has been done in the specific area of human excreta management; for it is not a very pleasant topic to study or discuss about. This very challenging area has been picked up by Dr Pathak in all his ventures through the different activities of Sulabh. To reach his goal and vision of empowering the scavengers, he has initiated a lot of research in the field of sanitation. Today, sanitation is very important not only to bring about awareness about the benefits of good sanitation but also the dangers of insanitation. Sanitation research also suggests new methods to improve and popularise sanitation measures.

In the past, government agencies have typically built sanitation infrastructure, but sanitation professionals are now concentrating on helping people to improve their own sanitation and to change their behaviour. Improved sanitation has significant impacts not only on health, but on social and economic development, particularly in developing countries. The health sector has a strong role to play in improving sanitation in developing countries through policy development and the implementation of sanitation programmes.

Adequate sanitation, together with good hygiene and safe water, are fundamental to good health and to social and economic development. Improvement in one or more of these three components of good health can substantially reduce the rates of mortality and the severity of various diseases and improves the quality of life of a huge section of the population, particularly children, in developing countries. Sanitation is the safe disposal of human excreta. The phrase "safe disposal" implies not only that people must excrete hygienically but also that their excreta must be contained or treated to avoid adverse effect to their health or that of other people.

The diseases associated with poor sanitation are particularly correlated with poverty and infancy and alone account for about 10 per cent of the global burden of disease. At any given time, close to half of the urban populations of Africa, Asia and Latin America have a disease associated with poor sanitation, hygiene and water. Of human excreta, faeces are the most dangerous to health (Hotez 2007). Diarrhoeal diseases are the most important of the faeco-oral diseases globally; causing around 2.5 million deaths annually, many of them among unde-five children in developing countries.

Systematic reviews suggest that improved sanitation can reduce rates of diarrhoeal diseases by 37 per cent. The studies conclude that diarrhoeal disease rates could be substantially decreased by interventions designed to improve the sanitary and general living conditions of households. Further, observational studies of infants' faeces disposal practices highlight the importance of the safe management of both adults' and infants' faeces.

Neglected tropical diseases, that do not result in mortality, cause substantial Disability-Adjusted Life Year (DALY) losses in developing countries (Hotez 2007). Many of these diseases have a faeco-oral transmission pathway. Thus, improved sanitation could contribute significantly to a sustained reduction in the prevalence of many of these diseases. Unfortunately, the current policy focus in most parts of the world is on treatment by medication, rather than good sanitation system.

With 4.2 million deaths each year (1.6 million among children under five years), acute respiratory infections are the leading cause of mortality in developing countries. Although sanitation is not directly linked to all acute respiratory infections, studies report that 26 per cent of acute lower respiratory infections among malnourished children may have been due to episodes of diarrhoea. Thus, sanitation could be a powerful intervention against acute respiratory infections. Poor sanitation, hygiene, and lack of clean water are responsible for about 50 per cent of childhood and maternal underweight status, primarily through the synergy between diarrhoeal diseases and undernutrition, whereby exposure to one increases vulnerability in the other.

In addition to its impact on health, improved sanitation generates both social and economic benefits. Householders understand these wider benefits but scientists have only recently begun to study individuals' motivations for improving sanitation and changing sanitation behaviour. While the main goal of agencies' sanitation programming is to improve health, householders rarely adopt and use toilets for health-related reasons. Instead, the main motivations for sanitation adoption and use include the desire for privacy and to avoid embarrassment, wanting to be modern, the desire for convenience and to avoid the discomforts or dangers of the bush, and wanting social acceptance or status. Furthermore, for women, the provision of household sanitation reduces the risk of rape and/or attack experienced when going to public latrines or the bush to defecate, and for girls, the provision of school sanitation facilities means that they are less likely to miss school by staying at home during menstruation (Mara 2010).

The economic benefits of improved sanitation include lower health system costs, fewer days lost at work or at school through illness or through caring for an ill relative, and convenience time savings. In total, the prevention of sanitation, and water-related diseases could save some $7 billion per year in health system costs; the value of deaths averted, based on discounted future earnings, adds another $3.6 billion per year (Hutton 2004). Furthermore, in much of the developing world, at any time, around half the hospital beds are occupied by people with diarrhoeal diseases.

Currently, some 2.6 billion people lack access to improved sanitation, two-thirds of whom live in Asia and sub-Saharan Africa; 1.2 billion lack even an unimproved sanitation facility and must defecate in the open, of whom more than half live in India. Regional disparities in sanitation coverage are huge (WHO). Whereas 99 per cent of people living in industrialised countries have access to improved sanitation, in developing countries only 53 per cent have such access. In developing countries, urban sanitation coverage is 71 per cent while rural coverage is 39 per cent. Consequently, the majority of people lacking sanitation live in rural areas; this balance will shift rapidly as urbanisation increases. However, over the past two decades, provision of improved sanitation has barely kept pace with increasing populations while most other social services, including water supply, have outpaced population growth (Mara 2010).

Evolution of Toilet

We have only fragmentary information on the subject of toilets as it is a private secluded place to help the body relieve its waste. A brief history of toilets is presented in Chapter 7 as reported in different parts of the world. Sitting toilets in human history appeared quite early. In the remains of the Harappan civilisation in India, at a place called Lothal (62 kilometres from Ahmedabad in Western India) and in the year 2500 BCE, people had water-supplied toilets in each house which were linked with drains covered with burnt clay bricks. To facilitate operation and maintenance, it had man-hole covers and chambers. It was the finest form of sanitary engineering. But with the decline of the Indus Valley Civilisation, the science of sanitary engineering disappeared from India. In later years, the toilets in India remained primitive and open defecation became rampant (Pathak 1995).

Archaeological excavations confirm the existence of sitting toilets also in Egypt (2100 BCE). Though we have been able to mechanise the working of these toilets, the form and basic format of the toilet system remains the same. In Rome, public baths-cum-toilets were also well-developed. There were holes in the floor and beneath was flowing water. When the Romans travelled, they constructed toilets for their use. The pans were key-hole type so that the liquid and solid wastes were separated at the origin and disposal became easier. Excavations in Sri Lanka and Thailand too have brought out a contraption in which urine was separated and allowed to flow while the other portion was used at the same time for defecation.

Historical evidence exists that the Greeks relieved themselves out of the house. There was no shyness in using the toilet. It was frequent to see at dinner parties in Rome, slaves bringing in urine pots made of silver; members of the royalty used them but continued the play at the same time. Whatever little information is available about the history of toilets in India, shows they were quite primitive. The practice of covering waste with earth continued till the Mughal era, when in the forts of Delhi and Agra, one can see remnants of such methods to dispose of human waste (Ibid).

It was also popular in those days to emphasise the medicinal values of human waste. Urine was supposed to have many therapeutic values. Some quacks even claimed that by study of urine, they could confidently say whether a young girl was a virgin or not. It was also widely believed that the dung of a donkey mixed with nightsoil removed black pustule or the urine of a eunuch could help make women fertile. For oral care, it was advised to relieve oneself on one's feet because the "divine liquid" gives the required cure. In ancient Indian writings, there are stories about the strength of wrestlers. If a wrestler defecates too much, he is relatively weak because he cannot digest all he eats. Similarly, a perfect saint has no need to defecate, for he eats as much as he can digest or he is able to digest all that he eats. So not to defecate was considered saintly while in other societies not to defecate was considered manly. Blown Bettelheim states that men of the Chaga tribe blocked their anus during the ceremony of attaining manhood and pretended as if they did not defecate at all. This was also one way of establishing superiority over women. The ancient Greeks, it is reported, had similar beliefs. Swallowing something and not eliminating it was considered a source of power and authority.

The period between 500– 1500 CE was a dark age from the point of view of human hygiene. It was an era of cesspools and human excreta all around. Rich houses and forts in India had protrusions in which defecation was done and the excrements fell into the open ground or the moat below. The forts of Jaisalmer in India and big old houses on the banks of rivers bear testimony to this fact. In Europe, it was an era of chamber pots, cesspools and close stools. The toilets protruded out of the castles and the excrement fell into the river or surrounding ditches.

In the absence of proper toilet facilities, people had to defecate and urinate wherever they could. Defecating on the road, open spaces, or just easing oneself in the river was very common. While the authorities were educating people to have private places for defecating, and getting it cleaned, in actual practice there was total disorder. Squalor and filth abounded in cities. The social reformers advised people where to defecate, how to defecate in privacy and the need to control themselves when in company. Children were taught not to touch human waste.

The rich used wool or hemp for ablution while the poor used grass, stone, sand or water, depending upon the country and weather conditions or social customs. Use of newspaper was also common. In India, it is very common to use water for ablution. However, the hand one uses varies in various parts of India. While in south India, people use the right hand for eating food, it is considered disgusting to use the same hand for ablution with water. So the left hand is used for sanitary purposes. In most parts of north India, however, no such sharp distinction exists.

In each society, from time to time, the government felt the need to provide public toilet facilities to those who could not afford to have individual toilets. Public toilets have a long history in a number of countries and most of them were constructed and managed by municipalities. But there was all-round disgust with their poor maintenance, vandalism and lack of basic facilities. As hygienic conditions in public toilets were bad, people preferred to defecate in the open. This was true in most countries.

In order to improve sanitary conditions, governments in various countries resorted to legal measures. In India the first Sanitation Bill was introduced in 1878. It tried to make construction of toilets compulsory even in the huts of Calcutta. The Bill even proposed construction of public toilets at the cost of neighbouring houses. The Government of India enacted another Sanitation Act in 1993. Under this Act, construction of a dry latrine and its manual cleaning was made an offence.

In the past, latrines were tucked away in attics to keep them away from the noses and eyes of the family and society. In contrast, the 20th century has given pride of place to the toilet in the home. They are more opulent, more spacious than at any time in the past. While the provision of a toilet in the house solved the household problem of cleanliness, the challenge remained as to how to dispose of human waste in cities. This was also solved when the sewer system was introduced. In 1970, realising that sewerage facilities would remain out of the reach of society at large, Sulabh International introduced a pioneering twin-pit, pour-flush latrine and human excreta-based biogas plants. This gives an appropriate solution to dispose of and recycle human waste into fertiliser, electricity and gas. The Sulabh experiment became a success story and the technology is now well established and has been successfully functioning for almost half a century and is financially sustainable. At the household level, the TPPF latrine based on the Sulabh model has also been a success.

Reasons for Slow Progress

For many years, national governments, aid agencies and charitable organisations have subsidised sewerage and toilet construction as a means to improve access. This approach has resulted in slow progress for two main reasons. First, the programmes have tended to benefit the few relatively well-off people who can understand the system and capture the subsidies, rather than reaching the more numerous poor people. Second, such programmes have built toilets that remain unused because they are technically or culturally considered inappropriate or because the householders have not been taught the benefits of using them. For example, in India, many toilets are used as firewood storage or goat sheds and a recent study showed that about 50 per cent of toilets built by a large government programme are not used for their intended purpose (Sanam 2007).

Even when appropriate toilets are promoted, their technical specifications frequently make them prohibitively expensive. Another reason for slow progress is that disposal of children's faeces, the most vulnerable to faeco-oral disease transmission, is neglected and under-researched. A recent literature review that analysed a wide range of disposal practices for children's faeces and the health gains that can result from them, noted that this whole topic is significantly neglected.

Further, sanitation is not an inherently attractive or photogenic subject. Before the declaration of the International Year of Sanitation in 2008, sanitation specialists had failed to persuade politicians, the media and other influential people of the importance of the subject. However, in 2008, there were many political events related to sanitation, notably regional sanitation conferences across the developing world that resulted in Regional Sanitation Declarations, which have moved sanitation up the political agenda.

Trends in Sanitation Issues

Recently, there has been a shift away from centrally planned provision of infrastructure towards demand-led approaches that create and serve people's motivation to improve their own sanitation. Although sound technological judgement about appropriate solutions remains essential, appropriate programming approaches are now more important and contribute most to the success of sanitation work. Some of the prominent approaches or innovations that apply to both rural and urban sanitation are mentioned here (Mara 2010).

Sanitation Marketing

Sanitation marketing uses a range of interventions to raise householders' demand for improved sanitation. The approach involves understanding householders' motivations and constraints regarding sanitation adoption and use. These are then used to develop both demand and supply side interventions to ensure that appropriate sanitation products and services are available to match the demand.

Community-Led Total Sanitation

Community-Led Total Sanitation (CLTS) is a communication-based approach that aims to achieve ODF status for whole communities rather than helping individual households to acquire toilets. CLTS was developed in Bangladesh and uses external facilitators and community volunteers to raise community awareness that open defecation contaminates the environment and the water and food ingested by householders. It encourages a cooperative and participatory approach towards ending open defecation and creating a clean, healthy, and hygienic environment from which everyone benefits (Kar 2008). CLTS has spread from South Asia to Africa and South America in the past 10 years and appears to be highly successful in certain communities. The success or failure of CLTS may relate to its cultural suitability and the degree to which it addresses supply-side constraints in sanitation adoption.

Community Health Clubs

Community health clubs aim to change sanitation and hygiene attitudes and behaviour through community activities. The approach has proved effective and also economical in districts of Zimbabwe where villagers were invited to weekly sessions where one health topic was debated and then action plans formulated. It is believed that if a strong community structure is developed and the norms of a community are altered, sanitation and hygiene behaviour are likely to improve.

Sanitation as a Business

Traditionally, sanitation has been regarded as a centrally provided service with little role for the creativity of business. However, the increased demand created by sanitation marketing, CLTS and community health clubs can be met by the development of a vibrant local private sector for producing, marketing and maintaining low-cost toilets. The local private sector can also be encouraged to become involved in pit-emptying, sale of safely composted human excreta as fertiliser, generation of methane from biogas toilets and the operation of public toilets. Sulabh is a classic example in this context.

Approaches Emphasising Low Cost

Many sanitation advocates now place the affordability of the toilets at the centre of the planning process. A common strategy is to encourage people to start with the simplest type of improved pit latrine and then to progress over time towards higher-specification and higher-cost toilets on the sanitation ladder. The critical and most cost-effective step on this ladder, for both health and social reasons, is the first step from open defecation to fixed-location defecation; the subsequent steps up the ladder may yield smaller incremental benefits.

Approaches Specific to Urban Sanitation

Most successful demand-led approaches have been developed in rural contexts. Urban sanitation is much more complex, mainly because of higher population densities, less coherent community structures and the absence of opportunities for open defecation. Urban sanitation must extend beyond the household acquisition of a toilet to a systems-based approach that covers the removal, transport and safe treatment or disposal of excreta.

For on-site urban sanitation systems, pit-emptying services are common in middle-income countries where householders can afford the cost, but less common in poorer countries. For off-site or centralised systems, simplified or condominial sewerage systems, in which sewers are placed inside housing blocks and then discharge into conventional sewers, if there are any nearby, or led to a simple local wastewater treatment plant, can provide the same level of service as conventional sewerage but at around one-third to half of the cost.

In densely populated low-income urban areas, community-managed sanitation blocks, used only by community members who pay a monthly fee for operation and maintenance, are an option. Public sanitation blocks that can be used by anyone, normally for a small fee per use, can be an acceptable alternative provided that they are well operated and maintained and have 24-hour access. And, in less densely populated low-income urban areas, on-site sanitation options of the types described for rural areas are often applicable.

The lack of national policies is a major constraint to success in sanitation. Governments in general and health ministries in particular cannot play their key roles as facilitators and regulators of sanitation without policies that support the transformation of national institutions into lead institutions for sanitation, that increase focus on household behaviours and community action; that promote demand creation, and that enable health systems to incorporate sanitation and hygiene. Other constraints to success in sanitation are population growth and increasingly high population densities in urban and peri-urban areas of developing countries. Furthermore, most of the people who lack improved sanitation live on less than $2 per day, which makes high-cost, high-technology sanitation solutions inappropriate (Cairncross 2006).

Although macro-economic analysis shows that sanitation generates economic benefit, the benefit does not necessarily accrue to the person who invests in the improved sanitation. So the economics at the household level remain a constraint to success in sanitation, many people are simply unable or unwilling to invest, given all the other competing demands on their money.

Sanitation is a complex topic, with links to health and to social and economic development. It affects many but is championed by few. From the analysis of the situation, three major strategies can achieve success in sanitation (Mara 2010):

The most important of these strategies is political leadership, which is manifested by establishing clear institutional responsibility and specific budget lines for sanitation, and by ensuring that public sector agencies working in health, in water resources and in utility services work together better. The regional sanitation conference declarations released during the International Year of Sanitation, in which many government ministers were personally involved, were an important step forward. In addition, the biennial global reports on sanitation and drinking water published by WHO and UNICEF contribute towards political leadership and aid effectiveness by publicising the sanitation work of both developing country governments and support agencies.

The second strategy is the shift from centralised supply-led infrastructure provision to decentralised, people-centred demand creation coupled with support to service providers to meet that demand. This strategy is transforming sanitation from a minor grant-based development sector into a major area of human economic activity and inherently addresses the problem of affordability, since people install whatever sanitation systems they can afford and subsequently upgrade them as economic circumstances permit.

The third strategy is the full involvement of the health sector in sanitation. The health sector has a powerful motivation for improving sanitation, and much strength to contribute to achieving this goal. The health sector now needs to reassert its commitment and leadership to help achieve a world in which everybody has access to adequate sanitation.

Sulabh Research Application

Surrounded by latrines and soap dispensers, sanitation charity founder Bindeshwar Pathak is most at home in the toilet, which he vows to build in every impoverished home in India. Affectionately known as India's "toilet guru", Pathak, inspired by Gandhiji, has spent more than four decades working to improve sanitation in a country where half of the population relieves itself in the open. His study and insights have led him to initiate innovative methods and technology in sanitation systems. All these have much to do with his research in sanitation.

Two-Pit Toilet Technology

Pathak has already constructed 1.3 million toilets for households using his cheap, two-pit technology. Such toilets use less than a gallon of water per flush compared to 2.6 gallons (10 litres) for conventional latrines and do not require connection to underground sewer lines, which are nonexistent in most villages. Pit toilets also eliminate the need for the degrading task of manually removing toilet waste.

Pathak is determined to banish the need for such manual scavengers, who often scoop out excrement with their hands into wicker baskets. Born and brought up in an upper-caste Brahmin family, Pathak recounted, when he was a 10 year-old boy, how he was made to consume cow dung and urine as part of a purification ritual after he touched a woman who used to clean latrines. Pathak's charity has also harnessed "biogas" produced from human waste which is used to generate electricity to power the charity's offices. The gas has also been bottled for use as fuel for cooking.

Sanitation and Technology

The full range of technical options for providing adequate basic sanitation is still not widely known nor are the characteristics of the different options well understood. In particular, there is little appreciation of the long-term financial, environmental and institutional implications of operating and maintaining the various sanitation systems. As a result, in many cases, communities and local governments are choosing technical options that, in the long term, are unaffordable and/or unsustainable.

Challenges arise from the wide range of options available and the differing environments and conditions to which each is suited. Experience shows that it is important to allow local involvement in the choice of solutions, but with a full grasp of the requirements of each option. The options include the ventilated improved pit toilet in all its variations, composting toilets, separation toilets, dehydration type toilets, on-site wet systems such as aqua privies and septic tanks, and a range of full waterborne systems.

The choice of technology is not only based on the technical aspects of each technology, but also on such factors as the permanence of the settlement, financial costs and affordability, design life, expectations and preferences, institutional capacity, the potential for job creation and environmental considerations. This guideline will present the different technical, and to some extent financial, properties of the various technology options which have proved to be viable for large-scale use. The variety of proprietary systems are not named nor addressed individually, but usually can be classified as a member of one of the generic categories of sanitation systems addressed within this guideline.

Construction Requirements

There are a number of approaches to and requirements for the construction of the physical sanitation facilities that are not related to a specific technology choice. The approach adopted can lead to increased community participation and ownership, the enhancement of job creation and skills development, and contribute to the long-term sustainability of the facility. However, the approach must not result in the construction of poor quality facilities that the households and communities find inferior or unacceptable. It is therefore important that no matter what technology is chosen, the construction be done in a way that both promotes community ownership and job creation, and is a high-quality product that people will be proud of and that will function effectively according to the design principles during its lifetime.

Sustainability of Sanitation Systems

The sustainability of a sanitation system is usually the most important consideration when selecting a specific technology option for a community. Sustainability refers not only to measures to minimise breakdowns and costs in the operation of a scheme, but also refers to measures taken to maximise its positive social impact while minimising any negative environmental impacts. Some of the key requirements for promoting sustainability of sanitation systems and their relationship to choice of technology are:

1. User education and participation in technology choice

It is imperative that representatives of the community who will benefit from the sanitation project be consulted and fully informed of the sanitation technology options that could be considered. The representatives must be part of the decision-making process, and should in turn inform the residents of the options and choice. It is the responsibility of the local authority to ensure that the necessary level of user education on the proper use, care and maintenance of the selected sanitation technology is provided; this will vary depending on the system to be installed.

2. Health and hygiene promotion

It is the responsibility of the local authority to ensure that a health awareness programme is implemented followed by an ongoing programme of health and hygiene promotion is established. Any programme must focus on the particular needs of the different communities, in line with the level of service to be developed. Factors to be addressed by a programme of sanitation health and hygiene promotion should be formulated following a comprehensive participatory process.

Operation and Maintenance Availability

Households are responsible for the operation and maintenance of the sanitation system components located in their own premise, but the municipality may provide support for undertaking bigger tasks such as emptying pit or septic tank, moving top structures or unblocking sewers. It is the responsibility of the local authority to ensure that all transport, treatment and disposal facilities and equipment for handling sanitation wastes are appropriate to local conditions and of sufficient capacity to deal with the wastes associated with the level of service to be provided. The operation and maintenance requirements of the transport, treatment and disposal facilities and equipment and all their associated costs must be planned for.

It is the responsibility of the local authority to ensure that the recurrent costs of the level of service to be developed are identified in full during the planning stage. Along with any user education programme, issues around cost recovery awareness and the implications of non-payment must be addressed on an ongoing basis; this in itself constitutes an operation and maintenance cost.

The selection of an appropriate technology from a range of possibilities is the key to the successful and sustainable operation of any facility. Choice of technology is often considered a simple process, but is usually quite complex requiring careful assessment of factors, consultation with the beneficiaries and the operating authority, and an understanding of the integration of factors affecting the sustainability of a system.

Unsanitary conditions and contaminated drinking water have adverse effects on both the health of the human population and the environment. Approximately 40 per cent of the world's population does not have access to improved sanitation. In addition to the indignity suffered by those lacking sanitation facilities, millions of people in the developing world die each year from diseases contracted through direct and indirect contact with pathogenic bacteria found in human excreta. Infectious diseases such as cholera, hepatitis, typhoid and diarrhoea are waterborne, and can be contracted from untreated wastewater discharged into water bodies. More than half of the world's rivers, lakes and coastal waters are seriously polluted from wastewater discharge. The cost of inadequate sanitation translates into significant economic, social and environmental burdens (Sulabhenvis 2018). As the world attempts to realise these goals, we must evaluate new technologies, identify research gaps and critically discuss ways forward.

Available Low-Cost Sanitation Technologies

Recent studies in sanitation identified several low-cost sanitation technologies. These excreta disposal systems offer different degrees of user convenience, protection against the spread of diseases and water demand for their operation. They can be classified in several ways. A basic classification is based on whether the waste is disposed of within the site or is transported somewhere else. Under this classification, the technology is either on-site or off-site.

On-site sanitation systems include those in which safe disposal of excreta takes place on or near the plot or site of the toilet. Systems included in this classification are overhung latrines, trench latrines, pit latrines, the Reed Odourless Earth Closet (ROEC), ventilated improved pit latrines (VIP), composting latrines, pour-flush latrines and septic tanks.

Off-site sanitation systems include those in which excreta is collected from the individual toilets and carried away from the plot to be disposed of. Vault and cartage and the bucket latrine are included in this category. Some of these systems involve the use of water and are therefore classified as wet systems. Others disallow the use of water, even for hygienic purposes, and are therefore classified as dry systems (McGill 2018).

Another way of classifying sanitation systems is through their application as either individual household sanitation technologies or community sanitation technologies. Systems that are classified as household sanitation systems include the pit latrine, pour-flush toilets, composting toilets, aqua-privies and septic tanks, which are built in individual houses. Systems such as bucket latrines, vault toilets with vacuum-cart collection, communal toilets and sewerage systems are classified as community sanitation facilities.

Studies of appropriate technology for water supply and sanitation under the World Bank International Drinking Water Supply and Sanitation Decade (1980–1990) defined several comparative criteria to introduce the putative performance of these technologies. The general criteria include: water supply service levels, soil condition requirements, cost, housing density, complementary investments, reuse potentials, environmental factors; self-help potential; and institutional constraints.

Recent studies on sanitation in developing countries identify some special requirements needed in addition to the general criteria identified above. Nimpuno (1984) emphasises operation, costs, construction, water requirements and urban adaptability as special considerations in the selection of sanitation technologies in developing countries. For existing low-income settlements without adequate sanitation facilities, it is of great importance that small-scale, even individual, household installations are chosen, so that in time the individual provisions can be linked up to form a network, and the systems can be upgraded gradually.

Recommended Sanitation Technology Options

UNICEF's Latrine Technology Manual, has given a list of recommended sanitation technology options (Nyarko, et. al. 2018).

Dry On-Plot Systems VIP Toilet

a. Fixed top structure–pit emptied

Waste drops into the pit where the organic material decomposes and excess liquids percolate into the surrounding soil. Natural airflow through the top structure and moving across the top of the vent pipe removes smells and vents gases from the pit into the atmosphere. A darkened interior is maintained, causing insects entering the pit to be attracted towards the light at the top of the vent pipe and trapped by the fly screen. A separate hand washing facility is required.

The VIP should be located to prevent ingress of storm water into pit, as well as to prevent the contamination of local groundwater that is used for drinking. The system cannot accept domestic wastewater, nor can it be installed inside the house. Ensure that there is access to the pit for mechanical pit-emptying equipment, and availability of facilities for sludge treatment and disposal. Repair or replace damaged or worn materials to ensure the proper functioning of the toilet.

b. Movable top structure–pit not emptied

Operational and institutional requirements are as for fixed top structure above. There should also be land available to dig a new pit and move the top structure when the pit is full.

Dry On-Plot System Ventilated Improved Double Pit (VIDP) Toilet

The principles of operation are the same as for the VIP toilet. One pit is used until filled to within about half a meter of the top. The pedestal and vent pipe holes are to be completely sealed before the other pit is used. The contents of the first pit are dug out after a period of at least two years, once the contents have become less harmful. The first pit can then be reused when the second pit is full, while the second pit is allowed to stand and be emptied after two to three years.

The operational and institutional requirements are similar to those for the VIP toilet, except that promotion of manual emptying by the householder is required, and the safe use of the decomposed waste as a soil conditioner on the plot is possible. A suitable disposal site for the sludge should be available close to the structure.

Dry On-Plot System Composting or Desiccating Toilets

Waste is deposited in the chamber below the pedestal. For composting toilets, dry absorbent organic material, such as wood ash, straw or vegetable matter is added after each use to absorb odours, control moisture and facilitate biological breakdown (composting). In desiccating toilets, the solid wastes dry out rapidly through enhanced airflow or with the help of additional dry material like wood or coal ash. In these cases the urine may be separated from the solids to improve the rate of drying of the faeces. It is also called urine diversion system (UDS) toilets. The urine is separated or diverted through the use of specially adapted pedestals. The urine may be collected and used as a fertiliser, or drained to a soak pit where it will seep into the soil. In desiccation systems, ventilation systems are often enhanced to facilitate the rapid evaporation of moisture.

Composting or desiccating toilets do not accept domestic wastewater. It is important to teach and train the householder how to operate the toilet properly by, for example, manual "turning" of compost and removal of composted or desiccated material when required. A suitable disposal site or area for the desiccated or composted dry wastes is required, usually a garden compost heap or a pit where it can be buried.

Wet On-Plot System Aqua-Privy Toilet with Soak-Away

After use, the toilet pan or pedestal may be flushed with 1–2 litres of water.

Some pans have a tipping flap at the bottom that holds a small amount of water, opening when flushed. This flap acts as a seal between the pedestal and the digester. The wastes from the pan drop into a digester directly underneath the toilet, or just offset from the toilet structure. An aqua-privy requires an initial filling of the digester with water for the effective digestion of wastes and to keep the end of the pedestal chute submerged, and thus forms a rough water seal between the pan and the digester contents. The solid portion of the waste partly decomposes within the digester, while the liquids are displaced with each use. The displaced liquids flow to a soak-away. The digester requires desludging from time to time (usually between one and three years, depending on the volume of the digester).

The aqua-privy is appropriate where a flush type latrine is desired but only small volumes of water are available, usually carried by hand from a street or yard tap. The system can also accept domestic wastewater provided the soak-away is sized accordingly. For proper operation of the system, ensure access to the digester cover by mechanical equipment for the emptying of digester waste. In addition, it is necessary to provide an acceptable subsoil drainage system for excess liquids and the availability of sludge treatment and disposal facilities within the proximity of the settlement.

Wet On-or-Off-Plot Systems Septic Tank and Soak-Away

Human wastes from the toilet are flushed into a septic tank that acts as a settling chamber for the solids. The liquid is retained in the septic tank for at least 24 hours, or maybe up to 10 days. Domestic wastewater may also be drained into the septic tank, or alternatively directly into the soak-away. In the septic tank, solids settle down to the bottom where they undergo biological digestion. The liquids pass out of the tank and into a subsoil drainage system (soak-away). Digested sludge gradually builds up in the tank and requires eventual removal by tanker.

The septic tank and soak-away system requires a reliable household water connection. Specific design criteria must be applied to the settlement tank and soak-away system. This option is applicable only in areas of low settlement density and where soils have a high ability to drain effluent away. For the optimal functioning of the system, ensure access for the emptying of tanks by vacuum tanker, and the availability of sludge treatment facilities.

Wet Off-Plot Systems Small Bore Solids-Free Sewer

The principles of operation here are the same as for the septic tank and soak-away, except that the liquid effluent is conveyed by a system of small-diameter pipes to a wastewater treatment system (which may be located close to the community, or linked to the municipal works via existing sewerage pipelines).

As for a septic tank and soak-away system, a reliable household water connection is needed. For optimal functioning, ensure access for emptying of the septic tank, and the availability of sludge treatment and disposal. Routine maintenance of the pipe network is essential.

Wet Off-Plot Systems Full or Conventional Waterborne Sewerage

(An in-house full-flush toilet connected to a sewer (pipe) network which drains to a wastewater treatment facility)

Waste from the toilet is flushed, using between 6 and 13 litres of water per flush, into the sewer system for removal to a central treatment facility. A clean water seal is maintained in the toilet pan after each flush. Domestic wastewater is also drained into the sewers. The sewer system may require pump stations if the topography is not suitable for gravity transport of all the sewerage within the communities. There are several types of wastewater treatment facilities that treat the wastes to a suitable quality prior to discharge into a stream or for reuse in municipal parks and gardens.

The operation of full or conventional waterborne sewerage requires a reliable and uninterrupted household water connection and spatially regular permanent settlements. Stringent design criteria must be applied throughout the sewerage network to ensure the uninterrupted flow of wastes to the treatment works. Skilled, organised and effective operation and maintenance capability is required for sewers and the full functioning of wastewater treatment facilities.

Wet Off-Plot System Conventional Waterborne System with Shallow Sewerage

Waste from the toilet, and usually also domestic wastewater, is flushed into a sewer system, with an option of using low-flush pedestals to reduce the amount of water that is flushed. The internal sewer network is laid at a shallow depth (1–1.5m) with a flatter gradient, within the property of homeowners rather than in the street reserve. Householders accept the responsibility for maintaining the sewers that run through their properties, and are supported by making accessible pipe-clearing rods which people are trained to use when required. The bulk sewers are as for conventional sewer systems, and the treatment of the wastes is as for conventional sewerage.

The conventional waterborne system with shallow sewerage requires a reliable and uninterrupted household water connection. The sewer lines can, however, be laid out in a less formal or spatially regular pattern, and are thus suitable for less formal or denser settlements. Less stringent design criteria may be applied, but organised and effective operation and maintenance capacity within the community is required. This can be delegated to residents for the on-site portion of the sewers. Significant user education and acceptance of shared management of the system is critical. Skilled, organised and effective operation and maintenance capability is required for the functioning of the bulk sewers and the wastewater treatment facilities.

In actual sanitation projects, one of the causes of their failure is the overemphasis on technological installations at the expense of behavioural considerations such as latrine usage and upkeep and general hygiene practice of the users. In most of these projects, the stated priorities or goals often promote installation of facilities or numerical targets. Project planners pay little attention to the types of technologies acceptable to a given community, or to hygiene education needed to support the chosen option. Under these circumstances, it is more than simply a technical or economical analysis of the approach of providing adequate sanitation facilities. There is an element of deep-rooted cultural values which needs to be responded to in the process.

Among the various options of low-cost sanitation systems mentioned above, a few have been used in some coastal and waterfront communities. These systems include both individual and community systems (McGill 2018).

a. Communal toilets

The most common approach used to solve sanitation problems in coastal communities is the provision of communal toilets. This option has been considered as the only feasible and realistic sanitation improvement in high-density low-income urban areas built on tidal mudflats. Communal toilets or public toilets consist of a number of cubicles built on more stable ground shared by community members.

In the provision of communal toilets, problems were caused by technical requirements and socio-cultural in-acceptability of the facility. The public toilets built were not used much and did not function properly because the collection tanks were flooded whenever it rained. Since users had to pay to use the facility, many children defecated over open drains instead. In several cases, poor maintenance resulted in the facilities being abandoned. In the cases where the communal latrine did not function well, people continued to use the sea for sanitation. Another problem is the poor proximity of the facility to the users. The residents preferred to have latrines inside their houses, rather than use communal facilities which were distant from their homes.

b. Collection of night soil

In communities where communal toilets were not acceptable, individual facilities were preferred. The problem with the provision of individual toilets is the limited options for safe disposal of human waste, especially for those houses that are built on areas with high groundwater level and those submerged in water. With these conditions, the most ideal means is to collect the human waste and transport it to another site for treatment or disposal.

In China, human excreta was seen as a valuable source of fertiliser for centuries. Hence, excreta are still collected in buckets for reuse. Collection of night soil has been the traditional practice in the fishing village. In this village, due to the absence of running water and a sewer system, the traditional *matong*, wooden portable chamber pot, continues to be used to collect human waste. An integral part of the early morning scenes are the *matong* set by the doorstep of each household for collection.

This practice of collecting human waste demands the acceptability of waste handling among the community members. In communities where the sight and handling of excreta is rejected, the waste has to be disposed of quickly. In some communities, especially those located on marshlands, other options for sanitary excreta disposal have been tried, but due to the high groundwater level, problems occurred with the use of such systems. Sanitation technologies used in these communities involve on-site treatment such as the septic tanks.

c. Septic tanks

Septic tanks are comprised of a sealed tank having both an inlet and an outlet into which excreta is flushed from a conventional cistern flush toilet or a pour-flush toilet. The tank acts as a settlement unit in which solids settle down due to gravity. The solids undergo a process of anaerobic decomposition which results in the production of water, gases, sludge and a layer of floating scum. In settlements built on low-lying areas, septic tanks do not function properly since the subsoil structure is too impermeable for the leaching of the septic tank effluent. Being unable to permeate the soil, the effluent, still laden with pathogens, flows across the ground, thereby hastening the spread of disease and not allaying it. Low permeability is a problem for the subsurface effluent disposal system. Eventually, the surrounding soil will cease to absorb the effluent thereby causing failure in treating the effluent.

Another problem with the use of this system is the requirement for an in-house connection of water supply for the system to operate. In communities where the water supply is not accessible, this system is not feasible. But due to the limited water supply, saltwater from the sea was used instead. The use of salt water to flush latrines retards decomposition and soak away of sewage, hence making the system operate ineffectively.

With high groundwater level seen as a problem in the use of on-site systems, some sanitation technologies were designed for this condition. However, non-technical problems, such as implementation and usage problems, were identified with the use of such systems, as in the case of the cesspools.

d. Cesspools

The cesspool consists of concrete rings which are about 0.75 metre in diameter with small holes in the rings. The rings are stacked below the latrine floor and fixed above it is a ceramic toilet bowl with or without a water trap. The floor of the latrine is generally raised above the floor level to avoid overflow during the rains. The cesspool is widely accepted because of its ease of construction and low cost. The construction materials are available in prefabricated form and construction at the site takes only a few hours, and no special skills are required. Most of the households construct their own latrines.

The cesspool was designed for areas with a high groundwater level. It was launched as a low-cost solution for urban areas in Thailand in the early 1970s. The original design of the cesspool consists of two interconnected tanks: the first tank for settling solids, the second tank, the soakage, where purified effluent flows. The first tank has a vent pipe, since most of the biogas is produced here, and an inlet for the waste, a squatting plate with a water seal. Both tanks are made of concrete rings; the first one has a tight bottom, the second one has no floor. This design requires regular removal of sludge, but the system still percolates a considerable quantity of unstabilised organic matter and pathogens into the groundwater.

This system operates well in sites with a high groundwater level. The high groundwater level keeps the second tank filled with fluids, allowing secondary treatment of effluent before it soaks away. If there is low groundwater level, the overflowing fluids from the first tank will soak away into the ground before any secondary treatment takes place, resulting in considerable pollution. Despite the wide application and acceptance of the technology, sanitation and environmental problems occur in the actual installations of the cesspool. Other problems associated with simplified cesspools are improper construction of the tanks and absence of the vent pipe. Furthermore, dislodging of the built cesspool is a problem since most of the latrines do not have an off-set vault and no manhole is provided. Latrine owners would abandon it once it is full or would break the vault and replace it with a new one.

e. Composting toilets

In swampy and flood-prone areas, composting toilets are used and are considered to function well in such ground conditions. This system is a family unit consisting of two above-ground tanks for dry and anaerobic composting. The two watertight tanks serve by turns as receptacles for defecation and composting. Unlike other composting toilets, the composting process takes place without aeration or turning over of the material. Ashes are added to the fresh excreta to achieve suitable carbon-nitrogen ratio, to eliminate odour and prevent the presence of flies. The system also involves the separation of urine treatment to reduce acidity and humidity, and to lower the nitrogen content of the waste pile. The urine is placed in another container with either water or soil and ashes, which after a few days can be used as garden fertiliser.

The main advantages of this system are the non-disposal of waste into the ground and the possibility of building the vault above the ground, despite the adverse ground conditions. However, the success of this system relies on a high degree of user care and attention, where careful use and maintenance of the composting toilet is not difficult.

The problem with the low-cost options described earlier is that they are demanding from the user's point of view. In most cases, the users have to be involved in the maintenance and operation of the systems. In the earlier attempt to provide sanitation facilities for coastal and waterfront communities, the sewerage system was considered technically appropriate. Also, since it provides the 'flush and forget comfort' to the user, this approach supposedly simplifies the solution. However, the actual application of the sewerage system is found to be not at all feasible in all cases.

f. Sewerage system

The sewerage system is considered technically feasible in coastal and waterfront communities, but due to high capital requirements, and a large amount of water supply to operate the system, this option will remain inappropriate. Sewage is collected into a central tank and from there pumped into the municipal sewerage system. It is exceedingly doubtful whether the sewerage scheme will ever be made to work successfully.

All sanitation technologies can be described as being either "wet" or "dry": Wet technologies require water to flush faeces. Most urban sanitation in India is "wet", involving some form of flush toilet connected to a leach pit, septic tank or sewer. Dry technologies do not use water for flushing. They include a range of different types of traditional pit latrines, ventilated improved pits, as well as contemporary designs that promote the safe reuse of excreta.

Low-Cost Sanitation Methods

Low-cost sanitation options have significantly improved, especially for the reuse of sewage for agriculture or aquaculture. The scheme for Low Cost Sanitation for Liberation of Scavengers started from 1970 under the aegis of Sulabh. The objective of the scheme is to convert or construct low-cost sanitation units through sanitary two-pit, pour-flush latrines with superstructures and appropriate variation to suit local conditions and construct new latrines where households have no latrines and follow the practice of defecating in the open in urban areas. This would improve overall sanitation in the towns. The scheme also encourages adoption of new technologies like biodigesters and ecosan toilets by the implementing agencies.

Sulabh Shauchalaya—Low-Cost Sanitation

The Sulabh Shauchalaya is the logical outcome of the study, work and research of Dr Bindeshwar Pathak in his efforts to improve sanitation methods and to eradicate manual scavenging and open defecation. The Sulabh flush compost toilet is eco-friendly, technically appropriate, socio-culturally acceptable and economically affordable. It is an indigenous technology and the toilet can easily be constructed by local labour and materials. It provides health benefits by safe disposal of human excreta on-site. It consists of a pan with a steep slope of 25°—28°, specially designed, trap with 20 mm water seal requiring only 1 to 1.5 litres of water for flushing, thus helping conserve water. It does not need scavengers to clean the pits (Sulabhenvis 2018). There are two pits of varying size and capacity, depending on the number of users. The capacity of each pit is normally designed for the usage of three years. Both pits are used alternately. When one pit is full, the incoming excreta is diverted into the second pit. In about two years, the sludge gets digested and is almost dry and pathogen-free, thus safe for handling as manure. Digested sludge is odourless and is a good manure and soil-conditioner. It can be dug out easily and used for agricultural purposes. The cost of emptying the pit can be met partially from the cost of manure made available. The Sulabh toilet can also be constructed on the upper floors of buildings. It has a high potential for upgradation, and can later be easily connected to sewers when introduced in the area. Sulabh has so far constructed over a million individual household toilets in different parts of the country.

Operation and maintenance of a Sulabh flush compost toilet is very easy and simple. Before use, wet the pan by pouring only a little quantity of water. After defecation, pour 1.5 –2 litres of water in the pan for flushing. Pour about half a litre of water in the pan after urination. The pan should be cleaned once a day with a brush or a broom and with soap powder periodically. One of the pits is to be used at a time by plugging the drain of the other pit. Kitchen and bathroom wastewater or rainwater should not be allowed to enter the pits. Other solid wastes like kitchen waste, rags, cotton, sweepings, etc., should not be thrown in the pan, this could block the toilet. When the first pit in use is full, the flow should be diverted to the second pit and the filled up pit should be desludged after a 1.5 to two-year rest period. The first pit can then be put to reuse, when the second pit fills up.

To check pollution of drinking water sources, the pits in fine soils should be located at a minimum distance of 3 metres from open wells and shallow hand pumps, provided the groundwater table throughout the year is 2 metres or more below the bottom of the pit. If the water table is higher, the distance should be increased to 10 metres. In coarser soils, the same safe distances can be maintained by providing a 500-mm-thick sand envelope of 0.2 mm sand all around the pit and sealing the pit bottom with some impervious material like puddled clay, a polythene sheet, lean cement concrete or cement stabilised soil.

Normally, bacteria do not move beyond 3 metres horizontally in homogeneous soil and vertically they do not permeate more than 1 metre; however there can be marginal deviations depending upon the types and compaction of the soil. It may be noted that chances of groundwater contamination occur due to higher hydraulic load. Since in this system the hydraulic load is only 1.5–2 litres per use, there is no chance of groundwater contamination.

The cost of Sulabh flush composting toilets varies widely to suit people of every economic stratum. The cost ranges from ₹1,000 to 10,000 per unit. It depends upon the materials of construction of pits and the seat as well as the superstructure. The pits can be constructed with bricks or any locally available materials like stones, logs, burnt clay rings, concrete rings or even used coal-tar drums. The quality of the superstructure ranges from simple gunny bag sheets or thatches; to well-finished tiles, with RCC roof, doors, washbasin and other facilities. Cost also varies due to size and capacity of the pits, varying from two years' to 20 years' capacity for each pit. Keeping the basic design unchanged, Sulabh has a number of such toilet models for demonstration.

Manure from Human Excreta

One of the major difficulties in the use of human excreta as manure is the presence of bacterial and other pathogens. Human excreta contains a full spectrum of pathogens causing various infections. It should be free from pathogens before being used as manure. Another problem is psychological and religious taboos associated with it. The studies carried out by Sulabh have revealed that the content of a Sulabh toilet pit is almost free from pathogens when taken out after two years of resting. To make it completely pathogen-free, digested sludge is sun-dried for two to three weeks. During drying of sludge, big lumps are formed, making it difficult to mix into soil homogeneously. Sulabh developed a technology to granulate such dried lumps into small graded granules which look like processed tea leaves. Before granulating, it is processed in a ball mill to break it into small pieces. Then it is passed through the mass mixer where the moisture content of the manure is regulated by adding water. Such manure has a good percentage of plant nutrients. Besides, it increases humus and water holding capacity of the soil. Sulabh has carried out experiments to monitor its manurial effects on different vegetables and flowering plants. In all the cases tested, the effect of the manure on the growth of plants was very encouraging (Sulabhenvis 2018).

Compared to different sanitation systems available, the Sulabh system is innovative in several aspects. The technology is unique, as it requires very little water for cleaning and flushing, the cost of construction is low, and it requires very little space. Sulabh system is also cost effective as it guarantees maintenance of the facility for five years for private latrines and 30 years for public ones.

Sulabh International offers both private household latrines and public latrines. Combining action with education, Sulabh offers technological training programmes involving people in the construction of their own latrines, or those of their neighbours. Some of these training sessions are targeted specifically at adolescents.

The installation of public latrines begins with an invitation from a local authority or community-based organisation. Sulabh then surveys the area in order to identify the best site. The criteria involved in the site selection include availability of land (typically, it is a municipal park or government-owned vacant lot), convenience and accessibility of the site for the users, and the degree of need in the community. Similar to the private latrine approach, Sulabh installs the public latrines on-site through a participatory process which involves training for local youths, and then sets up a crew to maintain the latrines. Educating the community about the importance of using the latrines, and the implication for both their personal health and the urban environment, is an important part of latrine operations. Sulabh retrains those people formerly working as scavengers so that they may undertake new and more dignified vocations.

Sulabh's success is indicated by its spread to other areas. Impressed by its initial operations, the World Bank funded projects in five other states in the country. During its 20-year history, Sulabh International has built 6,60,000 private latrines and about 2,500 public latrine complexes in 584 towns in 18 states of India. With UN support, the latrine design, now slightly modified, was successfully constructed in 19 countries in Asia, Africa and Latin America. Most cities in developing countries can benefit from this innovation as they have large portions of populations that are cut off from formal services, while their public agencies are unable to afford more conventional systems. Sulabh provides a low-cost and self-help solution to residents who are increasingly forced to inhabit environmentally vulnerable areas.

Although the general advantages of Sulabh toilets are already stated earlier, the particular benefits of Sulabh toilets can be stated as:

- Hygienically and technically appropriate, and socio-culturally acceptable
- Affordable and easy to construct with locally available materials
- Design and specifications can be modified to suit householder's needs and affordability
- Eliminates mosquito, insect and fly breeding
- Can be constructed in different physical, geological and hydro-geological conditions
- Free from health hazards and does not pollute surface or groundwater, if proper precautions and safeguards are taken during construction
- Can be located within the premises as it is free from foul smell and fly/mosquito nuisance etc.
- Can be constructed on upper floors of houses
- Pits are generally designed for three-year desludging intervals, but if desired, it can be designed for longer periods or it can be reduced even to two years
- Maintenance is easy, simple and costs very little.
- Needs only 1 to 1.5 litres of water for flushing, while a conventional flush toilet needs 12 to 14 litres of water.

- Needs less space than a septic tank toilet system
- Does not need scavengers for cleaning the pits or disposal of sludge. This can be done by the householder
- Makes available rich fertiliser and soil conditioner.
- Can be easily connected to sewers when introduced in the area
- A low-volume flushing cistern can be attached to avoid pour flushing

Sulabh flush compost toilet does not cause water pollution. Depending on the availability of space, the shape of pits may be designed. It may be rectangular, circular or linear in shape. It fulfils all the seven conditions of a sanitary latrine laid down by the WHO (Wagner 1958: 39).

1. The surface soil should not be contaminated.
2. There should be no contamination of groundwater that may enter springs or wells.
3. There should be no contamination of surface water.
4. Excreta should not be accessible to flies or animals.
5. There should be no handling of fresh excreta; or when this is indispensable, it should be kept to a strict minimum.
6. There should be freedom from odours or unsightly conditions.
7. The method used should be simple, and inexpensive in construction and operation.

Special Features of Sulabh Technology Eco-Friendly Technology

The Sulabh technology is socially acceptable, economically affordable, and technologically appropriate and does not require scavengers to clean the pits and has been implemented in more than 1.2 million houses all over India, liberating over a million scavengers.

Sulabh Public Toilet Complexes

Construction and maintenance of public toilets at public places and in slums on "pay-and-use" basis is a landmark of Sulabh in the field of sanitation. It is an important activity of Sulabh in the field of community health and hygiene and environmental sanitation. So far, it has constructed or is maintaining over 8,000 such public toilet complexes in different parts of the country, where maintenance is provided round the clock. These complexes are located at public places like bus stands, hospitals, markets, etc. and in the slums.

For the construction, operation and maintenance of these complexes, the organisation plays the role of a catalyst and a partner between the official agencies and the users of the toilet complexes. Children and indigent persons are exempted from such charge. This is a unique example of partnership of local authorities, an NGO and the community.

Biogas from Public Toilets

Recycling and use of human excreta for biogas generation is an important way to get rid of health hazards from human excreta, besides promoting use of biogas for cooking, lighting and electricity generation. Biogas digesters, when attached to public toilet complexes, recycle human waste into biogas. The biogas from public toilets has multiple benefits improving sanitation, community health and hygiene, and the environment and providing dignity to women and girls, in addition to using biogas for different purposes. Production of biogas from public toilets and recycling and reuse of effluent through a simple and convenient method is major breakthrough in the field of sanitation and community health.

Sulabh Effluent Treatment (SET) System

After a series of experiments, a simple and convenient technology, the Sulabh Effluent Treatment (SET), was invented to further treat the effluent of the biogas plant. The technology is based on sedimentation and filtration of effluent through sand, an aeration tank and activated charcoal followed by exposure to ultraviolet rays. The treated effluent is colourless, odourless and pathogen-free with biochemical oxygen demand less than 10 mg per litre and is safe for discharge into any water body without causing pollution. It can also be used for cleaning of floors of public toilets in water-scarce areas.

Sulabh Technology Reduces Greenhouse Gas Effect

In addition to conserving and reusing water the system has an additional in-built advantage of reducing a greenhouse gas effect arising out of carbon dioxide and methane production due to degradation of human waste. Due to the design of the leach pit of the Sulabh toilet in households, the carbon dioxide produced is diffused in the soil through honey combs and does not escape into the atmosphere. Because of anaerobic digestion of human waste during biogas production, methane is produced that is used for different purposes. It is not left to escape into the atmosphere. Thus, both these technologies help in reducing the greenhouse effect and thus improving the environment.

Financial Viability of the Projects

Since human excreta is considered the most hated object in society, it was difficult for anyone to conceive of the financial viability of a project related to its disposal. However, Sulabh has made it financially viable. The cost of construction is met by the local body. The maintenance of toilet blocks and day-to-day expenses is met from the charging the users. Sulabh does not depend on external agencies for finances and meets all its financial obligations through raising internal resources. All the toilet complexes are not self-sustaining, particularly those located in slums and less developed areas. The maintenance of such toilet complexes is cross-subsidised from the income generated from toilet complexes in busy and developed areas.

Elimination of Social Stigma and Psychological Taboo

Earlier, there was social stigma and psychological taboo attached to handling of human excreta. It could also be due to the fact that only people of the lowest economic and social strata were supposed to be associated with this job. Due to the efforts of Sulabh, and financial viability, people from higher social status now compete to take up sanitation projects without psychological reservations.

The task of total sanitation coverage in any country can be fulfilled only through close co-operation between local government and the community or local NGOs involved with such work. Neither government nor NGOs/CBOs can fulfil the task alone as the problem requires technical as well as social aspects to be tackled. Therefore, it needs a holistic effort to overcome the problem. The strategy developed by Sulabh can easily be replicated in other developing countries to improve the sanitation status and quality of life.

Sulabh International in collaboration with UN-Habitat Nairobi, has trained professionals from 14 African countries for capacity development towards achieving the MDG for sustainable development in water and sanitation. Sulabh technologies have received worldwide recognition. Sulabh has signed an MoU with Ethiopia to provide its expertise to improve sanitation, health and hygiene. It has trained more than 50,000 people to work in the construction and maintenance of community toilets in India.

Sulabh Rural Sanitation

Sulabh has taken up a programme for rural sanitation in 350 districts of the country, where volunteers have been trained in the technology, methodology implementation and follow-up work. Masons have been trained. Toilet pans and water seals have been made available at various centres so that people of the area can have the facility to construct toilets to suit their income and choice.

A campaign has been launched to make people in rural areas aware of the fact that they should not go barefoot for open defecation; should put soil on human excreta after defecation so that flies do not sit on excreta and, in turn, on food, which is the main cause of diarrhoea, dysentery and cholera. Literature has been published in 18 languages of the country and distributed by social workers. Mass communication workers perform dramas, mono acts and hold painting competitions in schools to promote awareness. A full-fledged two-hour feature film has been made to make the people aware of the importance of sanitation. The film also provides entertainment. In rural areas, most children suffer from worm infestation, viz., hookworm, roundworm and tapeworm.

Most schools in rural areas do not have toilets for children. Consequently, boys and girls face difficulties. This increases drop-out rates, particularly of girl students. Apart from the government programmes, Sulabh has initiated a programme to get toilets constructed in schools by taking donations from private individuals as well as NRIs. Teachers and students are also taught how to keep the toilets clean. Children are given responsibility by turns to maintain the toilets and teachers also inspect and supervise by turns. The number of toilets is as per the strength of the students. Various programmes such as health check-up camps, and rural sanitation have been taken up in villages. For the speedy implementation of sanitation programmes in rural areas, Sulabh has made the following proposals:

1. A nationwide campaign to make people aware of the adverse effects of open defecation. People should be instructed not to go barefoot while going for open defecation.

2. People going for open defecation should be educated to put soil on excreta after defecation.
3. Sulabh has prepared 46 designs. The choice of designs should be left to beneficiaries who will take a decision, keeping in view their resources.
4. Possible help either in the form of subsidy or loan or both should be extended to all beneficiaries who want to have toilets in their homes irrespective of income groups.
5. The role of NGOs is very crucial in the implementation of the sanitation programme throughout the country through house-to-house contacts and follow-up.
6. The NGOs should be identified either by the state governments or the district administration. The selection of NGOs should be based on their experience, expertise and infrastructure.
7. The NGOs identified for implementation of the programme should be given proper training in various aspects of the programme.
8. The entire range of training starting with IEC implementation and follow-up should be given to the same NGO.
9. The NGOs selected for sanitation work should be allowed 15 per cent of the estimated cost of the IEC activities, including implementation and follow-up services. In addition, 10 per cent of the project cost should be allowed for training and support services. For setting up sanitary marts and production centres, subsidy as admissible under the Government of India Sanitation Programme should also be paid to the NGOs.
10. Interest-free bank loans should be provided to all beneficiaries who want to have toilets in their houses.
11. A nationwide campaign should be launched through the media for generating demand for safe hygienic toilets. Apart from a door-to-door campaign, it will be the responsibility of NGOs to publish literature in local languages and make them available to the people.
12. The implementation of the programme will require social mobilisation on a large scale which will include people belonging to various groups. Politicians and policymakers will have to be involved in a big way so that they can take interest in policy decisions in favour of sanitation programmes. The social mobilisation would

also include village elders, doctors, lawyers and school teachers; print media, radio and television.

13. School sanitation will form an important component of the programme as it is through school teachers and students that the message of sanitary toilets will reach the villages.
14. Public toilets in rural areas should be constructed near panchayat bhawans, village markets, health centres, bus stands and other public places where people congregate in large numbers.
15. The following recommendations of the Planning Commission in the Tenth Five Year Plan were made for implementation of the rural sanitation programme successfully.
    a. Under the existing arrangement subsidy is available only for substructure. The Planning Commission has recommended that the subsidy should be inclusive of sub and super structure for the basic twin-pit, pour-flush system.
    b. The subsidy for low-cost household toilets is to be given to rural families below the poverty line and it should be at par with subsidy in the urban households. The Planning Commission has recommended that the present subsidy level should be increased to 50 per cent.

Sulabh Urban Sanitation

Of the many things that can make for healthy cities, clean living conditions are very important. Sanitation is a basic condition for development. It is not only the problem of maintaining cleanliness, it is also an economic and social problem of raising production and promoting a good life. A lack of proper sanitation contributes to the death of millions of children below the age of five every year; and about 50 diseases are associated with poor sanitation. Sanitation-related diseases are among the major causes of death in India and in most other low-income countries.

A concern for sanitation involves not only the waste disposal systems, water supply and sewerage networks but also our rich ecological heritage. Our cities and towns are not clean—the garbage heaps, the large number of people defecating in the open or urinating against the walls, degraded land and destroyed forests—all indicate ill-health for the people living on the fringe. Modern civilisation has increased, rather than lessened, the problem of scavenging and open defecation. With the rapid expansion in urban populations, the scope for open defecation has been reduced and, today, large sections of this population live in slums. Comparable problems exist in many other megacities. In a UNDP-assisted survey of 210 towns in 11 states and three union territories of India, it was found that only 27 per cent of people in 12.8 million households had sanitary facilities and one-third of all households (10.4 million) had no toilet facilities at all.

Sulabh developed a low-cost, affordable, culturally appropriate technology that did not need emptying by scavengers—the Sulabh two-pit, pour-flush water-seal toilet system. This system has been installed in more than one million households and is used in over 3,000 community toilets. It is now being used by about 10 million people every day. The World Bank, UNESCO and other agencies and institutions in India and abroad have approved Sulabh technology for adoption in South Asian countries. Sulabh toilets function independently of the city sewerage system and, to that extent, the rivers are not polluted. Nor is there a need to build treatment plants or expand the sewerage network, both of which are very expensive.

Toilet Museum and Importance

The Sulabh International Museum of Toilets in Delhi, established in 1992, is run by Sulabh International, and is dedicated to the global history of sanitation and toilets. Dr Pathak's objective in establishing this museum was to highlight the need to address the problems of the sanitation sector in the country, considering the efforts made in various parts of the world in this field since the third millennium BCE.

The museum has three main sections—Ancient, Medieval and Modern. In the 'Ancient section, the story unfolds with the sanitation arrangements of the Harappan settlements of around 3,000 BCE. The excavated main sites of that civilisation at Harappa and Mohenjo-Daro in modern Pakistan, and Dholavira and Lothal in Gujarat province of India have remnants of wells, bathing tanks, both over-ground and underground drains, toilets, soak-pits, roads and lanes. The W.C. toilet at Mohenjo-Daro of 2,500 BCE is acknowledged as a championing work in the field of sanitation. The pucca wide underground drain of Dholavira in the citadel section of the township has manholes at regular intervals to monitor the flow inside. Simultaneously, the museum also displays sanitation arrangements of other ancient civilisations of Egypt, Babylon, Crete, Jerusalem, Greece and Rome.

During the Middle Ages, whether in India or elsewhere, kings and emperors used to live in big forts for security reasons. The museum displays toilets of Amber Fort of Jaipur, Akbar's fort in Fatehpur Sikri near Agra, Gingee Fort of Tamil Nadu and Golconda Fort of Hyderabad, Andhra Pradesh. In this section, one can also see the table-top toilet of England, the costly stones-studded bidet of Queen Victoria, highly decorated commodes from Austria and other cross-stools of that period in Europe.

The Modern section has interesting toilet-related cartoons, photographs of toilets from the catalogues of reputed sanitaryware manufacturing companies, public toilets of different countries and toilet jokes. The visitors in this section also see the toy-commode from China, the mobile toilet of Sulabh, the electric toilet from the US and the model of the world's biggest toilet complex at Shirdi in Maharashtra. The museum also exhibits some ultra-modern electronic toilets from Japan, South Korea and other countries.

The museum has a rare collection of facts, pictures and objects detailing with the historic evolution of toilets from 2500 BCE to date. It provides a chronological account of developments relating to technology, toilet-related social customs, toilet etiquette, prevailing sanitary conditions and legislative efforts of different times. It has an extensive display of privies, chamber pots, toilet furniture, bidets and water closets in use since 1145 CE to modern times. It also has a rare collection of beautiful poems related to toilets and their usage.

The pictures displayed in the museum make one aware of how the world looked when societies did not have the benefit of the water closet and the changes that have been brought about by its invention. Ornately carved and painted urinals and commodes attract attention and are a source of amusement to many. The models and pictures of medieval commodes are noteworthy. There is also a replica of medieval mobile commode in the shape of a treasure chest, which the English used while camping out for a hunt. One could imagine the shock registered by some unsuspecting highway robbers, if they made away with such "treasure chests", thinking it to be containing something costly.

The museum also showcases how the Roman emperors used to have toilet pots made of gold and silver. It has a rare record of the flush pot devised in 1596 by Sir John Harington, a courtier during the reign of Queen Elizabeth I. The museum displays the sewerage system of the Harappan civilisation dating back to 2500 BCE and maintains a detailed record of how modern toilet pans have emerged over a period of time.

The museum has a stock of interesting anecdotes and facts associated with the development of toilets. Tracing the history of toilets from the Indus Valley Civilisation in Lothal, 62 km from the city of Ahmedabad, India, where a highly developed drainage system existed, the museum also documents facts relating to the countries in Europe where most of the early technological developments in the evolution of toilets took place. The national flags of different countries from where the pictures of toilets have been collected, are also displayed. The museum has over the years proved to be a source of inspiration and a unique centre for raising awareness about proper sanitation and toilets around the world.

The Sulabh International Museum of Toilets is the brainchild of Dr Pathak. His painstaking efforts for marshalling even minute details about the development of toilet systems in the world led to the establishment of this unique museum in New Delhi. The exhibits, so collected, have been meticulously displayed chronologically. Thus, it showcases the development of toilet systems from the past 5000 years, to the end of the 20th century.

The main objective of the toilet museum is educative with a research value, including

i. educating students about the historical trends in the development of toilets;
ii. providing information to researchers about the design, materials and technologies adopted in the past and those in use in the contemporary world;
iii. helping policymakers understand the efforts made by their predecessors in this field throughout the world;
iv. helping the manufacturers of toilet equipment and accessories improve their products by functioning as a technological storehouse; and
v. helping sanitation experts learn from the past and solve problems in the sanitation sector.

The museum has exhibits from 50 countries, arranged sequentially. The museum's exhibits bring out the development of the toilet-related technologies of the entire gamut of human history, social habits, etiquettes specific to existing sanitary situation and the legal framework in different periods.

Unlike body functions like dance, drama and songs, defecation is considered very low. As a result, very few scholars documented precisely the toilet habits of our predecessors. The Nobel Prize winner for Medicine (1913) Charles Richet, attributes this silence to the disgust that arises from noxiousness and lack of knowledge about usefulness of human waste. Others point out that as sex organs are the same or nearer to the organs of defecation, those who dared to write on toilet habits were dubbed either as erotic or as vulgar and, thus, were despised in academic and social circles (Pathak 1995). However, as the need to defecate is irrepressible, so were some writers who, despite social as well as academic stigma, wrote on the subject and gave us at least an idea with regard to the toilet habits of human beings.

Toilet is a part of human hygiene which is a critical chapter in the history of human civilisation and which cannot be isolated or accorded an inferior position. Toilet is a critical link between order and disorder and between good and bad environment. This is what Dr Pathak has stressed in his works, involvement and commitment.

In India, the society is constantly threathened with health hazards and epidemics. Considering this fact, the subject of toilet is as important as other social challenges like literacy, poverty, education and employment. The subject of toilet is more important because lack of excremental hygiene is a national health hazard while in other problems the implications are relatively closer to only those who suffer from unemployment, illiteracy and poverty. Hence Pathak considers a study of the history of toilet as an important subject.

As long as man did not have an established abode, he did not have a toilet. He excreted wherever he felt like doing so. When he learnt to have a fixed house, he moved his toilet to the courtyard and then within his home. Once this was done, it became a challenge to deal with the smell and the need was felt to have a toilet which could intake human wastes and dispose of these out of the house instantly and, thus, help maintain cleanliness. Man tried various ways to do so. While the rich used luxurious toilet chairs or close stools, the poor defecated on the roads, in the jungle or straight into the river. It was only in the 16th century that a technological breakthrough came about which helped human beings to have clean toilets in houses. This breakthrough did not come about easily and the human race had to live in insanitary conditions for thousands of years.

Chapter 11

FUTURE OF SANITATION

Sulabh sanitation has its own history of origin and growth, beginning from the efforts of Bindeshwar Pathak in Patna, Bihar. Research on sanitation technology has helped its expansion and invention of versions suitable for places, culture and geographical conditions. In the preceding chapters we have seen the different phases of sanitation. But what is the future of sanitation? In spite of government efforts and the working of NGOs it is estimated that in India more than 50 per cent of the population does not have access to clean and safe sanitation. Manual scavenging and open defecation still continue for various reasons.

In this respect, there are certain challenges faced by sanitation. The first challenge for countries seeking to solve the problem of access to sanitation is to define what sanitation really means. The second challenge is to decide what aspects are the most important. In other words, what aspect of the problem is going to be dealt with as a priority? This problem is not simple and many professionals confuse the two steps. With respect to defining sanitation most professionals would agree that sanitation as a whole is a large concept (Nagla 2015) which covers:

1. Safe collection, storage, treatment and disposal/reuse/recycling of human excreta (faeces and urine)
2. Management/reuse/recycling of solid wastes (trash or rubbish)
3. Drainage and disposal/reuse/recycling of household wastewater (often referred to as sullage or grey water)
4. Drainage of storm water
5. treatment and disposal/reuse/recycling of sewage effluents
6. Collection and management of industrial waste products and

7. Management of hazardous wastes (including hospital wastes and chemical/radioactive and other dangerous substances)

For countries with very low access to basic sanitation, increasing the effectiveness of management of excreta at the household level may have the biggest health implications and it may be the biggest challenge. For this reason, some countries may legitimately decide to focus their efforts at this level in the short term. In other cases, specific inter-linkages between elements of sanitation mean that a more complete solution may be better. In this case, there will probably need to be some interventions to improve management of solid wastes and storm water drainage, otherwise the sewers won't work.

Yet some countries or communities may try for a more complete solution which includes a focus on protecting the environment from contamination. It will be possible to start with an "ecological" approach to sanitation which seeks to contain, treat and reuse excreta where possible, thus minimising contamination and making optimum use of resources. The key issue here is that each community, region or country needs to work out what is the most sensible and cost effective way of thinking about sanitation in the short and long terms and then act accordingly. Flexibility and pragmatism should be the priority; and both professionals and politicians need to try and see past experiences and ideas developed elsewhere. A pragmatic local approach with an eye to wider environmental issues is likely to result in more progress than blind adherence to a rigid global definition.

In this direction, Dr Pathak envisaged sustainable technology for a better environment, healthier society and human dignity through Sulabh technologies.

For individual houses, the Sulabh two-pit, pour-flush, on-site technology is appropriate, affordable and eco-friendly. Sulabh helps in construction of these toilets and conversion of dry toilets to pour-flush toilets in individual houses, to prevent defecation in the open and eliminate manual scavenging.

For public places, high-rise buildings, places of congregation and non-sewered areas, Sulabh constructs and maintains public toilets on a long term "pay-and-use" basis, to provide a sustainable sanitation solution. Biogas digesters attached to public toilets recycle human excreta into biogas for further use. This promotes environment improvement as well as provides human dignity. Other technologies are for wastewater treatment through duckweed with direct economic returns from pisciculture and composting of solid wastes through Sulabh Thermophilic Composting Treatment (STAC).

Sulabh's methodology propagates and implements the above technologies. This is done by education and motivation of beneficiaries; going house-to-house, giving information to them, motivating, educating and training them. People are to construct toilets themselves, or Sulabh will design it and construct it for them. Implementation, maintenance and follow-up are done by members of Sulabh.

Regarding construction and maintenance of public toilets, the land and funds for construction are provided by the local bodies and then leased to Sulabh for monitoring. But, recently, the government gives land and construction is done under the Build-Operate-Transfer (BOT) system. Sulabh follows a whole-town approach and cross-subsidises the funds. This is developing a model on how NGOs should work in partnership with government agencies and local bodies on the one hand and people on the other. Sulabh has developed various strategies towards meeting the MDG on sanitation with involvement of all stakeholders and in partnership with government, local bodies and communities.

ECOSOC and Sulabh International Social Service Organisation plan to work together to help in empowering people throughout the world to achieve the MDG on sanitation. The project is innovative and unconventional as in the sustainable technologies developed by Sulabh, complete recycling of human waste takes place and it provides an alternative to the old technologies of sewerage and septic tank systems which are costly to construct, difficult to maintain and pollute the environment.

The development of these technologies have shown how to eliminate defecation in the open and remove the practice of manual cleaning of human excreta and also enabled women to use toilets with dignity and safety while girls have secured the benefits of toilets in schools. There is reduction in mortality rate of children because of diarrhoeal diseases. Untouchability and social discrimination have been reduced in society by liberating and rehabilitating scavengers.

The cost associated with the development and implementation of Sulabh activities is much lower than that involved in conventional styles of human waste disposal, which are expensive and unaffordable. Sulabh's technology-based human waste disposal systems lead to decentralised on-site human waste disposal besides being appropriate and affordable, even for the poorest of the poor, enabling them to easily adopt them and find a sustainable solution as compared to defecation in the open.

Hence, there is a need to motivate, educate and train people explaining the benefit of sanitation for a better environment, healthier society and human dignity. Human excreta has been implicated in the transmission of many infectious diseases including cholera, typhoid, infectious hepatitis, polio, cryptosporidiosis, and ascariasis. For a sanitation system to provide the greatest health protection to the individual, the community and society at large, it must isolate the users from their own excreta; prevent nuisance organisms (e.g. flies) from contact with the excreta and subsequently transmitting disease to humans; and inactivate the pathogens before they enter the environment or prevent the excreta from entering the environment (WHO).

It is important to understand that sanitation can act at different levels, protecting the household, the community and society. In the case of latrines, it is easy to see that this sanitation system acts at a household level. However, poor design or inappropriate location may lead to migration of waste matter and contamination of local water supplies, putting the community at risk. In terms of sewage, the containment may be effective for the individual and possibly also the community, but health effects and environmental damage may be seen farther downstream of the original source, hence affecting society (WHO).

Furthermore, the health impact of inadequate sanitation leads to a number of financial and economic costs including direct medical costs associated with treating sanitation-related illnesses and lost income through reduced or lost productivity and the government's costs of providing health services. Additionally, sanitation also leads to time and effort losses due to distant or inadequate sanitation facilities, lower product quality resulting from poor water quality, reduced income from tourism and clean-up costs. Increases in female literacy (due to increased school attendance where proper sanitation facilities exist) contribute to economic growth.

Many people do not realise the health and economic benefits to the individual, the community and to society from improving sanitation. The high cost of improving sanitation is often cited as a barrier to implementing sanitation projects. Improving sanitation is often low on the list of priorities. There are so many other pressing needs for the attention of governments like food supply, education, medical treatment and dealing with war and conflict. Most people are aware that poor sanitation has a health impact, but there is a lack of awareness of the extent of ill-health that it causes.

On the other hand, human society has developed very different socio-cultural responses to the use of untreated excreta. This ranges from deep disgust to practical preference. While determined partly by survival economics, these cultural differences apply to many water-deficient poor countries, as well as to water-rich areas. This results from the strongly held view that human excreta, especially faeces, is repugnant and best kept away from the senses of sight and smell. Products fertilised with raw excreta are regarded as tainted or defiled in some way. These views are less rigid in the case of using excreta in compost and sludge for agriculture, but still pose a barrier to use of waste.

Sanitation has been a neglected aspect of Indian public policy and society is the worse for it. It is not a silver bullet, but sanitation is the thread that connects some of our pressing social and health issues (as in Nagla 2015). Numbers do not always tell the story, but in the case of sanitation they put things in perspective in place. Women in more than half of India's homes have to step outside, often in unsafe circumstances, to attend to their basic needs. The proximate cause of horrific rapes was because victims had to step outside their homes. Women's safety has other dimensions also. However, tardy progress on sanitation just adds to challenges that women face. India's poor record in sanitation has adverse consequences in other areas too. Research on high malnutrition rates among Indian children shows open defecation plays a significant role in their stunting.

The Indian government has largely ignored the positive spinoffs of investing in improvement of public health facilities such as provision of clean drinking water and sanitation. These areas need a sharper focus as they are people-friendly dimensions of social infrastructure investments. The resources generated by governments on account of economic growth should be utilised to improve public health facilities as they link economic progress to a tangible improvement in the lives of ordinary Indians.

Sulabh Vocational Training Programmes

Development of skills is important for all but crucial for the less educated. For SCs, including the scavenging community, it has a pointed relevance. The Sulabh Vocational Training Centre aims to provide development and training in diverse skills to boys and girls from weaker sections of society, especially from scavenging households, so that they use their newly acquired talents to the fullest and achieve better economic and social adjustment. Its main objectives are to mobilise boys and girls from the weaker sections to enable them to pick up market-oriented trades and thus enable them not only to earn a living, but also to help them towards developing confidence, self-esteem and reliance, so that they can be absorbed in the national mainstream.

The courses are so designed that they help students acquire skills which help towards self-employment. There is a follow-up programme to monitor the progress of each student in later life. The first Sulabh Vocational Training Centre was set up at Patna in 1985. It offered vocational training to young boys and girls in several trades. By all accounts, it was a roaring success. Shortly thereafter, another centre in collaboration with the government of Maharashtra was set up in Mumbai. It offered adolescents vocational training programmes in keeping with market demands in the Mumbai area. It has been quite successful and continues to attract the attention of both trainees and employers. Yet another centre was opened in Delhi in 1992. It offers one year's training in (1) English Stenography (2) Cutting & Tailoring (3) Beauty care (4) Computers, (5) Dress designing (6) Embroidery (7) English and Hindi Typing (8) Electrical work (9) and Audio-Visual work.

Teaching Sanitation

It is part of the vision of Dr Pathak that sociology of sanitation should be taught as a discipline in all the universities of India. Having been provided awareness at primary or other lower levels of the education system, students at higher education level and in the universities are in a position to carry out further research in the field. At present, 10 universities have introduced sociology of sanitation as a course at the post-graduation level. Some more universities have placed it in the syllabus scheme. Unfamiliarity with the nature of the discipline is partly responsible for it not being taken up as a subject for teaching.

The following topics may be compiled as a model syllabi if the course is taught:

Course Heading: Sociology of Sanitation

Unit—I: Introduction

a. Meaning, origin and scope of sociology of sanitation
b. Sociology of sanitation—issues and concerns for India
c. Significance of the study of sociology of sanitation

Unit—II: Philosophical roots of sanitation

a. History of sanitation in India
b. Changing concept of sanitation
c. Phenomenology of untouchability

Unit—III: Health and sanitation

a. Sanitation, hygiene and health
b. Health programmes and social legislation in healthcare in India
c. Sanitation policies and programmes; role of Sulabh and other NGOs

Unit—IV: Sanitation in India

a. Problem of environmental sanitation in India
b. Sulabh Sanitation Movement
c. Sanitation leaders: Mahatma Gandhi and Bindeshwar Pathak

Unit—V: Sanitation and society

a. Social construction of hygiene and sanitation
b. Scavenging castes and social deprivation
c. Sanitation and human dignity; dignity of women

With the help of subject matter experts, Sulabh has already brought out extensive literature on sociology of sanitation from different angles. Further, conferences, seminars and workshops conducted by the organisation have helped to generate new ideas and thinking on the subject. The research papers presented at these deliberations have become a source for further study and as study material for graduate students.

Research and Diploma Courses

Sociology of sanitation is the scientific study of sanitation in society. The study of sociology of sanitation reveals the depth and understanding of sanitation as a concept, method and perspective. The study of the subject should be taken in such a way that the reader will get all the answers to the problems or doubts regarding the subject. In the process of scientific study, social scientists gain knowledge of a particular subject and they are able to interpret that knowledge for better understanding of social problems. Thus, social scientists should consider sociology of sanitation as a subject of study and it should follow the methods of sociological research which will generate accurate knowledge about the subject.

Colleges and Universities

The Sulabh International Social Service Organisation is taking steps to initiate the opening of the *Sulabh International University of Sanitation* that will help in bringing hygiene and sanitation related awareness to the youth and the general public. Students passing out of the University will work as missionaries of sanitation that will result in a clean and liveable environment.

The University will be committed to excellence in research and development in environmental science and engineering, and will provide sustainable technological solutions to the environmental problems faced by governments, industries and society as a whole, especially the underprivileged people of India.

A dream project of Dr Pathak, the Sulabh International University of Sanitation, will also help the country to propagate the message of Mahatma Gandhi and Sulabh. It will be the first university of its kind in India. It will produce consultants and professionals to work in the field of development and public health, providing an in-depth understanding of how to deliver effective modern water supply, sanitation and other public health interventions in urban and rural areas in low-income and transitional economies.

The University will serve as an education and training resource centre for sanitation and environment management experts. With the visionary ideas of social scientist Dr Bindeshwar Pathak, the University will concentrate its efforts in the areas of research and development, and provide public/private consultancy services as well as tertiary education.

The University will be dedicated solely to training and increasing the capacity of human resource to analyse, design and implement effectively the solutions that will help make not just India but the planet clean. It will have a strong focus on the development of practical and policy skills and will address the critical future challenges of climate change, population growth and urbanisation. Emphasis will be laid on technical interventions in water supply, sanitation and solid waste management.

The University will provide different courses for youth, consultants and professionals working in international development and public health. These courses will train students in the essential skills and knowledge required to plan and implement, along with communities, water supply and sanitation projects and programmes worldwide, particularly in less developed countries. What will make it stand out will be its outreach to practitioners, using its knowledge base and applied research to develop the capacity of individuals and organisations throughout the world, promoting the integration of social, technical, economic, institutional and environmental activities as a prerequisite for development.

REFERENCES

Abad, R. 1991. "Squatting and Scavenging in Smokey Mountain" *Philippine Studies* (39); 267-285.

Ahmed, S. 2005. "Flowing upstream: Towards Gender Just, Equitable, and Empowerment Water Management", in S. Ahmed (ed.) *Flowing Upstream: Empowering Women through Water management Initiatives in India* (1-50), Ahmadabad: Centre for Environment Research.

Akram, Mohammad. 2015. *Sociology of Sanitation*. Delhi: Kalpaz Publications.

Ambedkar, B. R. 1948 (2008). *The untouchables*. Delhi: Siddharth Books.

Ambedkar, B.R. 1936. *Annihilation of Caste* (The Annotated Critical Edition). New Delhi: Navayana.

Angelakis, Andreas N. and Joan B. Rose 2014. *Evolution of Sanitation and Wastewater Technologies through the Centuries*. London: IWA Publishing Alliance House.

Anon,. 1891. "Disposal of Refuse in American Cities." *Scientific American* (65): 136.

Anon,. 1941. *The Story of Papermaking*. Chicago: J. W. Butler Company.

Aquarooms. 2013. *The History of the Toilet: Sanitation's Ups And Downs*. https:/ aquarooms. me

Bansal, Samarth. 2016. *What numbers tell us about Open Defecation in India*. https://www.thehindu.com

Barker, Kim. 2006. India's lowest slowly rising. *The Political and Business Daily*. http://www.sulabhinternational.org.

Barringer, E. 1954. *The Story of Scrap*. Washington, DC: Institute of Scrap Iron & Steel, Inc.

Bartone, C. 1988. "The Value in Wastes." *Decade Watch* (September): 2-4.

Berman, P. et al. 1994. "The Household Production of Health: Integrating Social Science Perspective on Micro-level Health Determinants", *Social Science and Medicine*, 38, 2, 205-215.

Bhol, Aditya. 2015. *Let's celebrate Gandhi by purging manual scavenging.* https:// www.dailyo. in

Bilitewski. B. J. Hardte and K. Marck. 1994. *Waste Management*. Berlin: Springer Verlag: Hughes.

Birdbeck, Ch. 1978. "Self-Employed Proletarians in an Informal Factory: The Case of Cali's Garbage Dump." *World Development* (9-10): 1173-1185.

Blumenschine, R. 1986. *Early Hominid Scavenging Opportunities: Implications of Carcass Availability in the Serengeti and Ngorongoro Ecosystems*. Exford. England : B. A. R.

Blumenschine. R. and J. Cavallo. 1992. "Scavenging and Human Evolution." *Scientific American* (October): 90-96.

Boot, M. and Cairncross, S., 1993. *Actions Speak: The study of hygiene behaviour in water and sanitation projects*. The Hague, The Netherlands: IRC International Water and Sanitation Centre and London UK: The London School of Hygiene and Tropical Medicine.

Bourne, P. G. 1984. *Water and sanitation: Economic and sociological perspectives* Orlando: Academic P.

Bray, W. 1968. *Everyday Life of the Aztecs*. New York: Dorset Press.

Burawoy, Michael. 2005 "For Public Sociology". *American Sociological Review*. 70: 4–28.

Burkert, W. 1992. *The Orientalising Revolution: Near Eastern Influence on Greek Culture in the Early Archaic Age*, Cambridge USA: Harvard University Press.

Cairncross, S, and Valdmanis V. 2006. Water supply, sanitation, and hygiene promotion. In: Jamison DT, Breman J.G., Measham A.R., et al., (eds). Disease control priorities in developing countries, 2nd ed. New York: Oxford University Press; 2006. pp. 771–792.

Cairncross, C. et al. 1996. "The Public and Domestic Domains in the Transmission of Disease", *Tropical Medicine and International Health*, 1, 27-34.

Carcopino. J. 1941. *Daily Life in Ancient Rome: The People and the City at the Height of the Empire*. New Haven: Yale University Press.

Cassen, R. 1978. *India: Population, Economy, Society*, London: Macmillan.

Castillo, H. 1990. *La Sociedad de la Basura: Caciquismo Urbano en la Ciudad de Mexico*. Mexico City: UNAM,

Cavill, Chambers, Vernon. 2015. *Sustainability and CLTS: Taking Stock Frontiers of CLTS: Innovations and Insights Issue 4*. IDS. p. 18.

Charles, K. Humphrey. 2010. *Safeguarding Sanitation In High Population Density Urban Settlements: A Case Study of Kibera Slums Nairobi*. https://ir-library.ku.ac.ke

Cipolla, Carlo M. 1980. *Before the Industrial Revolution: European Society and Economy* (1000-1700), London: W.W. Norton and Company.

Cointreau, S. 1990. *Recycling From Municipal Waste: How Do Industrialize and Developing Countries Compare*? New York: United Nations.

Coles, A and Wallace T. 2005. *Gender, Water and Development*. Oxford and New York: Berg.

Conant, Jeff. 2005. *Sanitation and Cleanliness for a Healthy Environment*, USA: Hesperian Foundation

Cowell, F. 1961. *Everyday Life in Ancient Rome*. New York: G.P. Putnam's Sons.

Curtis, Valerie. 1998. *The Dangers of Dirt: Household Hygiene and Health*, Wageningen: Grafish Service Centrum.

Dakshinamurty, Sonti. 1962. *Introduction to preventive and Social medicine: An Epidemiological and Social Medicine*, Kakinada: Educational Enterprises. pp.198-202.

Davis, K. 1951. *The Population of India and Pakistan*, Princeton N.J.: Princeton University Press.

Demko, G. and M. Jackson (eds.) 1995. *Populations at Risk in America: Vulnerable Groups at the End of the Twentieth Century*. Boulder, Colorado: Westview Press.

De Pree, Max. 2004. *Leadership Is An Art*. US: Currency Publisher.

Dittmer, Alison. 2009. *Towards total sanitation Socio-cultural barriers and triggers to total sanitation in West Africa*. London: Durham Street WaterAid. UNICEF.

Douglas, M. 1966. *Purity and Danger: An Analysis of Concepts of Pollution and Taboo*, London: Ark

Downs, Mary and Martin Medina. 2000. A Short History of Scavenging *Comparative Civilizations Review*. Volume 42; No 42. Article 4. Available at: https://scholarsarchive.byu.edu

Dumont, Louis. 1980. (1966) *Homo Heirachicus: The Caste System and Its Implications*, Complete revised English edition, Chicago: University of Chicago press.

Dunn, Ch. 1972. *Everyday Life in Traditional Japan*. Tokyo: Charles E. Tuttle Co.

Dutt, Ela. 2008. Sulabh International Is Fulfilling Mahatma Gandhi's Dream of Universal Sanitation. *News India Times*. Sulabh International Social Services (SISS).

Emirates Today E-Paper. 2007. Forsaking a Centuries-Old Dirty Task for a Clean One

Forster, E. M. 2001. "Preface". *Untouchable*. Mulk Raj Anand. New Delhi : Penguin. v-viii. Print.

Frederic, L. 1972. *Daily Life in Japan at the Time of the Samurai: 1185-1600*. New York: Praeger Publishers.

Friedelander, L. 1968. *Roman Life and Manners Under the Early Empire*. New York: Barnes & Noble.

Furedy, Ch. 1990. "Social Aspects of Solid Waste Recovery in Asian Cities." *Environmental Sanitation Reviews* Bangkok: Asian Institute of Technology.

Furedy, Ch. 1990. "Waste Recovery in China" *BioCycle* (June): 80-84.

Furedy, Ch. 1984. "Survival Strategies of the Urban Poor-Scavenging and Recuperation in Calcutta." *GeoJournal* (8): 129-136.

Furedy, Ch. 1984. "Sociopolitical Aspects of the Recovery and Recycling of Urban Wastes in Asia" *Conservation & Recycling* (7): 167-173.

Gans, Herbert J. 1999. A Sociology for Public Sociology: Some Needed Disciplinary Changes for Creating Public Sociology; in *Handbook of Public Sociology* by Vincent Jeffries (Ed) USA: Rowman & Littlefield Publishers, Inc.

Gans, Herbert. J. 1999. *Popular culture and high culture an analysis and evaluation of taste*. New York: Basic Books.

George, Rose. 2008. *The Big Necessity: The Unmentionable World of Human Waste and Why It Matters*. Metropolitan Books.

Glassner, B., and Freedman, J. A. 1979. *Clinical sociology*. New York: Longman.

Gleick, Peter H. 2002. "Estimated Deaths from Water-related Diseases 2000-2020". *Pacific Institute Research Report*, Pacific Institute for Studies in Development, Environment and Society.

Gonzalez, J., M. Cadena and M. Suremain. 1993. *Estudio Sobre los Circuitos de Reciclaje de Desechos SUlidos en la Ciudad de Bogota-*. Bogota: ENDA-America Latina.

Gupta, Monica Das. 2005. World Bank economist. *Economic and Political Weekly*.

Hanley, S. 1997. *Everyday Things in Pre-modern Japan: The Hidden Legacy of Material Culture*. Berkeley: University of California Press.

Hasegawa, T. 1983. "New Evidence on Scavenging Behaviour in Wild Chimpanzees." *Current Anthropology* 24(2): 231-232.

Hering, R. and S. Greely. 1921. *Collection and Disposal of Municipal Refuse*. New York: McGraw Hill.

Honenberg, P. and L. Lees. 1985. *The Making of Urban Europe 1000-1950*. Cambridge: Harvard University Press.

Hotez, P.J., Molyneux D.H,, Fenwick A, et al. 2007. *Control of neglected tropicaldiseases*. N Engl J Med. 357:1018–1027.

Hutton, G., and Haller H. 2004. Evaluation of the costs and benefits of water and sanitation improvements at the global level. Geneva: World Health Organization; 87.

Ibbetson, Denzil. 1974. *Panjab castes*. Delhi: B.R. Pub.

Indorf, A. 1994. *Occupational Health Hazards of Recycling Workers at the Bonanza Landfill in Venezuela*. Worcester, MA: Clark University. Master's Thesis.

Jain, Pankaj. 2014. *Drinking Water Annual Report*. New Delhi: Ministry of Drinking Water and Sanitation (*MDWS*).

Jarman, J. 1997. 'Water supply and sanitation' in J. Beall (ed.), *A City for All: Valuing difference and working with diversity*, Zed Books, London.

Jeffery, Roger. 1988. *The Politics of Health in India*, London: University of California Press, p.40

Jha, Hetukar. 2015. *Sanitation in India*. Delhi: Gyan Books.

Jha, Neena. 2004. (Ed) *Sanitation: Gandhian Thought and Philosophy on Sanitation* New Delhi: South Asia NewsNetwork International.

Johns, Hannah. 2012. *Stigmatization of Dalits in Access to Water and Sanitation in India*. New Delhi: National Campaign on Dalit Human Rights (NCDHR). www.ncdhr.org.in

Jutti, Petri S. and Katri J. Wallenius. 2005. *Kaivot Ja Kaymalat: Johdatus Historian Esimerkkina Sumoi* (A Brief History of wells and Toilets—The case of Finland), Tempere University press, ePublications, Tampere.

Kadence Themes,. 2018. *The History of Sanitary Sewers – Word Press Theme*. http://www.sewerhistory.org.

Kar, K., and Chambers J. 2008. Handbook on community-led total sanitation. London: Plan International UK; 51

Katzaman, M. 1988. "From Horse Carts to Minimills." *The Public Interest* (92): 121135;

Ketkar, S.V. 1990. *History of Caste in India*. Delhi: Low Price Publications.

Kulkarni, Sudheerna. 2012. *Music of the Spinning Wheel*. New Delhi: Amaryllis. Kumar, Ganesh S., Sitanshu Sekhar Kar, and Animesh Jain. 2011. *Health and environmental sanitation in India: Issues for prioritizing control strategies*. Indian J Occup Environ Med. 15(3): 93–96. https://www.ncbi.nlm.nih.gov

Lambert, Tim. 2018. *A Brief History of Toilets*. http://www.localhistories.org

Lena, H. 1990. *Historia del Papel en Mexico y Cosas Relacionadas* (1525-1950) Mexico City: Porrua.

Lipsett, Ch. 1974. *100 Years of Recycling History: From Yankee Tincart Peddlers to Wall Street Scrap Giants*. New York: The Atlas Publishing Co.

Lorenz. 2014. *History of Toilet*. https://neoignitionmarketing.wordpress.com

Malhotra, Aditi. 2015. *Five Things Mahatma Gandhi said about Sanitation*. The Wall Street Journal. https://blogs.wsj.com.

Mara, Duncan., Jon Lane, Beth Scott, and David Trouba 2010. *Sanitation and Health*. https://www.ncbi.nlm.nih.gov/pmc/articles

Mathews, Elsa. 2015. *Building a Life Beyond Manual Scavenging*. HTTP://WWW.KASHMIRTIMES.IN.

McGill. 2018. *Low-Cost Sanitation Systems used in Coastal and Waterfront Communities. Minimum Cost Housing Group*. https://www.mcgill.ca.

McLaughlin, T. 1971. *A Social History as Seen Through the Uses and Abuses of Dirt*, Dorset Press.

Medina, M. 1997. *Scavenging on the Border: A Study of the Informal Recycling Sector in Laredo. Texas, and Nuevo Laredo*, Mexico. New Haven: Yale University.

Medina. M. 1993. *Municipal Solid Waste Management in Developing Countries.* Chapel Hill: University of north Carolina.

Mehta, Jubin. 2017. *Six sanitation start-ups in India that are creating impact by making toilets* accessible. https://yourstory.com.

Melosi, M. 1981. *Garbage in the Cities: Refuse, Reform, and the Environment,* 1880-1980. College Station: Texas A&M University Press.

Melosi, M. 1987. "Out of Sight, Out of Mind, The Environment and Disposal of Municipal Refuse, 1860-1920." *The Historian* 621-640.

Mencher, J.P. 1974. The Caste System Upside Down or not-so-Mysterious. *Current Anthropology*. Vol. 15, No. 4, pp. 469- 493.

Merton, R.K. 1957. *Social Theory and Social Structure*, New York: Free press of Glencoe, pp. 131–194.

Milet, Bas Van, Spaargaten, Gert et. al. (2010) *Social Perspective on the Sanitation Challenges*, Springer.

Mills, C. W. 1959. *The sociological imagination*. London, United Kingdom: Oxford University Press.

Misra, Smita and Bishwanath Goldar (2008), "Likely Impact of Reforming Water Supply and Sewerage Services in Delhi". *Economic and Political Weekly*, Vol. XLIII, No. 41. pp. 57-66.

Mullegger, E., Langergraber, G. and Lechner, M. 2011. "Sustainable sanitation Practice, Planning Tools: Sustainable Sanitation Practice", *EcosanClub*, Issue 7.

Munsell, J. 1980. *Chronology of the Origin and Progress of Paper and Papermaking.* New York: Garland Publishing Co.

Nagla, B K. 2015. *Sociology of Sanitation*. Delhi: Kalpaz Publications.

Nagla, Madhu. 2013. *Gender and Health*, Jaipur Rawat Publications

Narayanan, K.S. 2013. *Toilet Tales from Far and Wide*. http://www.thesundayindian.com

National Informatics Centre (NIC),. 2015. *Freedom from Manual Scavenging*, Press Information Bureau Government of India. New Delhi.

Navayana. 2014. *But can we sweep caste away?*. https://navayana.org

Nelson, Erica Lee. 2006. Affirmative action in India flips caste roles. *The Washington Times* www.washingtontimes.com

Nimpuno, Krisno. 1984. "Viable Low Cost Sanitation Options", in *Water and Sanitation: Economic and Sociological Perspectives*, ed. Peter G. Bourne, Florida: Academic Press Inc. p.266-267

Nyarko, Kwabena Biritwum., Richard Buamah, Francis K.N. Nunoo., et al. 2018. *Latrine Technology Manual*. UNICEF. https://www.unicef.org

O'Connell, Kathryn. 2014. "What Influences Open Defecation and Latrine Ownership in Rural Households?: Findings from a Global Review" *world band group*. https://www.wsp.org

Pacey, A. 1980. Rural Sanitation. London, UK: Intermediate Technology Publications.

Pais, Richard. 2015. *Sociology of Sanitation*. Delhi: Kalpaz Publications.

Pandve, H.T. 2008. 'Environmental Sanitation: An Ignored Issue in India', *Indian Journal of Occupational and Environmental Medicine*, 12 (1): 40.

Park, J.E. and K. Park. 1977. Text book on *Social and Preventive and Social Medicine*, Jabalpur: Banarsidas Bhanot Publishers. P.94, 222,

Pathak, Bindeshwar. 1995. *History of Toilets, exploring history of sanitation & hygiene*. http://www.sulabhtoiletmuseum.org

Pathak, Bindeshwar. 1996. *Road to freedom: A sociological study on the abolition of scavenging in India*. Delhi: Motilal Banarsidass.

Pathak, Bindeshwar. 2003. *Sulabh Sanitation Movement*. New Delhi: Sulabh International Social Service Organisation.

Pathak, Bindeshwar. 2015. *Sociology of Sanitation*. Delhi: Kalpaz Publications.

Plumbing and Mechanical. 1994. *Who Invented The Water Closet?* http://www.repwars.com.

Ponting, C. 1991. *A Green History of the World: The Environment and the Collapse of Great Civilizations*. New York: Penguin Books.

Praeger, Dave (nd), *Poop Culture: How America is shaped by its Grossest national product*.

Prashad, Vijay. 2000. *Untouchable Freedom: A Social History of a Dalit Community*. New Delhi: Oxford University Press.

Price, J., Straus, R. A., and Breese, J. R. 2009. *Doing sociology: Case studies in sociological practice*. Lanham, MD: Lexington Books.

Purohit, Makarand. 2015. *Water Untouched: A film on Dalits' lack of access* http://www.indiawaterportal.org

Ramaswamy, Gita. 2005. *India Stinking: Manual Scavengers in Andhra Pradesh and their work*. New Delhi: Navayana.

Rastogi, Siddhartha Kumar. 2011. *A Case Study of Sulabh International Social Service Organisation*. Ahmedabad: Indian Institute of Management.

Rathi, Shubhangi 2015. *Importance of Gandhian thoughts about Cleanliness*. https://www.mkgandhi.org.

Rathje, W. and C. Murphy. 1993. *Rubbish! The Archaeology of Garbage*. New York: Harper Collins.

Reid, D. 1991. *Paris Sewers and Sewermen*. Cambridge: Harvard University Press.

Risley, H. H. 1891. *The tribes and castes of Bengal Anthropometric data*. Calcutta: Printed at the Bengal Secretariat Press.

Rosen, G. 1958. *A History of Public Health*. New York: MD Publications.

Routray, Parimita; Schmidt, Wolf-Peter; Boisson, Sophie; Clasen, Thomas; Jenkins, Marion W. 2015. "Socio-cultural and behavioural factors constraining latrine adoption in rural coastal Odisha: an exploratory qualitative study". *BMC Public Health*. 15: 880.

Royse, D. 1987. "Homelessness among Trash Pickers." *Psychological Reports* (June): 808-810.

Sanan, D. and Moulik S.G. 2007. Community-led total sanitation in rural areas. An approach that works. Washington, DC: Water and Sanitation Program; 12.

Sanchez, M. 1993. *El Papel del Papel en Nueva Espana*, 1740-1812. Mexico City: INAH.

Saxena, Ashish. 2015. *Sociology of Sanitation*. Delhi: Kalpaz Publications. Selsky, A. 1994. "Desperate Poor Praying on the Dead to Stay Alive." *Laredo Morning News* (July 24): A-19.

Sengupta, Sushmita and Rashmi Verma. 2018. *Sanitation will remain a mirage even after India stops defecating in the open*. https://www.downtoearth.org.in

Sharer, R. 1994. *The Ancient Maya*. Stanford: Stanford University Press.

Sicular, D. 1990. *Scavengers, Recyclers and Solutions for Solid Waste Management in Indonesia.* Berkeley: University of California Press.

Singh, Rajeev Kumar and Ziyauddin. 2000. "Manual Scavenging as Social exclusion: A Case Study", *Economic and Political Weekly*, Vol. XLIV, Nis 26 and 27, pp. 521- 523.

Sinha, Snigdha. 2015. *Making Bharat Swachch since 4 decades, in conversation with the Sulabh Shauchalya man – Dr Bindeshwar Pathak.* https://yourstory.com.

Srinivasan, Krithika. 2006. "Public, Private and Voluntary Agencies in Solid Waste Management: A Study in Chennai City", *Economic and Political Weekly*, Vol. XLI, No. 22, pp. 2259-2267.

Srivastava, B.N. 1997. *Manual Scavenging in India: A Disgrace to the Country.* Concept Publishing Company (P) Ltd. p. 178.

SSVK, 2013. *Manual Scavenging In India: The Practice, the Remedial Initiatives, the Shortcomings & the Challenges.* Samajik Shaikshanik Vikas Kendra (SSVK) Lok Shakti Bhawan Parmanand Path, Bihar. https://www.ssvk.org.

Stamp, Jimmy. 2014. *From Turrets to Toilets: A Partial History of the Throne Room* https://www.smithsonianmag.com

Sulabh International. 2012. *Sulabh international Toilet Museum in New Delhi. Sulabhinternational & filed under.* http://www.sulabhinternational.org

Sulabh International. 2013. *Sociology of Sanitation, Conference Proceedings.* New Delhi: Sulabh International Social Service Organisation.

Sulabh International. 2016. *Sulabh Sanitation Campaign* "How to Make India Free From Open Defecation by 2019. Sulabh News. http://www.sulabhinternational.org

Sulabh International. 2018. *Education of the Children of Scavengers.* http://www.sulabhinternational.org.

Sulabh International. 2018. *Sulabh Story in Brief.* http://www.sulabhinternational.org.

Sulabhenvis. 2018. *Low-Cost Sanitation. Envis Centre, Ministry of Environment & Forest,Govt. of India.* http://www.sulabhenvis.nic.in

Sutcliffe, A. 1984. *Metropolis* 1890-1940. London: Mansell.

Tebyan. 2010. *Sanitation in ancient Rome.* https://english.tebyan.net.

Thome-Kozmiensky. 1982. (ed.) *Recycling in Developing Countries.* Berlin: E. Freitag-Verlag.

Thompson, H. 1879. "Disposal of City Garbage at New Orleans." *Sanitarian* (7): 545.

Toilet Paper History. 2018. *Who Invented Toilet Paper*? http://www.toiletpaperhistory.net.

Ujang, Z. (ed.) 2003. *Environmental Biotechnology: Advancement in Water and Wastewater Application*, IWA Proceedings, Malaysia.

United Nations Children's Fund (UNICEF) 2008. *Sustaining the Sanitation Revolution—India Country Paper: SACOSAN III*. UNICEF. New Delhi: UNICEF.

United Nations in India. 2015. *Breaking Free: Rehabilitating Manual Scavengers*. http://in.one.un.org.

Vails, O. 1980. *La Historia del Papel en Espana*. Madrid: Empresa Nacional de Celulosas.

Vogler, J. 1984. Waste Recycling in Developing Countries: A Review of the Social, Technological, and Market Forces. In J. Homes (ed.) *Managing Solid Waste in Developing Countries*. New York: John Wiley & Sons, Ltd.

Wagner, E.G. & J.N. Lanoix. 1958. *Excreta Disposal for Rural Areas and Small Communities*. WHO, pp. 39

Wagner, E. G., & Lanoix, J. N. 1960. *Evacuation des excreta dans les zones rurales et les petites agglomérations*. Geneve: Organisation Mondiale de la Santé.

Water Aid, FANSA and WSSCC. 2011. *South Asian people's perspective on sanitation: Synthesis review*. Report South Asian people's perspective on sanitation Synthesis review Bangladesh, India, Nepal, Pakistan and Sri Lanka.

Water and Forestry. 2018. *Sanitation Technology Options. Water Affairs and Forestry Department*. http://www.susana.org

Weeks, L. 1969. *A History of Paper Manufacture in the United States*, 1690-1916. New York: Burt Franklin.

WHO and UNICEF. 2017. *Progress on Drinking Water, Sanitation and Hygiene: 2017 Update and SDG Baselines*. In WASH data reports page. Geneva: World Health Organization (WHO) and the United Nations Children's Fund (UNICEF).

Williams, G. 1981. *The Age of Miracles- medicine and Surgery in the Nineteenth Century*, Chicago, IL: Academy Chicago Publishers.

World Bank. 2016. *Ending Open Defecation and Achieving a Clean and Healthy Rural India.* http://www.worldbank.org

Yadav, Anurag. 2004. "Loo and Behold; A Toilet Museum!" April, *The-south Asian.com.*

INDEX